Food, Health, and Culture
in Latino Los Angeles

Rowman & Littlefield Studies in Food and Gastronomy

General Editor: Ken Albala, Professor of History,
University of the Pacific (kalbala@pacific.edu)

Rowman & Littlefield Executive Editor: Suzanne Staszak-Silva
(sstaszak-silva@rowman.com)

Food studies is a vibrant and thriving field encompassing not only cooking and eating habits but also issues such as health, sustainability, food safety, and animal rights. Scholars in disciplines as diverse as history, anthropology, sociology, literature, and the arts focus on food. The mission of Rowman & Littlefield Studies in Food and Gastronomy is to publish the best in food scholarship, harnessing the energy, ideas, and creativity of a wide array of food writers today. This broad line of food-related titles will range from food history, interdisciplinary food studies monographs, general interest series, and popular trade titles to textbooks for students and budding chefs, scholarly cookbooks, and reference works.

Food, Health, and Culture in Latino Los Angeles

Sarah Portnoy

ROWMAN & LITTLEFIELD
Lanham • Boulder • New York • London

Published by Rowman & Littlefield
A wholly owned subsidiary of The Rowman & Littlefield Publishing Group, Inc.
4501 Forbes Boulevard, Suite 200, Lanham, Maryland 20706
www.rowman.com

Unit A, Whitacre Mews, 26-34 Stannary Street, London SE11 4AB

British Library Cataloguing in Publication Information Available

Library of Congress Cataloging-in-Publication Data Available
ISBN 978-1-4422-5129-8 (cloth : alk. paper)
ISBN 978-1-4422-5130-4 (electronic)

♾™ The paper used in this publication meets the minimum requirements of American
National Standard for Information Sciences—Permanence of Paper for Printed Library
Materials, ANSI/NISO Z39.48-1992.

Printed in the United States of America

Contents

Acknowledgments

As Los Angeles' poet laureate Luis Rodriguez said, "I have a love/hate relationship with L.A." Somewhat unenthusiastically, I moved to Los Angeles in 2007 from San Francisco, bemoaning leaving a city of breathtaking beauty and the Bay Area that I had come to call home. Over time, I grew fonder of Los Angeles as I discovered the hidden charm beyond its endless freeways, billboards, and strip malls. As I became more familiar with the city, I discovered its different cultures that come together in a haphazard way, as *LA Times* food writer Jonathan Gold said. Not every about the city is so enchanting, however. I have also witnessed the racial and economic inequalities in which wealthy residents live surrounded by beaches, grocery stores, and yoga studios, while low-income residents live in food deserts without safe parks or sufficient grocery stores, and an excess of liquor stores and fast-food restaurants. This is the side of Los Angeles that is not as easy to love; however, it is the side of Los Angeles that has inspired me to teach food justice through community-based courses at the University of Southern California. So, my heartfelt thanks go to the city of Los Angeles itself for inspiring me to unearth its treasures as well as its misfortunes.

My next thank you goes to the many people whose stories have touched me and whose hard work often goes without esteem: the *vendedores ambulantes* (street vendors), the *loncheros* (Latino food truck owners), community garden activists, nonprofit organizers, and city residents who struggle to feed their families.

I would like to thank all the chefs who made time for me to interview them: Jaime Martin del Campo and Ramiro Arvizu of Casita Mexicana and Mexicano, Rocío Camacho of Rocío's Mexican Kitchen, Armando Palmer of Guisados, Ray García of Broken Spanish and Broken Spanish Taquería, Carlos Salgado of Tacos María, Wes Avila of Guerrilla Tacos, Daniel Snukal and Josh Gil of Tacos Punta Cabra, and Gilberto Cetina Jr. of Chichén Itzá. I would also like to thank the nonprofit leaders who shared information with me about their organizations: Dana Rizer of Groceryships, Irene Peña of Proyecto Jardín, and Neelam Sharma of Community Services Unlimited.

I would like to thank Bill Esparza, the L.A. food writer and Latino food blogger. Bill has single-handedly brought attention to many of L.A.'s small family restaurants. When I first had the idea to teach a class on Latino food culture in Los Angeles in 2010, I reached out to Evan Kleinman of KCRW's *Good Food* to ask her who to speak with for ideas. She answered, "Bill Esparza." Bill has lectured every semester in my class, taken my students and me on food tours of Tijuana, and happily answered all my questions. A real mensch.

This project would not have been the same without the collaboration with my former student Ebony Bailey. Ebony took many of the photos for the book. Her images have brought my words to life and it has been fun to work with her. I would also like to thank my former student Laura Reilly for her help with proofreading the entire book, and my former student Will Chandler who did an independent study with me.

To the University of Southern California, and particularly my colleagues in the Department of Spanish and Portuguese, thank you for giving me the freedom to create food studies courses and for your support.

Last but not least, I would like to thank my husband, Ben Singer, and children, Salomón and Arturo, for their support and patience during what must have felt like an endless process. Ben also drove around East L.A. with me surreptitiously snapping photos of street vendors and trucks. Salomón and Arturo, *gracias*, for accompanying me on endless excursions to eat Mexican food all over the city.

Introduction

The Mexican Gastronomy Bug

When I graduated from Emory University in 1995, I moved to Seville, Spain, to teach English, immerse myself in Spanish culture, and take a few graduate courses at the University of Seville. One course in particular had a lasting impact on me. It was on oral traditions in Andalusia, specifically the *Romancero*, the Hispanic ballad tradition that has its roots in late medieval Iberia and crossed the ocean with the *conquistadores* and soldiers of the Conquest. As part of the course, my classmates and I spent several days in remote villages searching door-to-door for elderly informants who recalled *romances* they had learned from their mothers or grandmothers. Later, during my doctoral program at UC Berkeley I studied medieval Spanish literature and folklore. I continued to research Spanish ballads, but I began looking at how they had survived and transformed in Latin America. I did extensive fieldwork in Cuba and the Mexican state of Michoacán, where I found that many of the same ballads existed as children's songs and Mexican *corridos* (ballads). Later, I wrote a dissertation about the roles of powerful women in ballads, *corridos*, and *narco-corridos* (drug-smuggling ballads).

In 2002, during my fieldwork in the Mexican state of Michoacán, I got to know the regional cuisine as I ate my way through market stalls and family-style restaurants that served cheap *comida corrida* (multicourse meals) in the cities of Morelia, Uruapán, and Apatzingán. I enjoyed regional dishes such as *sopa tarasca* and Michoacán-style tamales. This was my first true exposure to regional Mexican cuisine beyond the Tex-Mex I knew from my youth in Houston and childhood trips to Matamoros, a Texas border city. A few years later, I met my husband, Ben Singer, a Mexico City native who had moved to San Francisco to start a chain of Mexican-style pharmacies in the Bay Area. Ben and I visited his family in Mexico City where I was amazed not only by the city's incredible variety of street food but also by the sophistication of its exquisite high-end restaurants. We sampled *tacos de canasta* (soft, steamed *tacos* sold on the street) near the Zócalo, the city's main square, and enjoyed modern Mexican cuisine at Pujol, Chef Enrique Olvera's world-renowned restaurant. We traveled to a beach town on the Riviera Maya on the Yucatán Peninsula where we spent time with my husband's extended family, eating Mayan dishes such as *panuchos* and *pescado tikin-xic* from roadside stands and restaurants. We honeymooned in Oaxaca where we tried as many of the region's different *moles* as possible and sampled mescal, a spirit made in Oaxaca from fermented agave. We visited Oaxaca's Central Market where we watched cacao being ground into chocolate in large metal grinding machines and visited markets in Oaxacan villages where vendors greeted us cries of "Tamales, *tortillas, chapulines* (grasshoppers)!" I became fascinated by Mexico's diverse gastronomy, one that was designated by UNESCO as part of the Intangible Cultural Heritage list in 2010. This complex cuisine was very different from the Tex-Mex of my Texas upbringing. There were no combo plates or fajitas. Instead, each region's cuisine was distinct and used a variety of chilies and corn I had never known existed. Many people still worked collectively and used tools such as the *metate* (grinding stone) to make fresh *tortillas* every day. I was only at the beginning of my culinary journey, but I had already caught the Mexican gastronomy bug.

In 2007, I moved from San Francisco to Los Angeles, where I started a teaching job at the University of Southern California (USC). In a short time, I discovered that Los Angeles has a very different vibe from San Francisco. It has a much bigger Latino population and the Latino communities are not as confined to certain areas as they are in the Bay Area. As I drove around this huge metropolis, I was struck by how pervasive Latino culture was in Los Angeles. There were rainbow-colored umbrellas signaling Latino fruit vendors at nearly every major intersection. White catering trucks selling *tacos* and *cemitas* (thick sandwiches made on challah-like bread with sesame) dotted the landscape. As I commuted to USC from my home in Venice, I passed Oaxacan *panaderías*, Salvadorian *pupuserías*, *carnicerías*, and endless *taquerías*. I spent a few years exploring the city's Latino culinary landscape, discovering the restaurants and *taquerías* of East L.A., Boyle Heights, and beyond. I found that in close proximity to the USC campus, a short distance from downtown, there were myriad representations of Latino culinary culture: Oaxacan, Yucatecan, Salvadorian, Argentine, Peruvian, Latin-Asian fusion, etc.

Contemporary Los Angeles can increasingly be considered a part of Latin America. Only 200 miles from the Mexican border, it has the largest and most diverse population of Latinos in the United States—and is said to have the second largest population of Mexicans outside of Mexico City. At the same time, you could say that Los Angeles is a city that the border crossed after Mexico lost California in the Mexican-American War to the United States, having first been part of Spain, and later Mexico, before California became the thirty-first state in 1850. Today, there are 4.9 million Latinos living in Los Angeles County, roughly 9% of the nation's overall Latino population. According to the Pew Research Center, 78% of the Latinos living in Los Angeles County are of Mexican origin, while the next largest Latino-origin groups are Salvadorian with 8% and Guatemalan with 5%.[1] Los Angeles also has the largest population of Oaxacans outside of Oaxaca City, the region's capital. An estimated 80,000 Oaxacans have emigrated from this largely indigenous southern state to Los Angeles in the past few decades. These populations make Los Angeles a city with a very different Latino makeup than Miami with its Cuban and South American populations or New York City with its historic Puerto Rican and Dominican populations. While there are small numbers of Latinos in Los Angeles from the Caribbean and South America, it is still very much a Mexican city.

As I explored Los Angeles' different manifestations of Latino cuisine, I became fascinated with the exploding field of Food Studies. As a folklorist, food studies' multidisciplinary approach appealed to me since it allowed me to work in different disciplines. Like the *romances* or ballads, food seemed like an excellent tool to research and teach about a culture. In 2011, I developed a community-based course, "The Culture of Food in Latino Los Angeles," in which students examine the intersection of food and topics such as discrimination, authenticity, gender roles, art, and public policy. The course allows students to engage in local Latino communities and learn how cuisine—and culture—adapts and evolves in a new environment as a result of migration, new cultural norms, the size of the immigrant community, and the availability of ingredients. As part of the class, students visit restaurants, markets, *loncheras* (stationary food trucks that are a subsector of food trucks), and street vendors, and write about their experiences in weekly Spanish-language blog posts.

During excursions with students to visit restaurants, food trucks, and markets in Los Angeles' Latino neighborhoods, I became increasingly aware of the limited number of options for buying fresh, affordable food in low-income, urban communities known as food deserts. For example, South L.A., home to over 1.3 million people, has 60 full-service grocery stores that average 22,000 residents in contrast to 11,000 residents per supermarket in affluent West L.A.[2] Most of the available produce in these communities comes from corner stores where it is expensive and often of poor quality. As I became more aware of the challenges low-income, minority communities face, I became very interested in the field of food justice as a tool for change. Food justice refers to the right of communities to have access to healthy, affordable, culturally appropriate food regardless of race, socioeconomic class, gender, or ethnicity. Food justice advocates strive to protect the rights of people who live in food deserts and farm workers and enable people to make a difference. Food justice advocates to make a difference in their local food system. They recognize that many voices have been left out of the mainstream food movement. Nationally, the food movement has exploded in the past ten or fifteen years. In bestselling books and documentaries, journalists and activists speak of the importance of eating locally. Journalist and activist Michael Pollan frames eating locally as a moral and political act. The food movement has created a monumental change in response to our environmentally unsustainable and physically unhealthy global food system. However, it has not addressed the structural inequalities and inefficiencies in the food system that leave 48 million people or 14% of Americans food insecure every year, according to the U.S. Department of Agriculture.[3]

In 2014, I developed a second course, "Food Justice" in Latino Los Angeles that takes a critical look at the issues affecting the health of Latinos in Los Angeles and Mexico as well as local food justice movements. Students visit community and school gardens, local farmers markets, a café that employs former Latino gang members, illegal street vendors, and the Grand Central Market in downtown Los Angeles. In the past, my food justice students have participated in projects to support Proyecto Jardín, a community garden in Boyle Heights, a low-income Latino community. Currently, students are volunteering with various South L.A. food justice organizations. These experiences teach my students about the challenges Latino communities face and show them that access to healthy food is part of a larger structural problem of access to affordable housing, transportation, safe parks, and other basic human rights.

Over the years, I have gotten to know many of the people on different ends of the food spectrum, everyone from well-known chefs to leaders of food justice organizations. These relationships have shaped my knowledge of Latino food culture *and* food justice. As I developed the idea for this book, I wanted to write about both sides of the culinary coin, topics that at first glance seem so disparate, but are actually quite connected. I wanted to tell a story that would show everyone from foodies to food justice advocates that the topic of Latino food in Los Angeles is about so much more than just the best late-night taco truck. In this study, I hope to shed light on the richness of Latino cuisine as well as the complexities of the local food system; I want to demonstrate that, despite the expansion of Latino cuisine's popularity in Los Angeles and the celebrity of some Latino chefs as purveyors of healthy, fresh food, there is a stark divide between the quality and healthfulness of what is available at the restaurants of elite chefs versus what is available to many urban, low-income Latinos. Ironically, while chefs serve "authentic" cuisine to affluent diners, low-income immigrant families eat at McDonald's because they live in neighborhoods with limited dining options. At the same time, Latino food has become strongly favored across non-Latino populations hungering for an authentic dining experience.

The first chapter portrays the history of Los Angeles' Latino (primarily Mexican) culinary culture, one that spans everything from regional Mexican cuisines and "old-school" Mexican-American restaurants to Mexican street food. I begin by chronicling the early history of the *tamaleros*, the tamale wagons, in the late nineteenth and early twentieth centuries. I examine the discrimination the Mexican tamale men faced in a changing Los Angeles, a city that, in the span of decades, had gone from being a Mexican *pueblo* with a majority Mexican population to a city with a majority Anglo population. This chapter explores the perception of the Anglo population that Mexicans (and to some degree, their food) were unsanitary and dangerous. Instead of celebrating Los Angeles' early Mexican past, the Anglos in power replaced it with one that appeared Spanish—that is European and of elite status. Late nineteenth-century cookbooks printed in Los Angeles refer to Spanish cuisine, even though the recipes themselves are Mexican. Early Mexican restaurants catering to Anglos adopted a whitewashed, idealized version of Mexico and Mexican food for a diner that wanted an exotic experience without having to visit a part of the city populated by working-class Mexicans and Mexican-Americans. El Cholo Spanish Café, the second-oldest Mexican restaurant in the United States, opened in the 1920s selling Mexican food to Anglo diners seeking an "authentic" culinary experience.

Culinary historian Jeffrey Pilcher explains that historically Mexican food in Los Angeles has varied depending on the part of the city in which it was located. Taco shops that developed in the 1950s and 1960s were primarily located in non-Latino areas.[4] The fast-food *tacos* popular among Anglos bore little resemblance to their ancestors across the border—or, for that matter, across the city. A Taco Bell taco is a classic example of the Mexican-American food known across the United States—and even abroad—today. Critics have long argued over the authenticity of creations such as the Taco Bell taco and other Mexican staples in the United States. At first, I saw these U.S. adaptations as "inauthentic," but over time, I came to understand that authenticity is something dynamic that changes according to time and place.

The next chapter explores the contributions of regional Mexican cuisine and its influence on non-Latino chefs. During the 1980s and 1990s, Mexican cuisine in Los Angeles was beginning to expand beyond the Mexican-American fast-food staples of the previous few decades. During this period, tens of thousands of Oaxacans immigrated to Los Angeles and other parts of Southern California. This chapter provides a background on Oaxaca's unique cuisine and the role it has played in shaping Los Angeles' Latino "foodscape." Next, I profile several important Latino chefs and discuss their contributions to the development of Latino cuisine in Los Angeles.

I describe the challenges faced by Rocío Camacho, the only Latina chef in recent decades to have broken traditional gender barriers and to have received acclaim from food critics. Mexican cuisine was not the only one to expand in Los Angeles during the 1980s and 1990s. The arrival of a large number of Salvadorian immigrants during this period brought about an increase in Salvadorian restaurants. This Central American cuisine has been present in Los Angeles for a much shorter time and, as a result, has not become as familiar to non-Latino diners as Mexican cuisine.

Finally, I examine the recent elevation of Latino cuisine through the innovations of a group of young Mexican-American chefs in Southern California whose style of cooking has been named "Alta California Cuisine." Unlike previous generations of Mexican and Mexican-American chefs, this new generation of classically trained chefs is not trying to recreate the traditional dishes their mothers and grandmothers made. Instead, they are creating dishes that are influenced by Mexican traditional cuisine but rooted in Los Angeles. They use fresh, seasonal produce, local seafood, and import high-quality corn for their *tortillas* from small, Mexican family farms. They are a generation that does not believe that high-end Mexican cuisine must be served in a formal restaurant setting. Instead, Chef Wes Avila serves tacos made with high-quality, seasonal ingredients from a graffiti emblazoned truck.

Avila's truck Guerrilla Tacos represents the evolution of the *lonchera*, a mobile food truck that first appeared in Los Angeles in the mid-1970s to serve lunch to Mexican construction workers. The third chapter examines the *lonchera,* the modern-day iteration of the late nineteenth-century tamale wagon. Over time, *loncheras* became a place to get a quick, affordable meal in Latino neighborhoods and other areas of the city. Nowadays, *loncheras* are a staple of street corners in Latino neighborhoods and major intersections in the city. Thousands operate throughout the city both day and night and many Angelenos swear allegiance to a particular truck. *Loncheras* form a vital part of the city's identity, contribute to its economy, and create employment for immigrant families.

Despite the *loncheras'* vital role in the formation of modern-day Los Angeles' "foodscape," critics, primarily city officials and restaurant owners, have criticized them with much the same language they used about the tamale vendors nearly a century earlier. They have accused them of having unfair advantages over brick-and-mortar restaurants, being a public health endangerment, and contributing to crime and blight. This chapter looks at the recent challenges the truck owners have faced in attempts by city officials to regulate them. A 2008 city ordinance stated that if the *loncheras* parked for longer than thirty minutes in a residential zone or sixty minutes in a nonresidential zone they could receive a $1,000 fine and six-month jail sentence. At a time when downtown and surrounding areas were going through gentrification, the ordinance was intended to remove these "eye-sores." The "Taco Truck War" of 2008 demonstrates that although racial divisions are still present in twenty-first-century Los Angeles, increasingly different populations are willing to come together to fight a common cause. The ordinance angered the young Anglo professionals who ate regularly at the trucks. They created a petition and launched a website with the battle cry "Carne asada is not a crime." An unlikely alliance of truck owners and the Anglo foodies worked together to advocate for social justice and preserve the food truck industry.

The *loncheras* are the not the only form of street food integral to the city of Los Angeles. Another type of Latino microenterprise operates on the city's sidewalks, the *vendedores ambulantes* (Latino street-food vendors). The fourth chapter discusses the evolution of Latino street food in Los Angeles and the vendors' ongoing fight for legalization. Street food is and has always been a staple of Mesoamerican culture and still permeates the sidewalks of Mexico today. The Los Angeles Bureau of Street Services estimates that there are fifty thousand vendors operating annually in the city, around ten thousand of whom sell the street food for which Los Angeles is famous: bacon-wrapped hot dogs, sliced fruit, *raspados* (shaved ice), and *quesadillas*. Yet, Los Angeles is one of only ten major U.S. cities where it is illegal to sell food on sidewalk. Nonprofit organizations have been working to legalize street food in Los Angeles for decades. In 2013, a working group of the Los Angeles Food Policy Council submitted a proposal to the city council to legalize street vending. Since then, the leaders of the movement have held demonstrations at city hall and engaged in a social media campaign on Twitter and Facebook, but street vending remains illegal.

This chapter tells the story of one particular street-food vendor Caridad Vásquez, and her fight for legalization. Vásquez has been working as a street vendor since she arrived in Los Angeles in 1995 from Mexico. She had grown up selling tamales on the streets in Mexico. When she came to the United States she began selling food on the streets of Boyle Heights, an area close to downtown Los Angeles. Over the years, Caridad has had her cart and her livelihood taken away as a result of police crackdowns. In 2008, Caridad joined the Los Angeles Street Vendor Campaign and has become an outspoken advocate for street-food legalization. Nevertheless, street-food vending remains illegal in Los Angeles and vendors continue to be harassed and victimized. Caridad's story is part of a larger story of a disenfranchised, immigrant group trying to use their cultural heritage to make a living and participate in the public sphere.

The fifth chapter tells the story of a fictionalized character Marina Gutierrez, a low-income Latino mother struggling to provide fresh, healthy, culturally appropriate food to her family in a food desert. Marina's story reveals the challenges of our industrial food system, one in which processed foods are heavily subsidized, while fresh fruit and vegetables are unaffordable or not easily available in low-income areas. This chapter also examines the consequences of lack of access to healthy food: the dramatic rise in food-related diseases, particularly diabetes and obesity, which plague many low-income, minority communities. I look at why diabetes afflicts Latinos to a greater extent, and examine the effects of acculturation on Latino immigrant families. Finally, I explain how, during the second half of the twentieth century, as a result of racial discrimination and white flight in communities such as Marina's, grocery stores closed down and, over time, became populated by liquor stores, vacant lots, and fast-food restaurants.

In the face of this crisis, Latinos in Los Angeles are creating solutions that are both traditional and novel. In recent years, a food justice movement that seeks to transform the food system from farm to table has grown globally. The sixth chapter examines local food justice initiatives in Los Angeles' Latino communities. I look at how, in Latino neighborhoods of Los Angeles, in particular Boyle Heights and South L.A., grassroots organizations are working with the community to improve residents' food sovereignty through the expansion of farmers', markets for low-income shoppers, new community markets, corner store conversion programs, a moratorium on new fast-food restaurants, innovative nutrition programs, and urban agriculture programs. I profile the work of Homeboy Industries, the largest and most successful gang intervention, rehabilitation, and reentry program in the world. Homeboy helps many former gang members and recently incarcerated Latinos reenter society and turn their lives around through food production. I examine other new programs that have been effective at creating change, such as Groceryships, a new nonprofit organization that is taking a completely different approach to improving health in the community. Staff and volunteers work with small groups of South L.A. residents to improve health and diet through a peer-led education and support program. I also discuss other initiatives, such as the fast-food moratorium, that have met with resistance and been less successful.

The final chapter is dedicated to urban agriculture in Latino Los Angeles. Urban agriculture is one important way to improve access to healthy, fresh produce in low-income communities. The renaissance of urban farming in the United States in the past twenty years has led to many initiatives that have been very important for Latino communities. School gardens, community gardens, and urban farms are not only great ways for low-income Latinos to grow their own produce, but they also allow them to connect to their agricultural roots. I look at three different examples of urban agriculture in Latino Los Angeles: the South Central Farm, an urban farm that was demolished in 2006; Proyecto Jardín, a community garden under threat of displacement in Boyle Heights; and the Garden School Foundation. The South Central Farm was the largest urban farm in the United States from 1994 to 2006. It began in South L.A. after the Rodney King riots. And served as an oasis in the middle of pavements, freeways, and bloody gang violence for 350 indigenous Mexican immigrant families. The site became embroiled in a land struggle with the former owner and in 2006 the city ruled to return the land to the former property owner. Despite massive protests, the garden was bulldozed.

Projecto Jardín is a one-acre community garden that was established in 1999 in Boyle Heights, a Latino neighborhood near downtown Los Angeles. Community members grow medicinal herbs and vegetables native to Mexico and Central American countries. The garden has spaces for exercise and cooking classes. Despite its importance to the community, the garden has been under threat of displacement from its landlord, White Memorial Hospital, since early 2016. Community members have rallied to the support of the garden. The "guardians of the garden" have been occupying the land 24 hours a day and young Latino community members have been using social media to publicize their cause, but the garden's future remains uncertain.

The Garden School Foundation is an excellent example of a low-income, predominantly Latino elementary school that has battled children's obesity and lack of access to healthy produce through the creation of a school garden program. Urban spaces like these are very important to Los Angeles' Latino communities. Despite the tragic history of the South Central Farm and the current standoff at Proyecto Jardín, the future of urban agriculture in Los Angeles seems bright. Through the awareness First Lady Michelle Obama has generated and the hard work of many local organizations, there is a growing interest in food justice at the national and local levels.

Since I began my career in literature and folklore, the fields of food culture and food justice are relatively new fields for me. My teaching and research have been influenced by the work of culinary historian Jeffrey Pilcher. His 2012 book *Planet Taco: A Global History of Mexican Food* was key to my understanding of the development of Mexican food in the United States and related issues of power, authenticity, and discrimination. While not an academic study, I also found the historical accounts in journalist Gustavo Arellano's 2012 book *Taco USA: How Mexican Food Conquered America* very useful. Unlike Pilcher and Arellano, however, I do not focus on Mexican food at the global or even national level. Instead, my study is narrowly focused on the city of Los Angeles. I bridge the topic of Latino food culture with social justice issues, including the discriminatory practices faced by Mexican food trucks and illegal street vendors. While there have been academic articles published on the plight of the vendors and the hardships faced by the *loncheras*, no one has devoted chapters in a book to both of these subjects. My goal is for this book to generate greater respect for Latino cuisine not only in elite restaurants but also on the city's streets and sidewalks.

Proyecto Jardín Gate exterior. Photo courtesy of Ebony Bailey.

The work of Allison Alkon and Julian Agyeman in *Cultivating Food Justice: Race, Class, and Sustainability* and Robert Gottlieb and Anupama Joshi in *Food Justice* have shaped my understanding of food justice. While much of my information comes from the newspaper or National Public Radio segments, the most valuable knowledge comes from the people who I write about themselves, everyone from chefs and activists to nonprofit leaders and community members. Through the many individual's stories I tell, I give recognition to otherwise unheard voices of those who have helped shape Latino Los Angeles. Finally, the broken food system is a problem for all of us, but it hits low-income and minority communities the hardest. Communities across the United States are coming up with ways to meet these challenges locally. This book brings together two different intersections of the terms Latino and food: the rise in popularity of Latino food culture in Los Angeles and the challenges faced by local Latinos to live in communities where there is access to healthy, affordable, and culturally appropriate food.

Chapter 1

From Tamale Wagons
to California Burritos

A History of Latino Food in Los Angeles

Twenty-first-century Los Angeles is a multicultural city of endless strip malls and flashing billboards where different ethnicities collide and overlap in a somewhat haphazard way, particularly in the densely populated areas where Koreatown borders the Salvadorian and Oaxacan corridors of the city. In this area, Korean-language advertisements for Korean barbeque seamlessly blend with ones in Spanish for Salvadorian *pupusas* (a thick, handmade corn tortilla stuffed with cheese and beans, meat, or other ingredients), Oaxacan *tlayudas* (a large, thin, crunchy tortilla covered with refried black bean puree, Oaxacan cheese, lettuce, avocado, salsa, and other toppings), or Peruvian *pollo a la brasa* (rotisserie chicken). It is a city that the Pulitzer Prize–winning food critic of the *LA Times* Jonathan Gold calls "a glorious mosaic" where distinct sights and smells overpower the senses and stimulate the palate and the imagination, inviting you to explore its crowded streets and the food from its endless variety of restaurants, markets, food trucks, and street-food vendors.

But Los Angeles was not always like this. This chapter describes the history of Mexican food in Los Angeles beginning in the late nineteenth century. I chronicle the history of the *tamaleros*, the tamale wagons, in the late nineteenth and early twentieth centuries and explore the perception of the Anglo population that Mexicans (and to some degree, their food) were unsanitary and dangerous. I show how the Anglos in power attempted to replace the Mexican past with one that was Spanish—that is, European and of elite status. I discuss the "staged authenticity" of early twentieth-century Mexican restaurants that were created to provide an exotic experience for Anglo diners, and talk about the Mexican fast food of the 1950s and 1960s that was created as a commodity for Anglo consumers. As this Americanized version of "Mexican food" became popular across the country, contentious debates over its authenticity took place among academics and journalists.

When Mexico lost the Mexican-American War in 1848, the two countries signed a peace treaty, the Treaty of Guadalupe Hidalgo, in which Mexico agreed to give up California and a large area comprising parts of modern-day Arizona, New Mexico, Nevada, and Utah. Soon after, in 1850, California officially became part of the United States. The Anglos who came to power at that time saw themselves as a superior race and the local Mexican population as an inferior and uncivilized people. As historian William Deverell posits in *Whitewashed Adobe: The Rise of Los Angeles and the Remaking of Its Mexican Past*, the troubling ethnic relations between the Anglos in power and the recently conquered Mexicans make up an important part of Los Angeles' history. Deverell explains that Los Angeles is a city that matured by "whitewashing" its Mexican past through the process of "covering up places, people, and histories that those in power found unsettling."[1] The newly arriving Anglo population used brick, a more resistant building material, to cover up the Mexican adobe, the clay material the Spanish had used to construct the original *pueblo*, El Pueblo de Nuestra Señora la Reina de los Ángeles de Porciúncula, in 1781. The whitewashing of a Mexican past was one way that "white Angelenos created distance (cultural or personal) between themselves and the Mexican past and the Mexican people in their midst."[2]

By 1876, the transcontinental railroad linked Los Angeles to the rest of the country and the city's population was transformed from one with a Mexican majority to one that was majority Anglo. The railroad facilitated migration to California from the rest of the United States, bringing an influx of eager midwesterners attracted to Southern California's agricultural opportunities.[3] As a result, Los Angeles' population grew quickly. In 1850, when California became part of the United States, Los Angeles had fewer than 2,000 inhabitants, the majority of whom spoke Spanish. Between 1890 and 1930, Los Angeles' population jumped from 50,000 to 1.2 million.[4]

As the new migrants discovered that Southern California was an agricultural paradise and came west to farm the land, there was an increased demand for Mexican agricultural workers. In *Becoming Mexican-American*, George Sánchez explains that migration from Mexico is not only "a twentieth century phenomenon." Ever since Mexico lost "its northern territories in the aftermath of the Mexican-American War, there had been movements of Mexicans into the United States."[5] However, the earlier numbers of Mexicans paled in comparison to the number of Mexican immigrants who migrated to California between 1900 and 1930. During these early decades of the twentieth century, there was a massive movement of people and families from Mexico to the United States as a result of the violence and economic hardship created by the 1910 Mexican Revolution. Approximately 1.5 million

Mexicans migrated to the United States, most to the Southwest.[6] A large number of these Mexican newcomers settled in and around Los Angeles and established Mexican communities. As Mexican immigration to Los Angeles increased, Mexican culture was strengthened and revived.

As new Anglo migrants arrived in downtown Los Angeles, they went in search of an affordable meal. Mexican tamale vendors were among the first to capitalize on the city's growing population. In his exploration of Mexican food in the United States, *Taco USA: How Mexican Food Conquered America*, journalist Gustavo Arellano explains that the origin of the early vendors is "murky," but that "newspaper accounts place them back as far as the 1870s."[7] These early newspaper accounts touted the city's tamales to out-of-town visitors to Los Angeles. A *Los Angeles Herald* article from 1880, for example, stated that "the experience of our Eastern visitors will be incomplete unless they sample a Los Angeles street tamale."[8] By the 1890s, the tamale vendors were based near the original El Pueblo de Los Angeles. They dominated the street-food scene of the downtown area. During this era, tamales became an integral part of the diet of working-class Americans. They were, according to Gustavo Arellano, "L.A.'s first street food fad" and America's first mainstream introduction to Mexican food.[9] In *Planet Taco: A Global History of Mexican Food,* historian Jeffrey Pilcher explains that the discovery of Mexican food occurred "in racial and ethnic borderlands between Mexico and the United States," primarily San Antonio and Los Angeles, cities where "Mexicans maintained a significant presence until an influx of Anglo migrants tipped the balance."[10]

During the late nineteenth and early twentieth centuries, political and social power was concentrated in the hands of a small group of Anglo Americans who "were anxious to impose coherence" on the Mexican outsiders as they fashioned Los Angeles into a new, modern city.[11] They saw the Mexican residents as a dangerous ethnic Other that needed to be controlled. In his history of Mexicans in early Los Angeles, historian William Deverell observes that Los Angeles is "a city constructed precisely around racial categories and racial exclusion."[12] As a result, as the metropolis expanded, Mexicans and other minorities were isolated to areas east of downtown through a process known as "redlining." Redlining was a policy introduced by the Federal Housing Administration in 1934 that used housing covenants to restrict "alien races" to specific neighborhoods by denying them loans from the bank when they tried to buy outside the confines of these areas.[13] During the 1920s and 1930s, for example, the area of Boyle Heights, located just east of downtown, was home to a diverse population of "alien races" of Jews, Russians, Japanese, and Mexican-Americans. Cesar E. Chavez Avenue, a main street that runs through and beyond the area, was originally called Brooklyn Avenue.[14] The largest Orthodox synagogue in the Western United States served an area that was once home to the largest Jewish neighborhood in the city. During World War II, the Japanese were sent to internment camps. Afterwards, most returned to Boyle Heights, remaining there until housing covenants were eased in the 1950s. In the years after World War II, the redlining restrictions eased for certain ethnic groups and Boyle Heights' Jewish community dispersed, moving to the Fairfax District and other areas on the city's affluent Westside. Mexicans, on the other hand, stayed behind and the area became populated primarily by low-income Mexicans and Mexican-Americans.

In a city that came of age in response to "Mexican ethnicity and Mexican spaces," the Anglos saw early Mexican street-food vendors as sensuous and dangerous. The discrimination toward Mexican vendors did not occur only in Los Angeles, but further south in San Antonio as well. Beginning in the 1880s in San Antonio, Mexican women known as "chili queens" served *chili con carne* in the city's main plazas. A stew of beans, meat, tomatoes, and peppers, it was a dish that emerged in southern Texas when the area was still part of Mexico.[15] Gustavo Arellano explains that the chili queens, early Mexican street vendors selling in public squares and markets, were given this name "to further embellish the dish's exotic quality."[16] Not only was the food exoticized, the chili queens themselves were also portrayed as sensuous, even dangerous Latin beauties "waiting to be tamed by Anglo men."[17] In Los Angeles, on the other hand, the early street tamale vendors were men. In *Taco USA*, Gustavo Arellano describes how by the beginning of the twentieth century, as the phenomenon of tamale vendors spread throughout the country, white Europeans and African-Americans were selling tamales on the streets of New York, Chicago, and San Francisco. This phenomenon was depicted in the image from a popular song "Here Comes the Hot Tamale Man," sung by an African-American jazz band in the 1920s with the instruments "mimicking the rolling strut of the vendor."[18] Like the chili queens in San Antonio, the sexuality of the tamale vendors was also viewed as suspect. Pilcher cites an article from the 1924 *LA Times* that describes how the colorful silk shirts of one male vendor attracted customers' attention.[19]

At the same time Americans were being introduced to Mexican food and the country was in the midst of a tamale craze, popular accounts depicted tamale vendors as deviant and dangerous, a force the Anglo establishment needed to control and outlaw. By the first decades of the twentieth century, cities were restricting or barring completely the sale of street tamales. In Los Angeles, the city forced cart owners to pay for operating licenses as a way to lessen their numbers. Vendors, in turn, formed "a mutual society" and hired lawyers to defend themselves.[20] These early tamale men are the precursors to the modern-day, illegal L.A. street-food vendors, discussed in a later chapter on the battle for their legalization. Like their predecessors, critics have also accused modern-day street vendors of being dirty, magnets for crime, unfair competition with local businesses, and a nuisance to the city. The discrimination faced by the early tamale men is a history that has continued to repeat itself in the obstacles faced by Latino immigrant entrepreneurs throughout the twentieth and twenty-first centuries.

By the early decades of the twentieth century, Mexican food in Los Angeles was no longer just street food. By this time, upper-class Anglos had become interested in Mexican cuisine. Instead of calling it "Mexican," however, they referred to it as Spanish cuisine as a way to distance themselves from the negative stereotypes associated with their neighbor to the South. At the time, French cuisine was considered elite, while anything Mexican was looked down upon as less sophisticated and backward. Despite the negative stereotypes, Anglo settlers to California adopted and integrated Mexican cuisine into their diets.

The failure of early Mexican restaurants in Los Angeles among Anglos demonstrates the elite status given to European, particularly French, cuisines. In 1881, across the street from Los Angeles' main plaza, Hilario Preciado opened a restaurant that was advertised in classified ads in the *LA Times* simply as "Mexican Restaurant," serving "*tamales, enchiladas, carne con chile*, and *albóndigas* (meatballs), along with Spanish, French, and American dishes."[21] Despite the desirable location, the "Mexican Restaurant" and others like it soon lost popularity with the Anglo elite and were replaced with French restaurants, status symbols for a city with a burgeoning culinary identity. Unlike the global cuisine for which Los Angeles is famous today, at the time the city's Anglo community did not embrace outside culinary influences, but instead saw them as foreign influences that "threatened the possibility of an indigenous and unified L.A. food identity," one that was slowly forming alongside the growing city.[22]

Late nineteenth- and early twentieth-century cookbooks printed in Los Angeles also provide evidence of the Anglo preference for European cuisines. Cookbooks such as *How We Cook in Los Angeles* included Spanish Departments as well as French and German ones.[23] While this fascinating recipe collection compiled in 1898 by the Ladies' Social Circle includes a few traditional Spanish dishes, most of the recipes were Mexican. These include "Frijoles, Frijoles con Queso, Chili con Carni, and Purslane Salad." Purslane, known in Spanish as *verdolagas*, is a Mexican herb traditionally used in pork stews and vegetable soups. It is an incredibly nutritious and affordable plant and is found at Hispanic markets. Yet, today it is not known to most Anglos, even Anglos who cook or eat Mexican food, so it is striking to find in an early Anglo cookbook. The use of this herb in a nineteenth-century Anglo cookbook shows the influence of Mexican cuisine on the Anglo population of the time, despite their disregard and even disdain for Mexicans themselves.

It was not until 1898 that a cookbook published in San Francisco presented Mexican cuisine in a more sophisticated light. Encarnación Pinedo's *El cocinero español* was the first Spanish-language cookbook printed in California and only the third in the United States.[24] Only a few copies of this collection of Mexican, Spanish, and European recipes have survived, but in 2005, Dan Strehl translated a selection from the book and published it as *Encarnación's Kitchen: Mexican Recipes from Nineteenth Century California.* Pinedo's contribution to our understanding of early Mexican cuisine in California is significant because, unlike the earlier cookbook with its "Spanish Departments," an Anglo did not write this cookbook of 1,000 recipes and it was not written for an Anglo audience. Instead, it is the work of an educated woman writing in Spanish at the end of the nineteenth century, the period following the conquest of Alta California, the name given to the Mexican territory that covers modern-day California.[25] Pinedo was from an elite *Californio* family, the name for people of Spanish descent born in California between 1769 and 1848. Many *Californios* received large land grants from Spain and later Mexico and flourished during the 1830s to the 1880s. Pinedo's writing is, in large part, a response to the discrimination the native *Californios* faced from the Anglos. Her work represents the historic struggle of Latinos to create an identity that is respected by the wider population, while still preserving their culture.

As ethnic studies professor Victor Valle explains in the introduction to *Encarnación's Kitchen*, Pinedo's grandfather was at the helm of one of the wealthiest of these families, but his land was seized and he was coldly murdered by "Yankee men" when California became part of the United States. The family fought for generations to regain their land, but never succeeded.[26] Many women in Pinedo's family married Anglo settlers, but not Pinedo. She did not marry and her writing shows a bitter dislike of English cuisine. Pinedo argues that English "food and style of seasoning are the most insipid and tasteless that one can imagine."[27] Pinedo's resentment toward the English is likely linked to her family's troubled history with settlers of English ancestry. As Victor Valle recounts in the introduction, when Pinedo's grandmother heard of her husband's murder, she used a "culinary insult": "The Gringos were a bloodless people. They lived on tea and potatoes."[28] Strehl explains that, on the other hand, Pinedo's recipes were "the descendants of Mexico's nineteenth-century cuisine, which, with its 'distinctive Spanish, Indian, and French influences,' provided a sophisticated contrast to the amateur cookbooks compiled by the wives of the first Anglo settlers."[29] Writing in Spanish and ignoring Yankee recipes was a way for Pinedo to preserve the recipes in her native language and resist the changes that forever altered her social status.[30] By choosing to write in Spanish, however, she excluded the Anglo population, since by the time she wrote her book Anglo speakers outnumbered Spanish speakers in California.[31]

The title Pinedo gave the work—*El cocinero español* (*The Spanish Cook*) shows a desire to stress her European heritage and downplay her *mestizo* one. It was also a way to place her work in the "culinary mainstream," which for Pinedo was Catholic Europe.[32] Many of the recipes in *El cocinero español* have Castilian-sounding names such as *aves en mole gallego* (fowl in a Galician *mole*), *guajolote en clamole castellano* (turkey in Castilian broth), and *guajolote en mole gallego* (turkey in Galician *mole*). While these dishes refer to Spain and the region of Galicia, they are actually fairly traditional Mexican dishes and recipes. Referencing Spain in the recipes was another way for Pinedo to distance herself from Mexico and reinforce her connections to elite Europe.

The desire to elevate one's social status through a connection with Spain was not limited to the *Californios*. It formed part of the Anglo Angelenos' creation of a mythical "Spanish fantasy past" in which they romanticized the nineteenth-century California rancho period. In the classic 1946 book *Southern California Country: An Island on the Land* Carey McWilliams describes California during this period as a land with sacred symbols such as "the Old Spanish Don sunning himself in the courtyard of his rancho."[33] American writer and activist Helen Hunt Jackson popularized this mythical version of Old California in her 1884 bestseller *Ramona*, one of the most widely read novels of the period. *Ramona* tells the story of a beautiful Scottish-Native American orphan girl who is raised on a Mexican rancho in California during the 1850s. When Ramona falls in love with a Native American man, she is forced to elope and they suffer great hardships. The publication of *Ramona* awakened an interest in the decaying, neglected Spanish missions and their history and led to the Anglo fascination with the early *Californios*, an interest that emphasized a Spanish, past and whitewashed the Mexican one. In *Southern California Country*, Carey McWilliams describes how Southern California's Spanish background was "rediscovered" during this period with a "false emphasis" and "crass motives."[34] The Anglo elite formed associations to preserve the California missions to make money from the "tide of tourists," who came in search of the mythical sites from the novel.[35]

The Anglo fascination with Southern California's mythical Spanish past was on the minds of Leslie Brand and railroad titan Henry Huntington when they purchased hundreds of acres of what had once been a Spanish ranch, Rancho San Rafael, an area that encompasses much of the Los Angeles areas of modern-day Glendale and Burbank.[36] In an effort to capitalize on the fascination with the Spanish missions and their adobe architecture, in 1905 Huntington and Brand had a nineteenth-century adobe home on the property restored. They turned it into a restaurant they called Casa Verdugo, and claimed the building was from the eighteenth century. As USC professor Josh Kun explains in *To Live and Dine in L.A.: Menus and the Making of the Modern City*, the book for an a 2015 exhibit of over 200 historic Los Angeles menus at the Los Angeles Public Library, Casa Verdugo was built to be "a tourist destination for culinary time-travel back to 'Old California'" complete with a "Days-of-the-Dons theme-park approach to dining" that came with "strolling mariachis and sour cream tortilla casseroles."[37] The Los Angeles Public Library exhibit included a copy of a menu of Casa Verdugo from 1913 that features dishes such as "Spanish meat ball," "steamed rice, Spanish," Mexican dishes, such as enchiladas, frijoles, fried green chili stuffed with cheese, tomato sauce, as well as Southern classics like "sweet potatoes, Southern Style."[38] Clearly, the restaurant was rooted in Southern California's Spanish and Mexican pasts and, as Josh Kun explains, in the "cultural mythology that fueled" Los Angeles' early twentieth-century growth.[39] In *Whitewashed Adobe: The Rise of Los Angeles and the Remaking of Its Mexican Past*, historian William Deverell describes how Southern California "came of age through appropriating, absorbing, and obliterating the region's connectedness to Mexican places and Mexican people."[40] An early twentieth-century restaurant such as Casa Verdugo is one example of a canvas upon which the city of Los Angeles whitewashed its Mexican past.

During the late nineteenth and early twentieth centuries, most Mexican immigrants to Southern California came from Northern Mexico. They brought their unique cuisine with them, one that reflects ranch culture with its popular meat dishes such as *machaca* (dried beef), *arrachera* (skirt steak), and *cabrito* (baby goat). Along with meat, the region has a variety of flour *tortillas*, a Northern Mexican staple that gave rise to the original burrito. A name that means "little donkey," the original burrito was a flour tortilla rolled up with beef—a far distant cousin of the contemporary California burrito, an overstuffed creation filled with rice, beans, guacamole, lettuce, and cheese. According to historian Jeffrey Pilcher, the burrito first appeared with a culinary reference in Feliz Ramos I. Duarte's 1895 *Diccionario de mejicanismos*, where he defined it as a "rolled tortilla with meat or other thing inside, which in Yucatán is called *cosito*, and in Cuernavaca and Mexico City, *taco*."[41] The fact that the once simple burrito has evolved into the creations found across the United States shows that cuisine is not at all confined by national borders, but instead travels and adapts to the customs and ingredients it finds.

It was not until the Mexican Revolution (1910–1930) that Mexican immigrants arrived from the center of the country. Gustavo Arellano describes how the "biblical wave of migrants from Central Mexico … introduced other Mexican delicacies to the city largely unfamiliar to the region: *birria* (goat stew), *menudo* (soup made from cow tripe), and different preparations of pork, chicken, and beef, best eaten snuggled in a tortilla: the taco."[42] The taco was not found prior to this period outside of Mexico since it is not of Northern Mexican origin. It originated in Mexico City at the end of the nineteenth century. According to Jeffrey Pilcher, during the late nineteenth and early twentieth century, under the reign of Mexican president Porfirio Díaz, the capital of Mexico exerted political and cultural control over the rest of the country. "The taco became a culinary and linguistic expression of this hegemonic power."[43] By the 1920s, Pilcher explains, "Migrants from Central Mexico had carried their *tacos* as far as California."[44]

In 1923, a small storefront restaurant serving Northern Mexican cuisine opened near Exposition Park, blocks from the USC campus. El Cholo, Los Angeles' oldest surviving Mexican restaurant and the second-oldest Mexican restaurant in the United States, has carefully crafted the story of the restaurant's founding on its website and menus. According to the website, in 1923, Alejandro Borquez and his wife Rosa, Mexican immigrants from Sonora, a region of Northern Mexico, opened the Sonora Cafe. Two years later, inspired by the drawing of the figure of a man who looked like a *cholo* (the word *Californios* used at the time for farm workers) on a customer's menu, Borquez renamed the restaurant El Cholo Spanish Café. Alejandro and Rosa served dishes associated with Northern Mexico that were familiar to Anglo diners such as tamales, enchiladas, and flour *tortillas*. The El Cholo restaurants are designed with an haute hacienda look. They have stucco walls with murals of flowers and tropical fruit. Photographs of famous athletes decorate the walls. El Cholo uses visual cues such as stucco and adobe that remind diners of the Spanish Fantasy Past, while the image of Mexico presented is one that is highly stylized and theatrical. The waitresses wearing stereotypical flowered Mexican dresses, the photos of revolutionary hero Emiliano Zapata or the framed poster that says "Visit Mexico" with the image of a pretty, young *señorita* holding a basket of fruit on the wall, all evoke an idealized version of rural Mexico. El Cholo proudly displays its original menu of "Spanish-Mexican food" on its website featuring dishes such as *enchiladas, tamales,* and *chile con carne.* Today, El Cholo is more popular than ever with six locations throughout Southern California. In an era of innovative, modern Mexican cuisine, El Cholo has maintained its popularity with its standard Mexican-American cuisine, combination plates of enchiladas and *tacos*, oversized margaritas, and heaping baskets of chips and salsa. It even touts its success as an Angeleno institution on its cocktail napkins that proclaim, "I cannot imagine Los Angeles without El Cholo." In an era of corporate restaurant groups, sixth-generation family members run the restaurants today.

I have been teaching a class on Latino food culture in Los Angeles for several years at the University of Southern California. Every semester I send my students to visit El Cholo as part of an assignment on the history of whitewashing in Los Angeles. Nearly every semester they come back disappointed with the lack of "authenticity" of the food and feel that the ambience is one that is artificially created for Anglo or non-Latino customers. They observe great disparities between Mexican restaurants in non-Latino areas and restaurants they visit in Mexican neighborhoods, such as East L.A. and Boyle Heights, that serve regional cuisine or family-style cooking. In *"Comida Sin Par*. Consumption of Mexican Food in Los Angeles: 'Foodscapes' in a Transnational Consumer Society," Sylvia Ferrero argues that the adaptation of cultural and ethnic identity for the expectations of the Latino customer is part of the "dual life" of Mexican food in Los Angeles, one in which there is one cuisine for Mexican diners in East L.A. and Boyle Heights and another that has been adapted to the tastes of Anglo diners in upper-middle-class areas.[45] Not surprisingly, El Cholo's restaurants are located in non-Latino neighborhoods, areas that were—and still are—not threatening to diners looking for an experience that is "authentic," yet comfortable. Ferrero argues that restaurants like El Cholo function as exotic "staged" tourist sites where non-Mexican diners go to have a "'real' experience of Mexican food" and where they are "treated as foreigners."[46] El Cholo's menu includes dates that show when a dish was invented at the restaurant. For example, the menu displays 1959 as the year Carmen Rocha started making nachos at El Cholo, a dish she learned in her hometown of San Antonio, a dish, according to Pilcher, that was invented on the U.S.-Mexican border in the 1940s.[47] This timeline is a way for the restaurant to create connections to its historical past and market itself as more authentic.

Websites such as Thrillist attract readers with simplistic articles such as "The 16 Best Old-School Mexican Restaurants in L.A.," in which they list without distinction "Old-School" Mexican restaurants that have been in the city for at least twenty-five years. Arbitrary, ill-informed lists such as this one often include El Cholo, Cielito Lindo, Tito's Tacos, and Border Grill, discussed in the next chapter. Cielito Lindo is a stand that has been serving *taquitos* covered in avocado sauce since 1934. According to the website, Aurora Guerrero came to the United States from her native Zacatecas with her three young children to join her husband in the late 1920s. In the early 1930s the family worked different jobs on Olvera Street until Aurora received permission from Christine Sterling, Olvera Street's creator, to start her own business. Aurora developed a recipe for *taquitos* with avocado sauce. The website explains that the *taquitos* were "cooked at home and bundled in cloth to be carried to Olvera Street by trolley." Today, Cielito Lindo still makes the taquitos the same way, but I always find that they taste as if they have been cooked ahead of time and quickly reheated, a suspicion substantiated by an National Public Radio (NPR) interview in which current co-owner Diana Guerrero Robertson says that the taquitos "start at our warehouse in Lincoln Heights, where we make our *tortillas* fresh."[48] Cielito Lindo is influential because it "unleashed the first taco trend in American history, taquitos, the taco's rolled-up younger cousin."[49]

Cielito Lindo is located on one end of Olvera Street, a pedestrian street located at the original El Pueblo de Los Angeles. While Olvera Street is a symbol of the city's long history of whitewashing its Mexican past, it also has a dual life is a symbol of the city's long history of whitewashing its Mexican past, but it also has a dual life. Christine Sterling, a wealthy Anglo woman, designed it as an "authentic" Mexican marketplace in 1929 as part of an attempt to save the neglected Avila Adobe, a building built in 1818 by the Mexican mayor of Los Angeles. Sterling marketed her campaign as a way to preserve a structure that had once housed famous Americans. Wealthy, Anglo donors pitched in to preserve a valuable part of Los Angeles' history.[50] Today, Olvera Street has a number of Mexican restaurants, stalls, and tourist shops that sell souvenirs and kitsch that ranges from *lucha libre* masks to tacky T-shirts and children's guitars. Although Olvera Street originally primarily catered to Anglo visitors, over the years it has also come to represent the epicenter of Mexican culture in the city. Every year, important Mexican religious and secular holidays such as *Día de los Muertos* and Mexican Independence Day are celebrated there. While on most weekdays and average weekends, Olvera Street resembles a Disneyland version of a Mexican, when the Mexican and Mexican-American population fills the area on holidays it feels incredibly lively and—dare I say—authentic, as the plaza fills with Mexican music and dancing.

Among those that write about Mexican food in the United States, there has been a contentious debate over the authenticity of Olvera Street and restaurants such as El Cholo and Tito's Tacos, a taco stand from the 1960s discussed below. Purists argue that hard-shell *tacos* with iceberg lettuce, cheddar cheese, and sour cream, such as those found at Tito's Tacos, are inauthentic, but authenticity is not a quality inherent to certain foods; it is one that is socially constructed. It is something dynamic that varies depending on available ingredients, changes in technology, social class, and the influences of trade and travel. When Mexican immigrants arrived in the United States in the early part of the twentieth century, they did not find the wide variety of ingredients one finds today throughout Southern California such as Mexican sour cream, *queso fresco* (a semisoft fresh Mexican cheese served crumbled), and fresh corn *tortillas*. Instead, as Pilcher explains, in the United States, widespread industrial flour production and a lack of corn mills made wheat cheaper than corn, the staple used in *tortillas* found throughout Central and Southern Mexico. As a result, *tacos* were made with flour *tortillas*. Cheddar cheese was far more abundant than Mexican *queso fresco* and fresh lettuce was readily available.[51] Chefs and home cooks adapted their dishes to the ingredients available in the United States and to the Anglo appetite for large plates of food with the creation of the combo plate. The combination plate was invented in San Antonio when a restaurant started serving entrees alongside rice and beans, foods you would never find together on one plate in Mexico. This evolution is part of the invention of a mass-produced version of Mexican food for the U.S. market, one that succeeded in establishing "Mexican" restaurants across the country.

Are restaurants such as El Cholo inauthentic or do they represent the evolution of a regional Mexican cuisine? In 2010, I heard a radio interview with the Pulitzer Prize–winning food critic Jonathan Gold in which a caller asked what he thinks of restaurants such as Tito's Tacos. Surprisingly, Gold said he did not consider these places to be inauthentic. Instead, he argued that Tito's Taco's and El Cholo are authentic representations of what Mexican food has evolved into over centuries of a Mexican presence in Southern California. In fact, Gold went as far as to say that he considers Southern California to be a region of Mexico unto itself. When I heard Gold say this, I pulled my car over and listened closely. At the time, this statement seemed outrageous to me, but, as critic E. N. Anderson has stated, labels for cuisines such as French, Italian and American are "notoriously ambiguous." As Anderson observes, it is not possible to define foodways by national borders, and that between countries that border each other by land, such as the United States and Mexico, there has been "constant influence and borrowing."[52]

Editor of the *Orange County Weekly* and author of *Taco USA*, Gustavo Arellano's view of authenticity is even more unorthodox than Jonathan Gold's. Arellano, who delights in provocative, outrageous statements, wrote in a 2010 article that his postmodern stance on Mexican food now includes

> every manifestation of Mexican food … from the rarest Oaxacan *mole*, to a TacoBell deluxe-whatever to the Kogi taco, all Mexican food that calls itself Mexican, that can trace some part of its heritage to meals that in one way or another originated in Mexico is Mexican *and* authentic. How can it not be? Mexican food in all its manifestations is just a tasty extension of what the legendary Chicano scholar Américo Paredes once deemed "Greater Mexico": the idea that Mexico and its culture doesn't stop at the border.[53]

After reading Arellano's boundary-pushing article and hearing him make this argument in person, I reconsidered my own stance on authenticity. His use of the legendary folklorist Paredes' term "Greater Mexico" made sense. After all, California had been Mexico before it was ever part of the United States, but that was over a 150 years ago. I questioned some of what Arellano considered Mexican food: Sonora hot dogs in Tucson, the Mexican Hamburger in Denver, Southwestern Frito Pies, etc., but, at the same time, my view of "authentic" Mexican food evolved and expanded. I came to understand that globalized Mexican food, like Chinese food in the United States, means very different things to different people. In Los Angeles, historically Mexican food has had very different identities, meaning one thing to Anglo diners seeking an exotic experience, something very different to Mexican-Americans, and still something else to recent Mexican immigrants. None of it is inauthentic; instead different groups of people have very different understandings of "authentic" Mexican food. While these differences have certainly diminished in the past decade, a view of authenticity continues to be shaped by each person's background and set of experiences.

In "Was the Taco Invented in Southern California?" Jeffrey Pilcher explains that historically Mexican food in Los Angeles has varied depending on the part of the city in which it was located. Pilcher argues that early "taco franchises succeeded not by selling fast food but by marketing a form of exoticism that allowed nonethnics to sample Mexican cuisine without crossing lines of segregation in 1950s southern California."[54] These early taco shops were part of the city's historic racial divisions and show how Mexican food developed differently along racial boundaries. During the 1950s, Pilcher explains, restaurants with the word *taco* were located primarily outside of East L.A. and Boyle Heights in non-Hispanic areas on the Westside and in the San Fernando Valley.[55] Non-Mexicans who hoped to make money on the demand for *tacos* opened the taco houses. Starting in the 1950s, rather than using a traditional tortilla for their *tacos*, taco houses fried it into a crispy hard shell, a defining characteristic of Mexican cuisine in the United States for decades to come.

The rise of taco shops in Los Angeles occurred at the same time as the rise of fast food in Southern California. Southern California's claim to fame in food history comes, in large part, from having birthed fast food during the mid-twentieth century. During the 1950s through the 1970s, fast-food hot dogs, hamburgers, and *tacos* became staples in the American diet. Many Americans flocked to affordable chain restaurants, such as McDonald's and Taco Bell, to eat what in previous decades they would have eaten at a cart, wagon, or stationary truck. In the process, street food was eclipsed by fast food for many Americans. As Farley Elliot explains in his history of Los Angeles street food, "These fast-food chains often co-opted the same meals that had previously been considered street food staples, homogenizing and commodifying them until they looked a far sight from the original product."[56] The taco shops were no exception.

Taco Bell is perhaps the best example of the commodification of Mexican food in the United States, a process that standardized food production and made it more efficient.[57] To make money from the craze for the new fast-food dining experience, Glenn Bell opened a few Bell's Burgers between 1948 and 1950 in Southern California. When he opened one in San Bernardino across the street from a Mexican restaurant, he noticed its perpetually long lines. Sensing a business opportunity, Bell wanted to sell *tacos*, but didn't know how to make them. As Gustavo Arellano explains in *Taco USA*, Bell would go across the street to Mitla Café, a still-running Mexican restaurant that opened in 1937, famous for its hard shell, ground beef *tacos* covered in cheddar cheese, and return to his kitchen to try to copy them. The owner finally invited Bell into his kitchen to teach him how to make the taco shells.[58] Eventually, Bell, the persistent entrepreneur, developed a wire basket he used to fry up to six *tortillas* at a time.[59] After a few failed attempts at opening hamburger chains, in 1964 Bell opened his first Taco Bell in Downey, in what was at the time a white, suburban area of Los Angeles, an area of the city that today is primarily Latino. The rise of Taco Bell at the same time and place as other American fast-food giants such as McDonald's and Carl's Junior brought "Mexican" food into towns and cities across the country. Bell cleverly constructed his restaurants with a Mexican "theme park image using faux adobe walls" and a "mission-style bell tower" that gave its customers a sense of the restaurant's authenticity.[60]

Alongside Taco Bell, other "Mexican" fast-food restaurants sprang up with the new American suburbs during the 1950s and 1960s in Southern California. Tito's Tacos opened in 1959, located in the predominantly Anglo Westside Culver City location, Henry's Tacos opened in Studio City in 1961, and Lucy's Drive Thru Mexican and American Food opened in 1969. These places catered to the demand for an Anglo version of Mexican food—the fried taco shell loaded with ground beef, beans, lettuce, cheddar cheese, and a dollop of sour cream. They were meant to appeal to an Anglo palate and used ingredients both readily available and familiar to non-Latinos, substituting Mexican *queso fresco* for cheddar cheese and Mexican *crema* for sour cream. A few of these Mexican-American SoCal nonchain fast-food restaurants still exist in Los Angeles and are just as popular. Why? Even if I find these *tacos* bland and greasy, they represent a nostalgia for "Old-School" Cal-Mexican cuisine. As Bill Esparza writes in his "Taco Encyclopedia," "The crunchy taco? You'll find these across the country, but the zealous followers of local legends Tito's Tacos and Henry's Tacos know that Los Angeles is the original home of this Americanized favorite."[61]

The owners of El Cholo, Taco Bell, and Tito's Tacos were not the only ones to successfully capitalize on the Anglo desire for "authentic" Mexican cuisine without having to enter Mexican neighborhoods. At the same time that "Mexican" fast food was taking off in popularity in the 1950s and the 1960s, Mexican full-service dining catering to wealthy Anglos emerged. One of the pioneers of Mexican full-service dining in California was El Torito, a national chain that was one of the first to successfully market itself to wealthy Anglo customers. In 1954 Mexican-American Larry Cano, a World War II vet and East L.A. native, took over a defunct tiki bar in Encino, California, and turned it into El Torito, one of the largest Mexican restaurant chains in the United States. Cano, Gustavo Arellano explains, was "one of the few Mexicans to have an impact on Mexican food trends in the United States—in an industry notorious for seeing *gabachos* make billions off meals they copied from Mexican cooks and restaurateurs."[62] El Torito and other Mexican restaurants of the era no longer labeled themselves as Spanish or constructed idealized versions of a Mexican countryside. Instead, Cano created a more upscale dining experience that catered to Hollywood stars and other industry executives from the suburbs beyond the Hollywood studios with tableside guacamole and frozen margaritas, a cocktail Cano claimed to have been the first to popularize in the United States in a 2011 interview with Gustavo Arellano. As Arellano explains in an article entitled, "El Torito Founder Is Still the Big Enchilada,"

> It was his company that customized California-Mexican cuisine for mainstream consumption, taking the meals out of the barrios and fast-food dives of Southern California and into sit-down restaurants in areas across the country where customers didn't know how to pronounce the meals they waited for in hour-long lines.[63]

By the 1980s and 1990s, Mexican-American cuisine had become a staple across Southern California. Fast-food outlets such as Del Taco and Taco Bell competed with one another while full-service restaurants such as El Torito offered a dining experience complete with frozen margaritas. The California burrito, a flour tortilla packed with meat, cheese, beans and guacamole, emerged in the 1980s. By the mid-1990s, Chipotle founder Steve Ells brought San Francisco Mission-style, burritos to the masses and burritos became a national trend. Fast, casual chains such as Baja Fresh, Qdoba, and Chipotle opened across the country.

At the same time that Chipotle-style burritos were spreading across the country during the 1980s and 1990s, regional Mexican cuisine and other Latino cuisines began to grow in Southern California as more immigrants came from Mexican states such as Oaxaca, the Yucátan, Sinaloa, and Jalisco, and from Central American countries such as El Salvador, exposing Anglos and Latinos alike to a greater variety of cuisines. Non-Latino chefs, such as Mary Sue Milliken and Susan Feniger, were exposed to new flavors and dishes and began to experiment with regional Mexican cuisines at their own restaurants. In the next chapter, I explore the impact of regional cuisines on Los Angeles' burgeoning culinary landscape and the groundbreaking work of certain Latino chefs. I end by discussing a new generation of young, classically trained Mexican-American chefs whose cooking has been defined as "Alta California cuisine." While these chefs are influenced by the traditional Mexican food of their upbringing, the high-quality ingredients they use and their innovative techniques set them apart. Although critics and diners alike have received these chefs' cooking with great enthusiasm, discrimination toward Mexicans and Mexican-Americans has not completely disappeared. Some diners still see Mexican food as low-class and something that should never cost more than a few dollars. Technology, however, has revolutionized the way younger generations view food and dining. Nowadays, many young people read about food on social media or blogs and are willing to drive to Latino neighborhoods to eat at their favorite taco truck or to try a wonderful *mole*. The next two chapters explore, in part, the evolution of the city's Latino restaurants and *loncheras* (taco trucks).

Chapter 2

From Border Grill to Broken Spanish

The Evolution of Latino Cuisine in Los Angeles

During the 1980s and 1990s, Mexican cuisine was beginning to expand beyond the Mexican-American fast-food staples of the past few decades. Nationally, chefs began offering more culinary experiences that reflected traditional, regional Mexican cooking. This chapter explores the contributions of regional Mexican cuisine and its influence on non-Latino chefs. During the same period, thousands of Oaxacans immigrated to Los Angeles. This chapter also provides a background on the Mexican state of Oaxaca and its unique cuisine. It discusses the groundbreaking impact of Guelaguetza, the first well-known Oaxacan restaurant in Los Angeles and profiles other important Mexican chefs in Los Angeles, such as Gilberto Cetina, Jaime Martin del Campo, Ramiro Arvizu, and Rocío Camacho. It describes the challenges faced by Rocío Camacho, the only Mexican chef in recent decades to have broken traditional gender barriers and to have received acclaim from the city's food critics.

Mexican cuisine was not the only one to expand during the 1980s and 1990s. The arrival of a large number of Salvadorian immigrants during this period brought about a dramatic rise in the number of Salvadorian restaurants and *pupuserías*. This Central American cuisine has been present in Los Angeles for a shorter time and, as a result, has not become as familiar to non-Latino diners as Mexican cuisine. Finally, this chapter examines the gentrification of downtown Los Angeles, the Grand Central Market, and the many restaurants that opened in downtown Los Angeles since 2009. The chapter concludes by exploring the recent innovations of a group of young Mexican-American classically trained chefs who have applied the techniques of their culinary training and have used Southern California's fresh produce to recreate the traditional cuisine of their upbringing.

Rick Bayless was a pioneer among the non-Mexicans who first brought traditional Mexican dishes to a non-Mexican public. In 1987, Bayless, an Anglo chef from Oklahoma who had fallen in love with traditional Mexican cuisine, published his first cookbook *Authentic Mexican: Regional Cooking from the Heart of Mexico* after spending several years living in Mexico. In the same year, he opened Frontera Grill in Chicago, a restaurant specializing in regional Mexican cuisine. Two years later Bayless opened Topolobampo, one of Chicago's first fine-dining Mexican restaurants. He is also well known for his Mexican food show, *Mexico: One Plate at a Time*, now in its ninth season. But Bayless has also been a controversial figure in the Mexican restaurant world. In 2010, he came to Los Angeles to help inaugurate his latest Mexican restaurant, Red O. In an interview with a local television station, Bayless stated that he was opening a restaurant in Los Angeles because he was intrigued about "how the true flavors of Mexico, from central and southern Mexico, would play in Southern California." This was a ludicrous statement about a region that had been part of Mexico and one that had received immigrants from these regions of Mexico for nearly a century, and it incited outrage among other chefs and food critics.[1] Bayless's comment provoked a heated Twitter battle with culinary giant Jonathan Gold. Most recently, he sparked indignation when he was quoted in an NPR piece on culinary appropriation saying that the people who think that he cannot cook Mexican food because he is white are racists.[2] Despite his repeated insensitive comments, Bayless's contribution to elevating Mexican cuisine nationally at a time when it was known to the mainstream for burritos and combo plates is undeniable. In fact, when President Obama was running for office, he told reporters that when he and his wife wanted a night out on the town they ate at Bayless' restaurant, Topolobampo. Bayless' status as the Obamas' favorite chef speaks volumes for what he has done nationally for the reputation of Mexican cooking.

Rick Bayless was not the only Anglo chef to generate a greater understanding of traditional Mexican cuisine in the 1980s and early 1990s. During the early 1980s, classically trained chefs Susan Feniger and Mary Sue Milliken, a Jew from Toledo, Ohio and an Anglo woman, respectively, were having eye-opening experiences with Oaxacan and Yucatecan cuisine in the kitchens of the upscale French restaurants where they worked, and later at their own restaurant, City Café. In 1985, Milliken and Feniger decided they wanted to learn more about Mexican cuisine firsthand, so they loaded up a Volkswagen bug and took a road trip to Mexico. According to their website, the pair of intrepid female chefs spent a few months learning the "recipes and techniques of market vendors and home cooks, from street corners in downtown Mexico City to back road family barbecues and taco stands along the beach."[3] When they returned to Los Angeles, they opened Border Grill, a restaurant that was groundbreaking in its elevation of Mexican cuisine at a time when most diners still conceived of it as frozen margaritas, tortilla chips, and fajitas. Their original menu featured regional cuisine such as *chile rellenos* (a stuffed pepper usually filled with meat or cheese) and *panuchos* (crispy fried corn *tortillas* split and filled with black bean puree and shredded turkey, lettuce, pickled red onions, and a slice of avocadoes— a Yucatecan dish rarely seen on mainstream Mexican menus today), dishes that expanded Angelenos' culinary horizons. In *Taco USA*, Gustavo Arellano says that Susan Feniger and Mary Sue Milliken, were responsible for pushing "non-Mexican Los Angeles into unfamiliar terrain."[4] After a few years, Feniger and Milliken relocated Border Grill to Santa Monica's 4th Street, the restaurant's location since 1989. The Santa Monica location is in the center of a major tourist destination and local shopping district, attracting lunchtime office workers, after-work happy-hour customers, and people out on weekend nights. Its neon exterior signage and the bright orange color and geometric designs of the interior are striking and make the restaurant feel lively and vibrant. There are graffiti-like faces, planets, and coyotes decorating the walls and ceilings. Border Grill also practices sustainable purchasing of ingredients, uses organic rice and black beans, and seasonal, locally sourced ingredients whenever possible, an easy task as they are located just steps away from one of the country's largest farmers' markets.

As female trailblazers, Feniger and Milliken contributed to changing Los Angeles' culinary landscape, not only in their restaurants but also on television. Beginning in 1995, they starred in nearly 400 episodes of "Too Hot Tamales," a Food Network cooking show that featured simple dishes from around the world. Many cookbooks and, later, a food truck followed. The Border Grill food truck is one of my favorite stops when shopping at the Wednesday farmers' market in Santa Monica for a quick gourmet taco. Writer Gustavo Arellano places Feniger and Milliken in the Diane Kennedy-Rick Bayless cosmos of authenticity: chefs who claim to replicate the "authentic" flavors and dishes of rustic Mexico. Jonathan Gold seems to echo Arellano's sentiments in a review of Border Grill when he says, "Not riffs on Mexican food, or chiefly reinterpretations of Mexican food, but the real thing."[5] But while they may have started out in the Kennedy-Bayless camp, I do not believe their assertions still hold completely true today. On a recent dining expedition, I found that while there were many Mexican regional dishes on the menu such as *cochinita pibil* (Yucatán slow-roasted pork), and *pescado veracruzano* (a classic fish dish made with tomatoes, capers, and olives), the menu also included pan-Latin adaptations such as "quinoa fritters" with Cotija cheese, a blend of Peruvian and Mexican ingredients, and plantain empanadas.

A few years after Border Grill took off in the mid-1980s, regional Mexican cuisine prepared by Mexican chefs began to gain a greater foothold in the

Angelino culinary landscape. Oaxacan cuisine is one of the best examples of a regional cuisine that started to appear throughout the city as more Oaxacans immigrated to Southern California. The southern state of Oaxaca is one of Mexico's economically poorest, but it is also one of its culturally richest with sixteen different cultural and linguistic groups that have their own distinct cuisines. Oaxaca is famous for its *moles, queso oaxaqueño* (a round, white, soft cheese), mescal (an alcoholic beverage made from the maguey plant), corn, and chocolate. The large populations of Zapotecs, Mixtecs, and other indigenous groups have shaped the cuisine over thousands of years. Mexican cookbook author and pioneering chronicler of traditional Mexican cuisine, Diane Kennedy profiled the cuisine in her 2010 book, *Oaxaca al gusto: An Infinite Gastronomy*. Kennedy, long considered the Julia Child of Mexico, spent decades traveling the Mexican countryside, meeting home cooks, and searching for recipes and new dishes after she moved to Mexico from England with her husband in 1957.

In *Oaxaca al gusto: an Infinite Gastronomy*, Kennedy discusses a few ingredients that are central to Oaxacan cuisine: corn, chilies, and chocolate. She explains that chocolate's integral role in Oaxacan social and religious customs makes it an essential ingredient.[6] It can be made with water, known as *agua de chocolate*, or milk and served as a frothy drink prepared with a wooden frother called a *molinillo*. Three thousand years ago, during the time of the Olmec civilization, women first began to grind cacao beans into a paste and mix them with water. Much later, during the Aztec civilization of the twelfth through the fifteenth centuries, *xocolatl*—the Nahuatl word for *cacao nibs*—was reserved as a drink only for the nobles, priests, and warriors and was served in ornate clay drinking vessels. In fact, cacao nibs were so valuable they were used as a form of currency. Chocolate also had medicinal properties and was reported to be an energy booster, mood enhancer, and even an aphrodisiac. Legend has it that Montezuma drank his chocolate "from a gold goblet because he believed it made him more charming and attractive to women."[7]

Although the Aztecs used chocolate only as a beverage, yet today it is a key ingredient in many *moles. Mole* represents the pinnacle of the Mexican cooking tradition and is considered by many to be Mexico's national dish, but few of its ingredients were indigenous to the New World beyond chilies and chocolate.[8] The first known *mole* was *mole poblano* from the colonial Mexican city of Puebla. As an iconic dish, *mole* has a creation tale. The story goes that in the late seventeenth century Dominican nuns at the Convent of Santa Rosa were busy preparing for the bishop's visit when chocolate accidentally spilled from a shelf into the pot below.[9] The reality, however, is not so simple. The ingredients for *mole* have both medieval Spanish and pre-Columbian roots. Today, there are has many regional varieties and some *moles* have as many as thirty different ingredients. It takes countless hours to pound and grind the spices, nuts, chilies, and seeds in a *molcajete* (Mexico's version of the mortar and pestle) or at a communal mill. Over time, the region of Oaxaca became famous is for its variety of delicious *moles* and came to be known as the land of the seven *moles*. Oaxacan *moles* include *mole negro*, the most widely known in the United States and reputedly the most complex, a sauce made with dark chocolate, cinnamon, cloves, cumin, cilantro, and herbs; *mole coloradito* is made with mashed ripe plantains along with many other ingredients; *mole amarillo* lacks chocolate, dried fruit, and other sweeteners, which makes it spicier than most and is thickened with *masa harina* (corn flour); while *mole verde* gets its flavor and color from pumpkin seeds, cilantro, tomatillos, and jalapeños.

As more Oaxacan immigrants arrived in Southern California during the 1980s and 1990s, *moles* and other Oaxacan specialties became more widely available to Mexicans and non-Mexicans alike, a dramatic shift from the racial divisions of previous decades. Oaxacan immigrants came to the Central Valley and Los Angeles during the 1990s in search of economic opportunity after the passage of the North American Free Trade Agreement (NAFTA). Oaxaca is one of the poorest states in Mexico and it has the largest indigenous population. Historically, other Mexicans have discriminated against Oaxacans for centuries for being indigenous and speaking native languages. Many of the Oaxacans who came to Los Angeles were often uneducated and spoke limited Spanish. They continued to face discrimination from other Mexicans in the United States and, as a result, formed their own separate enclaves on the city's Westside in Venice, Santa Monica, and Culver City. Today, all of Los Angeles is sprinkled with hundreds of Oaxacan restaurants, food trucks, and bakeries. My family's Sunday favorite is El Sazón Oaxaqueño, located in a small strip mall near our house next to a Oaxacan bakery that serves fresh *pan dulce*. It serves delicious, fresh *mole* enchiladas, *tlayudas* (a large, thin, crunchy tortilla covered with refried beans, Oaxacan cheese, lettuce, avocado and other toppings), and *empanadas de huitlacoche* (a pastry stuffed with corn smut), but there is nothing particularly unique about this restaurant. A Yelp search with the word Oaxacan food turns up 274 Oaxacan restaurants for Los Angeles, but there are probably far more. Los Angeles is home to approximately 70,000 Oaxacans, but other reports estimate the city's population to be as high as 200,000.[10] There is even a name for Los Angeles' Oaxacan community, Oaxacalifornia, a fitting title considering it is now the third most important center of Oaxacan cooking in the world, after Oaxaca City and Mexico City.[11]

Fernando Lopez was one of the Oaxacan immigrants who came to Los Angeles in the 1990s in search of job opportunities when the peso devalued, leaving behind his wife and daughters in Mexico until he could afford for them to make the expensive and dangerous journey. In 1994, Lopez opened a street stall selling Oaxacan staples in "the heart of the emerging Oaxacatown."[12] Sensing a business opportunity, Lopez decided to open Guelaguetza, a Oaxacan restaurant that would serve the growing community. The restaurant's name Guelaguetza refers to an annual festival that takes place in July in Oaxaca. The word in the Zapotec language means *offering*. The restaurant was an offering to the Oaxacan community at a time when there were no other restaurants of this level of sophistication specializing in Oaxacan cuisine. As Jonathan Gold explains, "When Guelaguetza came along ... it wasn't that local Oaxacan food had never existed, or that regional Mexican cooking had never existed here ... but that the cooking was fully formed, and available in what seemed like all its stunning range."[13] A couple of months after it opened, Jonathan Gold reviewed Guelaguetza for the *LA Times,* writing that "at Guelaguetza you'll find the sort of Oaxacan dishes you've only read about in travel magazines." These include *mole negro, mole coloradito, tlayudas,* banana-leaf-wrapped tamales, and *chapulines* (grasshoppers). Of all Guelaguetza's dishes Gold describes, it is his description of the black *mole* that would have inspired me to make an immediate trip to Guelaguetza in 1994.

> But the black *mole,* based on ingredients the restaurant brings up from Oaxaca, is extraordinary, rich with chopped chocolate and burnt grain, undertones of toasted chile, wave upon wave of textured spice ... and so much better than other *moles* locally available ... that it is almost like seeing a Diego Rivera mural up close for the first time after years of seeing nothing but reproductions.[14]

Gold's review established Guelaguetza's reputation among Anglo diners, although, interestingly, the Spanish-language media and non-Oaxacan Mexicans ignored the restaurant for many years.

After his initial success, Lopez made the bold decision to take over an "ornate, palatial building" that had housed a Korean restaurant in the middle of Koreatown, the largest enclave of Koreans outside Korea.[15] Even today, the large, bright orange restaurant seems out of place as you drive through Koreatown. Guelaguetza serves a variety of Oaxacan specialties, such as *mole negro, rojo,* and *coloradito, tlayudas, memelas* (toasted corn dough cakes topped with fresh ingredients), and *empanadas* (handmade corn tortilla folded and stuffed with cheese, squash blossoms, or other ingredients). Lines quickly formed outside the restaurant and, as Gustavo Arellano points out in *Taco USA,* it was not just Oaxacans coming to eat there. Many Oaxacans worked as nannies for wealthy American families and invited the Americans to try their food and see their culture. "Soon Mercedes and BMWs parked near *Guelaguetza.*"[16] Over the years, Fernando Lopez developed a mini-empire with six restaurants around the city. He also published a newspaper for Oaxacan immigrants in Los Angeles, *El Oaxaqueño*. But when the recession hit in 2008, he realized his business was overextended. He closed all his restaurants except the original flagship one and put his college-educated children in charge of the finances. Despite these challenging years, Guelaguetza is more popular than ever and its customer base has continued to expand. These days, young hipsters visit Guelaguetza in search of "authentic" *mole* and *chapulines a la mexicana* (grasshoppers sautéed with onions, jalapeños, and tomatoes). Bricia Lopez, the owner's daughter who now runs the restaurant, explained the appeal in an interview with the *New Yorker*. "Eating grasshoppers is a thing you do here," she explained. "Like, 'Oh, my God, I ate a grasshopper, *woo*.'" For the younger diners, there's more of a "cool factor involved."[17] On weekend nights, the Mexican community fills up the cavernous space with a crowd that comes to dance to the live music on its

Guelaguetza exterior. Photo courtesy of Ben Portnoy.

Guelaguetza Mural of Children. Photo courtesy of Ebony Bailey.

stage. Over the years, Guelaguetza has become a favorite weekend nightspot known for its lengthy list of Oaxacan mescal and chili-infused *micheladas.*

In an interview with the *LA Times,* Lopez's children said that despite so many years in the United States, Lopez never acculturated. He spent most of his time around other Oaxacans and wanted to reside again in his native land. Once his children were grown, he made plans to return to Oaxaca for good. Since he once ran a restaurant for Oaxacans homesick for their native cuisine in Los Angeles, when he returned to Mexico in 2014 he opened a restaurant for Oaxacans who had returned and missed American food, a California-style burger joint he called Pink Burger in his hometown of Mitla, a town with an archaeological site nearly an hour from Oaxaca City. While Lopez was back in Mexico, his restaurant received its highest American honor. In 2015, Guelaguetza was the first traditional Mexican restaurant to win a James Beard Classics award, a category the Beard Foundation recognizes for regional restaurants that have been in business for at least ten years and have made significant contributions to their community. Mexican food journalist Bill Esparza noted in the *Los Angeles Magazine* that it was the first time that an "authentic" Mexican food restaurant had received this prestigious award.[18] The reward recognizes not only the quality of Guelaguetza's food but also its role in creating a vibrant Oaxacan culinary culture in Los Angeles, one located in the heart of Koreatown, reflecting the diversity of cultures that make up Los Angeles.

Soon, other chefs were inspired by Lopez and Guelaguetza and opened restaurants featuring traditional regional Mexican cuisine. In 1999, Jaime Martin del Campo and Ramiro Arvizu opened La Casita Mexicana in Bell, a working-class Mexican neighborhood of Los Angeles. Both chefs hail from the Mexican state of Jalisco. Ramiro grew up in his grandmother's home in the town of Tecolotlán, Jalisco. In an interview, Ramiro recounted nostalgically how he helped his grandmother in the kitchen from a young age. He would kill the chickens, find the right leaves for her to prepare *tamales*, and bring her the *nixtamal* (limed kernels of corn ready to be ground into *masa*) to make *tortillas* for his grandmother's *cenaduría* (small family owned restaurant). Most of all, Ramiro said that he observed her secrets, her magic culinary art of making *tamales*, and learned a tremendous amount about cooking and eating well from her. When Ramiro was a teenager he moved to Los Angeles to be with his parents. They owned El Indio, a small Mexican restaurant and tortilla factory in Culver City in the 1970s where Ramiro's job was to count the *tortillas*. After graduating high school, Ramiro studied travel management at a technical school. He spent the next seventeen years working in sales for Aero México Airlines. Through his job with the airlines, he became well acquainted with Mexico's regional cuisines.

Ramiro's business partner Jaime grew up in the southern Jaliscan town of Tototlán. During college, he studied tourism because, at the time, it was the only way in Mexico to study cooking, his true passion. Eventually, Jaime went to work for the Indonesian airlines, Garuda. It was then that the two Jaliscan natives met in Los Angeles at one of Jaime's famous potluck parties. The Mexican dishes that Jaime made for the party really impressed Ramiro and he suggested to Jaime that they open a restaurant together that served some of the Mexican food that they missed living in Los Angeles. In 1999, Jaime and Ramiro opened a small restaurant in distant Bell because it was the only location they could afford. At first, they called their restaurant Cenaduría la Casita Mexicana, but later it just became La Casita Mexicana. Although the vibrant walls with brightly painted wooden fruit and decorative tiles made the space inviting, much of the local Mexican-American population was not familiar with many of the flavors and would complain. Jaime and Ramiro slowly educated their customers about traditional Mexican cuisine. Eventually, their customers developed an appreciation for their complex dishes and they began to serve specialties such as *queso azetca* (four different Mexican cheeses filled with poblano chili slices, cactus, mushroom, and Mexican herbs wrapped in plantain leaves), *chile en nogada* (a complicated dish of pepper filled with cream and pomegranates, said to be Mexico's national dish because it represents the Mexican flag with its red, green, and white colors), and tortilla chips served with three different *moles*, *mole poblano*, *mole verde* (a *mole* made with toasted ground pumpkin seeds, tomatillos, and a Mexican herb, *epazote*), and a pistachio *mole*. They prided themselves on only using high-quality, fresh ingredients. They grow the herbs and greens they use in a small garden behind the restaurant and make their own cheese and chorizo in house. In fact, during my interview at their restaurant, they showed me the big pots of bubbling chorizo on the stove in the kitchen.

When I asked Jaime and Ramiro why they do not specialize in regional Mexican cuisine as other Mexican chefs in Los Angeles have done, they replied that they consider themselves Mexicans before Jaliscans and while they do serve some specialties of Jalisco, their goal is to serve excellent traditional Mexican cuisine from many different regions. They consider it their job to promote Mexican gastronomy to as many people as possible. Their goal is to take diners on a culinary journey not only to Jalisco, but throughout Mexico. They have served as Mexican culinary ambassadors through their many years of television cooking programs. With their exuberant, warm personalities, Jaime and Ramiro became the darlings of Spanish-language media, appearing regularly on the food segment of first Univisión and later Telemundo's morning talk shows. The popular duo appeared for two seasons as the judges on "Top Chef Estrellas," the Spanish-language version of Bravo's long-running competitive cooking program. Jaime and Ramiro told me that in the near future they are going to be featured on a National Geographic program on Latino cuisine.

Chef Jaime Martín Del Campo of Mexicano. Photo courtesy of Ebony Bailey.

I first met Jaime and Ramiro when I contacted them about bringing my students to La Casita Mexicana for a cooking class and a meal in 2010. They invited me to come and meet them. As we chatted, servers brought out samples from nearly every dish on the menu, along with their wonderful churros for dessert. It was a culinary tour de force I will never forget. Since then, it has become one of my favorite Mexican restaurants in Los Angeles, one to which I return often with family and friends. Despite their fame among Mexicans of all different backgrounds, they still seemed pretty unknown to non-Latinos when I first started visiting in 2009, although they told me that some Anglo foodies started to make the trek out to Bell a few years after they opened. In 2012, thirteen years after opening, Jaime and Ramiro expanded their tiny restaurant by taking over the lease on an adjacent store. By this point, the restaurant had become a dining destination. The expanded restaurant with soaring ceiling and wooden beams was more festive and had room for a store that sells Mexican candies, *mole*, and Day of the Dead figures. For several years, I brought my students for cooking classes at La Casita Mexicana. Jaime and Ramiro enthusiastically told the students about each dish, how to prepare it, and showed them the ingredients. The students learned to make *tacos de canasta* (literally, basket *tacos*, the soft, steamed *tacos* sold on the streets in Mexico stacked in cloth covered baskets), *tamales*, and a few different *salsas*. They loved the hands-on experience and enjoyed a wonderful meal afterward.

After more than fifteen years at La Casita Mexicana, Jaime and Ramiro wanted to try something new. They had waited a long time and were ready for a new, more centrally located restaurant that would serve a wider community. In early 2015, they opened Mexicano, a large, upscale restaurant, and Flautas, a takeout stand, in the Baldwin Hills Crenshaw Mall in South Central, the center of a historically African-American community that in recent decades had become home to many Central American immigrants. In his review of Mexicano, Jonathan Gold calls it their "big-statement restaurant" but without some of the touches "that might not appeal to non-Mexican palates" found at La Casita Mexicana.[19] Gone were the tortilla chips served with three different *moles* as well as a few of my favorite dishes from La Casita Mexicana. For example, the *queso fundido azteca* made with four different Mexican cheeses and filled with *nopal* and *poblano chile* slices had been replaced with a plainer *queso fundido* (melted cheese dish). When I asked Jaime and Ramiro about the changes to the menu, they said that they needed to start out gently with their customers, just as they had done seventeen years earlier at La Casita Mexicana. They said that since several diners had complained about the *mole*, they had replaced it with a mild puree of pinto beans with a sprinkling of Cotija cheese, changes to the menu that were meant to attract a wider clientele. Jaime and Ramiro explained that for customers who are unfamiliar with traditional Mexican cuisine, their food is like Nahuatl, an exotic language that is hard to pronounce at first. So, they were introducing new dishes and flavors little by little. As I looked around the restaurant on a Saturday afternoon, I saw a more diverse clientele than at La Casita Mexicana. The customers were roughly 60% African-American and the other 40% were a mix of Anglos and Latinos. For the moment, Jaime and Ramiro are busy between the two restaurants and their television appearances. When I asked Jaime about his long-term plans, he said his dream was to have a Mexican cooking school in downtown Los Angeles where he could train future chefs in Mexican cuisine and cooking techniques.

Chichén Itzá is another L.A. restaurant specializing in traditional Mexican cuisine that opened around the same time as La Casita Mexicana. It is located inside the Mercado de la Paloma, a warehouse converted into a cooperative market with shops and restaurants located just blocks from the USC campus and a short distance from downtown Los Angeles. The restaurant is named for the famous Maya temple complex and most well-known symbol of Maya culture. Chef Gilberto Cetina owns Chichén Itzá and runs it with his son Gilberto Cetina Jr., who now operates the restaurant while his father spends part of the year back in Mérida. In an interview with Chef Cetina Jr., he told me that his father learned to cook from his mother in his hometown of El Cuyo, a small town located between Mérida and Cancun built to house the workers of an American wood mill company. The elder Cetina's mother

Chile relleno at Mexicano Restaurant. Photo courtesy of Ebony Bailey.

ran a *fonda*, a small, economical restaurant, and was known as the cook of the town. Later on, Cetina's family relocated to Mérida, the region's capital, where he trained as an engineer and began to raise a family. When Cetina decided to relocate his family to the United States in 1986, he chose a different career path. He worked in restaurants for many years where he learned about the business until he was finally able to open his own. Cetina Sr. grew up in both Mexico and the United States. He lived in Morelia until the age of six and later returned to Mexico with his family from the ages of thirteen to twenty, formative years for him; when I asked him if he identifies more as Mexican or American he replied Mexican without hesitation.

Since Chef Gilberto Cetina Sr. opened Chichén Itzá in 2001, he has been elevating Yucatecan cuisine to a level not found elsewhere in Los Angeles and probably few places outside of Mexico, for that matter. The Yucatán is known for its unique cuisine that has been shaped by its distinct Spanish, Maya, and Lebanese culinary heritages. The menu reflects these diverse culinary influences with dishes such as Lebanese *kibi* (ground beef and cracked wheat patties), *panuchos*, and tamales that are only found in the Yucatán such as *brazo de reina* (literally meaning queen's arm, a *tamal* filled with hard-boiled eggs) and *tamal colado*. Chef Cetina is not afraid to sprinkle his menu with Maya words such as *tikin-xic* (fish fillets marinated in achiote and lime juice), and *cochinita pibil* (a traditional, slow-roasted pork dish of Maya origin). I have found dishes there that I have only eaten at traditional restaurants or markets in the Yucatán, such as *papadzules* (*tortillas* moistened in a pumpkin seed sauce stuffed with hard-boiled eggs and topped with tomato sauce). Dining at Chichén Itzá makes me nostalgic for beach vacations with my husband's family in the Yucatán where we sit in the hot sun consuming large amounts of delicious, homemade *panuchos* and drinking cold beer. Apparently I am not the only one to feel this way. Pulitzer Prize-winning food critic Jonathan Gold wrote that after eating at Chichén Itzá he went home and booked—"actually booked-an air ticket to the Yucatán." Gold calls Chichén Itzá "the most serious Yucatecan kitchen in town." Clearly, Chichén Itzá has made quite an impression on Gold since the restaurant is always on his list of Los Angeles' "101 Best Restaurants."[20]

In our interview, Cetina Jr. told me that there had been Yucatecan restaurants in Los Angeles for quite a long time before they opened. He recounted that in the 1970s there was one called El Nuevo Yucatán and before that there was one in Pasadena, but until about ten or fifteen years ago these restaurants were little known beyond isolated pockets of Yucatecan immigrants. When I asked Cetina Jr. how he thought Chichén Itzá had contributed to elevating the level of regional Mexican cuisine in Los Angeles, he explained that he and his father have taken a lot of time to think about their execution of traditional recipes. He gave me the example of his innovative method of preparing one of their most elaborate dishes, *cochinita pibil*. Gilberto explained that he cooks the pork as "slowly as humanly possible." He marinates it for 24 to 36 hours and then puts it in a cold oven for ten hours with a tray of hot ashes underneath it. Cetina Jr. said that this process raises the temperature to 500 degrees, but then it quickly drops to 185 degrees. By cooking it this way, he mimics the traditional method of cooking *cochinita pibil* in a pit, a process that gives it smokiness and makes it more "authentic." The very word *pibil* is Mayan for "cooked underground." Gilberto developed this technique after he read about a high-end Yucatecan restaurant in Mérida that built an oven that mimics cooking underground with stones. While many Mexican chefs of his generation are embracing modern Mexican cuisine, Cetina Jr. says he prefers to serve traditional dishes. He says the changes he has made are in his cooking techniques, such as employing the sous-vide preparation, but that customers are not even aware of them.

When I asked Gilberto why he thinks there has been a rise in interest in regional Mexican cuisine, he said he thought that the food trucks were the ones to break the ice. He explained,

> You can get good food anywhere now. When people have visitors from out of town, they come here (Mercado de la Paloma) and the Grand Central Market. They are no longer looking for a high-end dining experience. Los Angeles really pioneered that shift. Now you can find a little hole in the wall with high-quality ingredients in an unpretentious setting.

As a result of this shift, diners have become more interested in regional cuisine. Cetina Jr. added with pride, "Los Angeles has embraced regional Mexican cuisine and Angelenos are hungry and eager to explore places such as Chichén Itzá." I have witnessed Chichén Itzá's growing popularity since I first ate there in 2008. Over the years, I have brought many groups of students to eat there. The chefs have done cooking demonstrations for my students and lectured them on Yucatecan cuisine. In recent years, Cetina and his son have published a cookbook—*Sabores Yucatecos: A Culinary Tour of the Yucatán*, bottled their own salsa, and taught regular cooking classes at the market. When I asked Gilberto why, given their never-ending lines, they do not expand to a bigger location, he said that they believe in the cooperative concept of the Mercado de la Paloma and want to support it. It offers moderate rent and small-business training and for people like his father, not trained in how to run a restaurant, this support was vital to their ability to succeed. However, he did say he is looking at opportunities to expand to a second location with a similar concept in the coming years.

During the weekdays, Chichén Itzá is packed at lunchtime with office workers and USC employees. On the weekends, I have noticed that it is more of a family destination, attracting both Latino families and non-Latinos. When Chichén Itzá first opened, their customers were almost exclusively Mexican and, in fact, Cetina Jr. said that 90% of customers were families of Yucatecan descent until word got out around USC, located just a few blocks away. Gilberto explained that USC has been fantastic for their growth and for spreading the word about Chichén Itzá to a different demographic. Over the years I have brought hundreds of students to eat there and they have returned with their friends. Others have done the same. Cetina Jr. also pointed out that over the last five years, their customers have become less Latino and more Anglo. While he feels indebted to the Yucatecans who supported the restaurant in its early years, he is thrilled with the recent success and looks forward to his next endeavor.

Another L.A. chef to feature regional Mexican cuisine at her restaurants is Rocío Camacho, a Oaxacan native of Mixtec origin, "an indigenous civilization distinguished by artistry, pride and independence." Traits that, journalist Daina Solomon notes in her interview for the *LA Weekly*, Camacho has exhibited at the many Mexican restaurants where she has worked since moving to Los Angeles at the age of nineteen.[21] I interviewed Camacho at her restaurant Rocío's Mexican Kitchen in Bell Gardens, a working-class Latino city in Los Angeles County. I have eaten at two or three of her restaurants over the past several years, driving long distances to try her food, but this was the first time I met her in person. She is a small, dynamic woman who was eager to share her story.

Rocío Camacho was raised in Huajuapan de León, Oaxaca, a small, rural city, where she learned to cook from her mother. Her mother had a *fonda* inside the market. As a young child Camacho would pester her mother, but eventually she started helping her make *chile relleno* and other dishes. For Camacho, learning how to cook from her mother *fue un placer* (was a pleasure). She learned to make several dishes that are typical of her region of Oaxaca, including *chilate*, a chicken soup with *chile* costeño (an orange-reddish colored chili of low heat related to the *guajillo* chili) and *chile ajo*, a stew of pork ribs with a chili and garlic sauce. Camacho arrived at Los Angeles in 1997 and began working at a restaurant in Bell Gardens. Next, chefs Jaime and Ramiro hired her to work at the brand-new La Casita Mexicana. She developed a warm relationship with the chefs during her apprenticeship. They gave her the freedom to cook Oaxacan dishes that were different from the Jaliscan ones from their own background. Camacho stayed at La Casita Mexicana for five years until she was hired to be the head chef at La Huesteca, an upscale restaurant in an outdoor Mexican mall. She worked there for seven years until she had the chance to run her own restaurant with a business partner.

In 2009, Camacho opened Moles La Tía in East L.A. At Moles La Tía, Rocío had the opportunity to be truly experimental. She made as many as twenty-five different *moles*, both traditional and invented ones, including *mole de mango*, passion fruit *mole*, *mole de finas hierbas* (fine herbs) with frog legs, *mole* with pistachios, toasted coffee bean *mole*, mescal, and even *nopal* (cactus) *mole*. Since *moles* require countless hours of preparation, this was no small feat. Camacho describes her time at Moles La Tía as a wonderful experience. It was when she first received widespread recognition for her cooking from the food critics. Jonathan Gold wrote in a 2009 review, "In just a few months, La Tía has already established itself as one of the most serious Mexican restaurants in Los Angeles" known for its "complexity and deftness, imaginative use of local and imported ingredients, and skill in translating traditional, Pre-Colombian flavors for the 21st-century palate."[22] Like his review of the black *mole* at Guelaguetza fifteen years earlier, Gold's review of Camacho's black *mole* lingers in one's memory for its sensuous and ekphrastic description. He describes it as "so dark that it seems to suck the light out of the airspace around it, spicy as a *novela* and bitter as tears, a *mole* whose aftertaste can go on for hours." It is a *mole* that is "so glossy and rich that I am always tempted to test its consistency by stabbing an index finger into it, and the resulting stain lingers as long as the empurpled digits of patriotic Iraqi voters."[23]

Jonathan Gold's review and others catapulted Moles La Tía to the attention of the Anglo market. Camacho told me that the Anglo market really

Chef Rocíio Camacho with the author.

appreciated her food and recounted with great pride the long lines of Anglo-Americans waiting for a table. "We even ran out of food," she said. Even though Moles La Tía was in Latino East L.A., she said there were always more Anglos dining there than Latinos. Camacho stayed at Moles la Tía for three years, but after she began to have problems with her business partner she decided it was time to leave. In 2012, she opened Rocío's Mole de los Dioses with a partner in Bell and soon after opened a second location in Sun Valley, a neighborhood in the far reaches of the San Fernando Valley. Anglo diners frequented the Sun Valley location and it got positive reviews. In 2014 Rocío's Mole de los Dioses was included in Jonathan Gold's list of top 101 restaurants. The restaurant's namesake *mole—mole de los dioses* (*mole* of the gods)—is named for a *mole* she prepares with *huitlacoche* (a fungus that grows on corn and is considered a delicacy in Mexico). This particular *mole* earned Camacho the nickname of the "goddess of *mole*" or "*mole* queen" among food critics.

During the summer of 2015, thieves broke into the Sun Valley restaurant and torched the kitchen, destroying hundreds of thousands of dollars of uninsured equipment in an act of arson.[24] Despite the latest setback, Camacho did not give up. Instead, she decided it was time to run a restaurant of which she was the sole proprietor. She had opened Rocío's Mexican Kitchen, a small restaurant with a takeout window near her home in Bell Gardens a month before the robbery. Bell Gardens is a city in Los Angeles County that is

Mole negro at Rocíio's Mexican Kitchen in Bell Gardens. Photo courtesy of Ebony Bailey.

95% Latino according to the latest census. Even though this time Camacho
is cooking for a Latino customer base, she continues to receive glowing
reviews from the media. Besha Rodell, food critic for the *LA Weekly*, wrote
a 2015 article titled "In a city with astoundingly good Mexican food, Rocío
Camacho's Mexican Kitchen serves some of the best."[25] I could not agree
more. Her *mole negro* was rich and spicy with a certain flavor I could not
place and did ask her to divulge. The *chile relleno* was light and flavorful and
the *tacos de cazuela*, shredded meat or chicken served in a small hot cooking
pot along with *salsas* and wonderful handmade *tortillas*, were flavorful and
innovative in its presentation.

Camacho is an interesting chef to profile because she is the only Latina
chef to have received this level of recognition in Los Angeles and because she
has worked her way up through the ranks of restaurant kitchens despite over-
whelming obstacles. Not only is she is a woman in a man's world, she is also
Mexican, indigenous, and speaks little English. She recounted to me, "Male
chefs have more opportunities than women. When I arrived at La Huasteca
I was told they would rather hire a man. But I can do the job of a man. I can
lift heavy soup pots and boxes." I asked her if she thought it would have been
easier to succeed as a woman in Mexico and she replied without hesitancy
that it has been more challenging in the United States than it would have been
in Mexico by leaps and bounds. "Mexico has many famous women chefs and
it was not as difficult for them as it was for me here. Friends suggested that
I come back to Mexico, but I wanted to stay here and keep trying." Camacho
seemed content running her small neighborhood restaurant during the day and
working evenings at a downtown Mexican restaurant, but I could see the glint
in her eyes. This is a tough, ambitious woman who knows that this is just a
temporary stop on her way to bigger plans and dreams.

A later but no less important player in the recent development of the
L.A. Mexican food landscape is Armando de la Torre. Armando had been
a very successful real estate agent in Los Angeles for decades when he
decided to open a Mexican restaurant in 2010. In an interview with Armando,
I asked him what inspired this midlife career change. He told me that at the
time he had just lost everything in a bitter divorce —"the big house, the
nice car, everything." When his new girlfriend asked him what he wanted
to do with the rest of his life, he told her that his dream had always been to
own a Mexican restaurant. She said he should do it. He was fifty years old
and had nothing to lose. Armando had grown up in Los Angeles eating his
mother's Mexican food and had always loved cooking. His mother was from
Hermosillo, a city in the northern Mexican state of Sonora near the border
with Arizona, and his father was from Aguas Calientes. Even though his
mother was from Northern Mexico, she prepared elaborate dishes from all
over Mexico for her five children: *mole, calabacitas, cochinita pibil*, etc.

Armando recounted that one of his fondest childhood memories was helping his mother in the kitchen. He recalls spending countless hours separating out the rocks from the beans to make *frijoles*. As an adult, he loved to cook for family and friends. He said that at parties he was always the one in the kitchen doing the cooking. During his divorce, he spent a lot of time at the restaurant of his close friend Ricardo Díaz, chef and owner of a few well-regarded L.A. Mexican restaurants. Díaz told him he would help him if he ever decided to open his own restaurant. A few months later, when there was a vacancy at a former restaurant space Armando's father owns in Boyle Heights, Armando decided to give the restaurant business a try.

Armando opened Guisados in December of 2010 in a small, bright orange space on the corner of busy Cesar Chavez Avenue in Boyle Heights. He named his restaurant "Guisados" for the name of a Mexican home-style stew known as a guiso. Guisados does not specialize in regional Mexican cuisine; instead, at first they served a very limited menu of Mexican home-style braises on handmade *tortillas* that included *calabacitas* (squash, tomatoes, bell peppers, and corn), chicken *mole*, *chicharrón* (pork rinds simmered in *chile*

Guisados wall stencil. Photo courtesy of Sarah Portnoy.

verde), and chicken *tinga* (a stew of tomatoes, onion, garlic, and chipotle). Boyle Heights was already packed with *taquerías* and Mexican restaurants, so how did Guisados set itself apart? It offered a unique concept, used social media to spread the word to the larger community, and created an inviting, modern space decorated with cool artwork from a rotating selection of local, up-and-coming artists. It also used fresh, homemade *tortillas* for its stews. The restaurant is located next to Carnitas Uruapan, a traditional Mexican butcher shop and *tortillería* owned by Armando's brother where they cook and grind the corn to make *nixtamal* used for *masa*. This gives Guisados easy access to daily, fresh *masa* for their handmade *tortillas*. The restaurant is not only known for its food but also for its memorable artwork. Armando's son, Armando Jr., stenciled much of the artwork on the walls at Guisados' various locations. At the Boyle Heights location, he painted a cow cut into all the different cuts of meat and stenciled the saying "In Tacos We Trust" above it. He stenciled a street sign that said "Boyle Heights" in black with paint dripping down below, an iconic image that has since been featured at a museum exhibit. Another piece of playful artwork features a family fleeing, as if they were running across the border, clutching Guisados *tacos* in their hands while the message painted above says, *No olvide su taco!* (Don't forget your taco).

Soon after opening, people began coming to check out the new hip *taquería*. The restaurant attracted doctors from the nearby hospital, but it took over a year before many local Mexican and Mexican-American residents were willing to try it. Guisados *tacos*—priced at $2.75 each—were and still are more expensive than the dollar *tacos* offered at nearby trucks and restaurants. While this has kept some Boyle Heights' locals from frequenting it, it allows owner Armando de la Torre to source high-quality ingredients and offer a selection of delicious, freshly made *agua fresca* (a water-based drink infused with fruit, seeds or flowers and sugar), including the popular Armando Palmero, a mix of lemonade and *jamaica* (hibiscus water) named after the owner that combines flavors in a way one Yelper described as "true euphoria." After Jonathan Gold reviewed the restaurant, Guisados got much busier overnight. Foodies and Mexican food aficionados from across the city lined up to try their *tacos*. I started eating at Guisados soon after it opened with my family and it quickly became our favorite weekend restaurant outing. Armando would always come by to chat with an extra taco for my kids.

When Armando's son told him he wanted to quit his marketing job and get involved with the restaurant, Armando decided to open a second Guisados. Armando Jr. had studied marketing in college and was already managing the restaurant's social media, a large part of their early success. In 2013, Armando opened a second location in Echo Park for his son to manage. The Echo Park location has been very successful with local residents who enjoy their *tacos* on its outdoor patio. By 2014, he opened a third location in downtown. The downtown location is sleeker, the music is louder, and its hip vibe matches the surrounding blocks of recently gentrified coffee shops, bars, and restaurants. The artwork on the walls here is edgier, while still maintaining its Mexican-American pride. A César Chavez quote on the wall reinforces Armando's philosophy that he is just trying to serve home-style Mexican food that reminds us of home: "If you really want to make a friend, go to someone's house and eat with him, the people who give you their food give you their heart."

The first time I took my USC students to eat at Guisados was an unforgettable experience. In his 2011 review of Guisados, Jonathan Gold described the *chiles toreados* as "less a side dish than a natural phenomenon, super-spicy serranos mostly, glistening and pungent, cooked with strands of onion and slyly boosted with a few slivers of what seems to be roasted habanero peppers." Gold goes on to say that you can get the chilies as a side or you can "jump in feet first" and get them "not just on a taco but *as* a taco." Gold had piqued my interest, but it was the following description of *chiles toreados* that convinced me to try them.

It is a taco that could go 15 rounds with Oscar De la Hoya. It is a taco that could play badass trumpet in a mariachi band and sing sweet love songs to your girl-friend. It is a taco that will sneak out of the house in the middle of the night to do things no taco should ever do, but you will always take it back, because you have tasted the complexity that lies three layers down.[26]

After that description, what choice did I have? I naively ordered even though the menu comes with a warning that I should have heeded: "this taco is extremely spicy." The sustained burning sensation on my lips was as unforgettable as the complex *guisos*. Armando talked to me about how important it was for him to serve *guisos* with layers of flavor. He commented that after Roy Choi started serving his unique combinations at Kogi in 2008, more Angelenos started looking for those layers of flavor in their food.

Guisados has clearly been unforgettable for many people, be it local residents or people from out of town who drive there after landing at the airport and reading about it on a list of Los Angeles' best *tacos*. Given his success, Guisados has grown quickly. In 2015 they expanded to West Hollywood and, as of our conversation in March 2016, Armando had signed a lease on a fifth location in Burbank. Armando expressed the fear that with so many locations he can't be in all the restaurants at once, but he knows, as a businessman, that it is smart to grow.

While regional and home-style Mexican cuisine was growing in Southern California during the late twentieth and beginning of the twenty-first centuries with restaurants such as Guelaguetza, La Casita Mexicana, and Chichén Itzá, it was not the only cuisine expanding during this period. Central American immigrants who arrived in Los Angeles in the 1980s in large numbers began opening more and more restaurants, bakeries, and market stalls. During the 1980s and 1990s, Salvadorian immigrants fled their country, escaping a violent civil war that raged from 1979 to 1992. To add to the upheaval, in 1986, a major earthquake struck San Salvador, the capital, killing many and leaving 200,000 people homeless. Tens of thousands of Salvadorians fled the instability. It is estimated that between 1981–2000 approximately a million Salvadorians came to the United States.[27] Many of these refugees came to Los Angeles and surrounding cities such as Long Beach and Santa Ana. While large numbers of Salvadorians reside in Houston and the Washington, DC, suburbs of Maryland and Virginia, the largest population in the country settled in the L.A. metropolitan area.[28]

Unlike the Mexican population, some of whom had resided in California for multiple generations, the Central American immigrants were newer arrivals and, as a result, formed their own separate enclaves. Since their cuisine is unfamiliar to those outside their communities, it typically has not gone through the same acculturation process as Mexican food. As one of my students pointed out, "There is no Pupusa Bell." Many of the Central American immigrants settled in South Los Angeles, an area that was once home to the largest African-American community in the West. The demographic transformation of South Los Angeles led to a shift in the neighborhood's culinary options. As the area evolved from being 80% African-American to one with a Latino majority, *pupuserías* replaced soul-food restaurants. Although it took a long time to establish, by 2012 the city of Los Angeles had an official El Salvador Community Corridor, a section near downtown that borders Koreatown. It is an area thick with Salvadorian stores, bakeries, and restaurants. *Pupuserías* and Salvadorian bakeries are not limited to this area, however. Many are located within blocks of the USC campus and I often recommend the inexpensive *pupuserías* to my students. For those of you who have not had your fill of *pupusas* in neighborhoods of suburban Maryland, Houston, or Los Angeles, *pupusas* are hearty stuffed and griddled disks made with the same *masa harina* (corn flour) as corn *tortillas*. They are most often filled with beans, cheese, chopped pork, *loroco* (a type of flower), and *revuelta* (a mix of beans, cheese, and pork) and are served with a Salvadorian cole slaw that goes on top, known as *curtido*, and a mild pureed red salsa. Typically, they cost around $2, so $5 can fill up even the heartiest of appetites. They also tend to be pretty formulaic, varying little from location to location.

Sarita's Pupusería in downtown's Grand Central Market maybe one of the few exceptions. On a recent trip to the market with my USC students, Sarita recounted that she began working in a jewelry stall at the market after immigrating to Los Angeles from El Salvador in 1980. When she heard a neighboring stall was up for sale in 1998, she scraped together the little money she had and opened a *pupusería* stall at the market. As the market grew into a foodie destination over the past few years and more non-Latinos began eating there, Sarita began creating *pupusas* with nontraditional, healthier ingredients such as squash, mushrooms, mozzarella, and basil. On a recent visit to the Grand Central Market with my USC students, Sarita spoke to them with great pride about the history of her business and how she has "persevered with discipline and vision." She generously served my students a sampling of free, tasty *pupusas*.

Sarita's Pupusería is located in The Grand Central Market, a large market that opened in 1917 to provide downtown residents a place to buy affordable produce—it was where the early tamale vendors set up shop when they were displaced in the early twentieth century. During a tour of the market, Joseph Shuldiner, the market's creative director, explained that during the early twentieth century wealthy Angelenos living in Victorian mansions on nearby Bunker Hill would go shopping at the market and other downtown stores. At the time, Shuldiner said, the market had almost one hundred stalls with whole aisles for meat, fish, and coffee roasters—he showed my students where you can still see the faint outlines of the stalls on the concrete floor today. By the 1960s, the Victorian houses had been mostly abandoned, so the city razed them to make way for future expansion. As the demographics of downtown became heavily Latino by the 1960s and 1970s, stalls opened in the market selling a variety of *moles*, dried chilies, medicinal herbs, and Mexican traditional candies such as tamarind lollipops (my children's first destination at the market). The market became a place where Latino shoppers would go to buy cheap produce or stop for a taco or bowl of *pozole* at lunchtime. Shuldiner explained that these long-term tenants are known as "legacy" tenants and he was trying to market them to a wider public. One of the older "legacy" stalls where Latinos have shopped for decades is Chiles Secos. They opened in 1975 and started off selling coffee, dried chilies, and rice. Later, they added a variety of *moles*, the food most prominently displayed in a glass case at the stall. They sell four different *moles* in a thick paste. Despite the market's current trend toward fancy signage, at this stall each *mole's* name is written in black marker on a piece of paper: *mole negro, mole verde,* and *mole colorado*, just as one would find at any market stall in Mexico.

Since 2013, the market has undergone a major transformation and ensuing gentrification. According to Shuldiner, when he was hired to transform the market, over half of the stalls were empty. The market was definitely not a dining destination. Over the past three years, Shuldiner and his business partner Kevin West have brought in new vendors such as Wexler's Deli, Belcampo Meat Company, and the extremely popular Eggslut. In a

Chiles Secos stall at Grand Central Market, downtown Los Angeles. Photo courtesy of Ebony Bailey.

Grand Central Market, Downtown Los Angeles. Photo Courtesy of Ebony Bailey..

very short time, the market has become a crowded, foodie mecca as new, artisanal vendors selling organic falafel sandwiches, pricey grass-fed beef burgers, and $6 almond milk lattes moved in. While the newer vendors are more expensive, the quality of the food has improved dramatically and, as Shuldiner explained, some of the older vendors have benefited from the changes. The owner of Villa Moreliana, a specialist in *carnitas* (slow-cooked pork from Michoacán, Mexico), was able to open a second stall in 2015, La Tostadería, a high-end *cevichería* that serves wonderful octopus, shrimp, and fish ceviche and only uses high-quality, sustainable seafood and fish. As a result, the Tostadería's prices are noticeably higher than the price at the average ceviche stand in Los Angeles. A shrimp or fish tostada costs $7 or $8 instead of $4. Sandra Felix, the chef, explained that, given the higher prices, their customers are primarily Anglos and Asian. The owner of Chiles Secos, on the other hand, told me that she has not benefited from the changes to the market. She said that now fewer Latinos come to shop, but added that a few non-Latinos ask her questions about the *moles* and occasionally buy them. In a presentation to my students, Shuldiner explained that his goal is to maintain the authenticity of the older stalls, while bringing in new ones to attract the attention of a wider customer base. As a result of the changes, the market is far more active and vibrant than it had been in decades. Sarita's Pupusería coexists in the same space with a high-end cheese shop. Sarita's no longer only attracts Latino diners looking for a quick, delicious meal, but also young hipsters and curious foodies in search of Los Angeles' best *pupusas*.

The Grand Central Market's transformation is representative of the recent gentrification of downtown Los Angeles. In 1999, the city of Los Angeles passed an "adaptive reuse ordinance" and "developers seized the chance" to attract new residents to restored historic buildings converted into apartments and condominiums.[29] The Staples Center opened the same year and a few years later, in 2003, Walt Disney Hall, a remarkable work of public architecture designed by Frank Gehry, opened. The past decade or so has seen a building renaissance in a downtown that previously had enjoyed little activity at the end of the workday. As historic buildings that had sat vacant for decades were converted into apartments and condominiums, people began to move downtown. The increase in housing in turn attracted new restaurants and nightlife to the area. As the gentrification spread, downtown became a popular dining destination. In 2009, Bottega Louie, a palatial, cavernous Italian restaurant and gourmet market sparked the renaissance of restaurants and bars along 7th street when it opened in a historic Beaux Arts building. In 2011, Chef Joseph Centeno opened Bäco Mercat, a restaurant known for its flatbread sandwiches or bäcos in Catalan, in the historic Old Bank District.

The restaurant quickly became a destination for downtown diners. Soon after, Centeno opened two more restaurants on the same block, including Bar Amá, his own interpretation of Tex-Mex cuisine as a native of San Antonio. Bar Amá is not only a fun place to get a margarita, it is also one of the few places in Los Angeles where a native Texan—such as myself—can eat Tex-Mex staples such as "queso," the melted Velveeta cheese dip with Ro*Tel diced tomatoes Texans consume while watching football. The chef, of course, uses real cheese and noncanned tomatoes. Centeno later opened a third, more upscale restaurant at the same time that a whole host of new cantinas and bars sprung up in downtown.

Of these recent arrivals, it was the restaurant Rivera that made the greatest contribution to elevating Latino cuisine in downtown Los Angeles. The opening of the sleek, high-end restaurant in 2009 contributed to the transformation of downtown from a gastronomic wasteland to a fine-dining destination. It was also a comeback for Chef John Sedlar who had left the culinary profession for fifteen years to serve as a spokesman for high-end tequilas. Sedlar was no newcomer to the L.A. food scene, however. He began to work at high-end Southern California restaurants in the early 1980s and opened his own restaurant Saint Estephe in 1985. The restaurant was originally conceived as a French restaurant, but it evolved into the birthplace of what came to be known as "modern Southwest cuisine."[30] Sedlar, who is a fifth-generation native New Mexican, became known as the "father of modern Southwest cuisine." At Saint Estephe, he combined the traditional foods of his childhood that he learned from his grandmother Eloisa—fiery chilies, earthy beans, and corn—with classic French techniques. Later, at his second restaurant Bikini in Santa Monica, Sedlar "cobbled together the first draft of pan-Latin fusion cooking several years before the style hit Miami."[31] Jonathan Gold calls John Sedlar "one of the most innovative chefs to ever wield a whisk in Los Angeles," while no less an authority than the late Craig Claiborne of the *New York Times* called Sedlar "one of America's treasures, a genius in the kitchen." *Food Arts* lauded him for "updating, upgrading and celebrating the foods of his Hispanic heritage."[32]

I was fortunate to get to know John Sedlar after I contacted him in 2010 to ask about taking my students to visit his gallery space that housed a unique collection of archival, fine-art photographs of Mesoamerica's pre-Hispanic ingredients and animals. The collection included incredible, blown-up photographs of iguanas; the hairless dog *Xoloitzcuintle*; *tortillas decoradas*; chocolate; and the *necuazcatl* (honey ant), an insect enjoyed as a sweet delicacy in pre-Hispanic Mesoamerica. He also had an impressive collection of artifacts of agricultural tools and cookware such as *metates* (a grinding stone), *molcajetes* (the pre-Hispanic version of the mortar and pestle), and contemporary *molinillos* (Mexican hot chocolate wooden frothers). My students truly had a unique experience when we visited this short-lived gallery space and saw these fascinating objects with the chef himself. Sedlar's long-term plan was to build a center for Latin culinary arts and history in downtown Los Angeles that would feature his collection and have a large open kitchen and dining space. He planned to call the space Museo Tamal: The Center for Latin Culinary Arts & History. I accompanied Sedlar to numerous fundraisers to try to attract major donors for the museum project, but unfortunately it did not come to fruition.

I ate at Rivera many times during the years it was open—moments I will treasure always. Going to Rivera was more than just eating out; it was a unique, multisensory experience. Apparently, I was not the only one to think this way. Irene Virbila, the former restaurant reviewer for the *LA Times*, wrote that she ate at Rivera more times than she needed to. "I couldn't help myself—Rivera's food is so utterly unique."[33] It was a place where art came to life both on the plate and in the space itself. As you approached Rivera, you looked into a long glass window that opened onto a sleek, elegant dining room. Once you entered, your eye was drawn to an electronic mural on the wall with different digital pictures that flashed abstract images, lizards, and Maya ruins that dissolved into one another. The adjacent bar featured beautiful bronze and leather tequila tasting chairs made in Brazil with an R designed along the side for Rivera. The restaurant had three different dining spaces with different menus and a different ambience for each space. Like a choose-your-own adventure book, your dining experience varied depending on which space you chose. Rivera's unique dining concept is best explained in Sedlar's own words on his website:

> When I opened Rivera in 2009, my culinary quest was to reexamine and redefine the five-millennia-deep Latin roots of modern Los Angeles cuisine. We traced those roots across three continents, each of which had a dedicated menu in one of Rivera's three dining rooms: Sangre (Spain), Samba (Central and South America), and Playa Bar (Mexico).

The Sangre dining room was more formal and was decorated with bullfighting paintings, meant to evoke the violent nature of Spanish culture. The room had a wall of tequila bottles made to look like shiny translucent bricks. Select guests had access to their personal bottles with a private key. The Samba lounge was more casual with a central long communal table, while the raw bar called Playa was a more lively space for a happy-hour or late-night cocktail with Baja Mexico seafood and other coastal Mexican dishes. If you wanted to know about a particular dish's history, you would call a designated phone number and Chef Sedlar would describe it for you, much as one finds today at art museums. Or, if you were as lucky as my students were for many years, the chef himself would give the cultural and culinary background of the dishes he chose for a curated meal he served to my class.

Sedlar's dishes were unique, artistic creations. One of the most beautiful foods I remember from Rivera was the *tortillas florales, tortillas* made from freshly ground *nixtamal* (limed corn kernels for grinding into *masa*). Each tortilla had flowers pressed into its surface. Over the years, Sedlar developed a technique that he called "Spiceology" in which he created elaborate drawings out of spices that reflected current political topics. One particularly memorable dish spelled out the word "Caution" in red spices with a family in flight, an allusion to the immigration debate that was taking place at the time. Even the names of the dishes elevated the cuisine. The Atlantic cod served with artichokes, chorizo, garbanzos, and spinach was called "horse latitudes" in memory of the horses that drowned when crossing the ocean "in the spirit of New World discoveries." Sedlar's "ensalada semana santa" (holy week salad) was inspired by Catholic and Moorish Spain with Seville oranges, garbanzos, beets, and Moorish spices. Instead of guacamole, Sedlar served a smooth Indian butter. When he opened Rivera, he was not just continuing his own culinary trajectory, but he was also inserting his place into a constellation of chefs experimenting with the boundaries of traditional Hispanic gastronomy. Sedlar was very aware of the innovations brought about by molecular gastronomy, a style of cuisine in which chefs borrow tools from the science lab that changed the way classically trained chefs conceived of their work and inspired extreme experimentation in the kitchen. In Mexico, Chef Enrique Olvera opened Pujol in 2000. Olvera gained recognition for

Xocolata at Rivera Restaurant. Photo courtesy of Ebony Bailey.

pushing the boundaries of traditional Mexican recipes by applying avant-garde cooking techniques to millennia-old indigenous practices and creating modernized versions of Latino cuisine that made Mexico City a culinary destination.

Sedlar hired Los Angeles' famous mixologist Julian Cox to curate the restaurant's cocktail list using top quality ingredients. These cocktails not only had exotic names and fresh ingredients grown on Sedlar's vertical, rooftop gardens, but some also recreated original, famous cocktails from Mexico and Latin America. "Tequila para mi amante" was a cocktail with strawberry-infused blanco tequila, acid phosphate, fresh lemon, and vermouth that dates to 1937 Mexico City, while "Hotel Nacional" was one of the signature drinks at Havana's Hotel Nacional de Cuba in the 1930s. My students of legal drinking age always loved to order the Barbacoa, a smoky, mescal-based drink made with chipotle, ginger, and beef jerky and served in a glass rimmed with powdered maguey worms. Sedlar even sourced his own *chapulines* from Guelaguetza restaurant to make in-house grasshopper salt for a drink he heard about while traveling in Oaxaca. The citrusy cocktail was inspired by the legendary sacrifice of a beautiful Zapotec princess, Donaji, whose story is reenacted each year at the Guelaguetza festival in Oaxaca. Sadly, Rivera closed in late 2015 when its popularity waned. Sedlar opened a new restaurant Eloisa in his hometown of Santa Fe and, as of yet, has not returned to the L.A. dining scene. Months after closing, the elegant Rivera space was transformed and later reopened later as the more casual restaurant Broken Spanish under the helm of chef Ray García.

Even though Rivera is no longer open, Sedlar's haute Latin cuisine set the stage for a new L.A.-based genre of cuisine that Mexican food writer Bill Esparza has named Alta California cuisine. Esparza defines Alta California cuisine as a style of cooking "from a group of Los Angeles-born *pocho* (Mexican-American) chefs rooted in the Latin cuisines of their youth, fine-dining experience in our California-cuisine kitchens, and the use of our abundant and diverse local products from L.A. farmers' markets."[34] Some writers have referred to this style of cooking as modern Mexican cuisine, but this designation is generally used to refer to the style of cooking of chefs such as Enrique Olvera in Mexico City. What these Alta California chefs are doing is something more uniquely Californian or Mexican-American, a reflection of their bicultural heritage and upbringing. Unlike previous generations of Mexican and Mexican-American chefs, this new generation of chefs is classically trained and is not trying to recreate the traditional dishes their mothers and grandmothers made. Instead, they are creating innovative dishes that are influenced by Mexican cuisine but rooted in Los Angeles. According to Esparza, this new generation of young chefs include Ray García of Broken Spanish and Broken Spanish Taquería, Carlos Salgado of Tacos María, Eduardo Ruíz of

Corazón y Miel, Daniel Snukal and Josh Gil of Tacos Punta Cabra, and Wes Avila of Guerrilla Tacos, a "roving modernist" taco truck that will be discussed in the next chapter. The work of this new generation of chefs is making the present day, Esparza insists, the most interesting time, and Los Angeles the most interesting place, for a unique interpretation of Mexican cuisine.

Ray García is one of the most respected young chefs in contemporary Los Angeles. He first became known for his California farmers' market-inspired cooking at Fig, a restaurant inside the high-end Fairmont hotel in Santa Monica. When Rivera closed in late 2014, García was asked to lead the effort to revive the former Rivera space.

In an interview, García told me that taking over the Rivera space gave him "the perfect opportunity to have a continuation of the conversation of more progressive Latin cuisine in our city" that Chef John Sedlar had been having far before modern Latin cuisine was a trend. García named his new restaurant Broken Spanish, a name that refers not only to his heritage as a third-generation Mexican-American, one who speaks "broken Spanish," but also to his ability to update traditional Mexican cuisine with other culinary influences. Broken Spanish gave García the chance to create dishes that went far beyond his East L.A. Mexican-American roots, placing him among the stars of the new Alta California category. García explained that for the first time in his career he was conceiving of and preparing dishes he could connect with on a personal level. As García stated, "Opening Broken Spanish was an opportunity for me to connect to something that goes deeper" and "allowed me to work off my natural palate as opposed to what I was trained to do." García described to me how he applies his classical chef's training to a dish such as the *chicharrón* (fried pork rinds) they serve at Broken Spanish. "The actual *chicharrón* is elaborately prepared and more closely parallels Italian *porchetta* than Mexican *chicharrón*." This dish "taps into my experience over the last twenty years. The steps in preparing it are French technique, but made through the lens of a third generation Mexican-American."

At the same time that the Rivera space became available, the space that had once housed Mo-Chica, a small downtown Peruvian restaurant, opened up. García jumped at the chance to create a sister *taquería* to his flagship restaurant, Broken Spanish. Like Broken Spanish, B.S. Taquería also uses unexpected ingredients such as the *lardo* and Manila clam taco, a dish Jonathan Gold named one of the ten best dishes of 2015. The title of Jonathan Gold's review of B.S. Taquería points to the innovations García has introduced at both of his restaurants: "B.S. Taqueria has a few twists even for this taco-centric city." In his review, Gold wrote that Chef García "has come into his own, proposing a bold, new style that is less Mexican than it is Mexican-American, channeling the food experiences of the Eastside through his hard-won classical technique."[35]

During our interview, I asked García about the rise in popularity of Broken Spanish and the food of other Southern Californian Alta California chefs over the past few years. He responded: "Many people are connecting with it and are excited to learn this style." García discussed the younger generation's interest in the new culinary style:

> This is a source of pride for me at Broken Spanish as I see it as the place where the next generation comes to learn about Alta California or Modern Mexican cuisine in the same way that Spago was influential twenty or twenty-five years ago. It is the first generation where people are eating with an appreciation of ingredients and techniques. It is easier to explain what we are doing to this generation of millennials than to older people like my own mother who still don't understand my approach.

When I asked García what he thought had inspired his restaurant's popularity, he explained that generational changes and an increased spending ability among a growing Latino population in the city has created a market for a consumer that may not have been there before. While in the past, García believes that the term modern Mexican cuisine would have been an "oxymoron" since Mexican food had not changed very much in Los Angeles, over the past five years Angelenos' ideas about Latin cuisine have evolved greatly. At the same time, the way the world looks at Mexican cuisine has changed as it has become increasingly global in nature. García mentioned the example of the world-famous Danish chef René Redzepi of Noma who named Mexican cuisine as his favorite food in 2014.

I recently ate at García's Broken Spanish and Broken Spanish Taquería for the first time. The space is more informal, brighter, and more open than Rivera. The sleek, luxurious ambience of Rivera has been replaced with cement tiles, a wood interior, Mexican ceramic dishes, and hanging plants. When I asked García why the space had been redesigned to be more informal, he said he wanted to create a more inviting and welcoming environment. He explained that when Sedlar opened Rivera in 2008 he had different challenges with people's perceptions of Latino cuisine than he, García, has today. Sedlar used the restaurant's setting to elevate the cuisine so that it represented "luxury and class," but, in the process, "had removed a bit of the warmth." Broken Spanish's approach was to create a "warmer space and open it up to more light." As for the menu, at first glance, the dishes seem fairly traditional, but most come with the twists that Gold pointed out in his review. We began our meal with *tortillas*, *carnitas* fat, and *queso fundido*. García's thick blue corn *tortillas*, made with heirloom corn he sources from Mexico, were one of the highlights of the evening. The *queso fundido* was prepared with *bacalao* (salted cod), an interesting variation that gave it an unexpected salty flavor. The *chile relleno* was stuffed with kale, potatoes, lemon, and an onion puree sauce. The most memorable dish of the evening was the *cabeza*, a fully cooked lamb head with pickled onions and cabbage. This dish was worth ordering for the spectacle of seeing half a cooked lamb's head on a plate. It reminded my Spanish dining partner, Ángel, of a dish his grandmother used to prepare. We all watched as Ángel tore the head apart, juice from the brain splattering across the dish and ate the meat, fat, eye, and brain with great gusto. Ángel described every bite of the lamb's head as "significant and deliciously unique." It seemed pretty gutsy to put this humble dish on the menu of an upscale, modern restaurant. When I asked García about this decision, he said that it is a dish from his childhood that he really wanted to have on the menu. He told me that his grandmother used to make it for family celebrations or perhaps when there was nothing else to eat. García added that it is definitely not a part of mainstream food memories, but it is warm, inviting, and exciting to see. "No other restaurant in Los Angeles serves lamb's head in a broth." He added, "Some diners enjoy tapping into that memory, while others want to learn and grow." Given his wide range of culinary genres, García has definitely expanded Los Angeles' foodscape and, with his plans to expand his *taquerías* to more locations around the city, will continue to serve "authentically inauthentic" cuisine in the years to come.

Along with Ray García, Mexican food critic Bill Esparza also named chefs Josh Gil and Daniel Snukal to the category of Alta California cuisine, much to their consternation. Gil and Snukal own Tacos Punta Cabras, a Santa Monica-based Baja-style *taquería*. Josh Gil grew up in Rosarito, a region of Baja, Mexico, known for its fish and shrimp *tacos* and other exquisite seafood dishes. He first learned to cook while helping his mother prepare meals for the family. After coming to the United States, Gil worked as a chef at several fine-dining restaurants in Los Angeles. He and co-owner Daniel Snukal, another chef who had worked in fine dining, met in 2008 and began a catering service together. In 2010, they started hosting underground dinners at a Santa Monica restaurant space. After three years, the owner suggested they take over the space full time and, without giving it much thought, they said yes. They didn't know exactly what type of restaurant they were going to put into the space—only that it would be seafood driven. They knew, however, that there was no Mexican restaurant like what they had in mind in Santa Monica. The Venice/Santa Monica area of Los Angeles, where I have lived since migrating south from San Francisco in 2007, has an overabundance of "it" restaurants, but is pretty sparse when it comes to interesting Mexican restaurants. So, I was happy to discover Tacos Punta Cabras had opened not far from my home.

I interviewed chefs Josh Gil and Daniel Snukal in 2016. We ended up in a long conversation on their views of Mexican cuisine in Los Angeles and the work of other chefs. They were happy to talk and were extremely opinionated. They told me that they were constantly driving down to Baja or to the Eastside of Los Angeles for good Mexican food. They discussed their favorite spots for different kinds of seafood in Tijuana, Rosarito, and Ensenada. When I asked them to compare those places with Mexican restaurants in the United States, they said that the places in Baja excel because they specialize. They are known for one or maybe two things. In the United States, on the other hand, we suffer from the "Cheesecake Factory" syndrome—restaurants have biblically long menus in an attempt to please everyone, while excelling at nothing. Many Mexican restaurant menus suffer from this phenomenon instead of specializing in what they know how to do best. Inspired by Guisado's success with a limited menu of home-style Mexican cuisine, Daniel and Josh decided to apply their experience with fine-dining techniques and Mexican street-food knowledge to a Baja-themed concept: fish *tacos*, fresh ceviche, and seafood cocktails. Tacos Punta Cabras opened in 2013 in a stretch of Santa Monica on a nondescript block over a mile away from the city's shopping district, Third Street Promenade. They named it for one of their favorite Baja surfing spots called Punta Cabras (Goat Point) south of Ensenada. As I am also always in search of a good Baja-style fish taco (fish *tacos* that are battered and fried, served with a cream sauce and cabbage), I was thrilled when I tasted theirs. Daniel and Josh told me that they pride themselves on using only high-quality ingredients. They use organic, sustainable, non-GMO ingredients whenever possible. They make their *salsas, agua fresca*, and *tortillas* fresh in the restaurant every day. In fact, they have fresh *masa* delivered daily to the restaurant and experimented with their tortilla recipe for months before finally perfecting it. They are licensed as a *tortillería*, so you can buy handmade, GMO-free *tortillas* there. When I asked them if it was worth the additional labor cost to make such high-quality *tortillas*, they responded that customers should be able to get *tortillas* not made by Mission, a major U.S. manufacturer of *tortillas*. Their comment reflects a larger trend among chefs in the United States to source high-quality *masa* from Mexico, as evidenced by the rapid growth of Masienda, a new company that is working with 5,000 smallholder farmers in Mexico, guaranteeing them a fair price and distributing the corn to chefs in the United States.[36]

Bill Esparza labels Daniel and Josh's food as Alta California cuisine, putting them in the same category as Wes Avila, Carlos Salgado, Ray García, and others. Specials on the menu such as unagi tostada with avocado, fried egg, and a spicy eel glaze; homemade shrimp and oyster sausage with curry cream green papaya salad; and the king mushroom taco with bonito and seaweed show their ability to play with different genres and create unexpected flavor profiles. Yet, they vociferously told me that they "hate" the categorization and think the term Alta California cuisine is "weird and horrible."

They say that they are not at all a uniquely Los Angeles phenomenon. Instead, they are "working with staples of the Mexican diet." "There is nothing we are doing here that doesn't rely on techniques that aren't ancient. We are not modern in that sense," Josh says. "What about the cauliflower ceviche?" I ask. Daniel responds that they make it the same way as if it were seafood, but use a vegetable instead. They say that they despise the Alta California designation because they have a "total disregard" for those that are trying to blow you away with their cooking. Their goal is just to do something good, but that they don't need to be labeled the best anything. Daniel exclaims, "Do we make the best tostada? Who cares? We do street food, that's what we do." They add that they don't like the "best" label because it implies they are better than others. "We try to be honest and do a product, we are not in it to make it better."

Despite their resistance to being labeled, what they do share with the other chefs is their classical training and their use of high-quality ingredients. When I asked them about their hopes for the future of Mexican food in the United States, they said they hoped it could be more appreciated and that people would be willing to pay more for high-quality Mexican food. "People will pay four times more for a bowl of pasta than they will for a good taco. It's a cultural stereotype we have to overcome." They think that the trucks and restaurants selling $1 *tacos* just add to the stereotype of Mexican food as cheap and, therefore, not as respected. "The guys selling *tacos* for $1 kills everything. You can't have GMO-free corn and make our own *agua fresca* for those kind of prices." When I asked Daniel and Josh about their future plans, they said that they want to open a similar concept "with a mom and pop feel" and stay by the beach. They recently opened a tiny Mexican burger joint named Hamburguesa Punta Cabras in downtown serving "nostalgia food," but it didn't work out. The space had problems and they quickly backed out of their lease. It seemed a minor setback for them. Given their combined experience and great collaborative relationship, I am sure they will continue to play a role in Los Angeles' Mexican culinary landscape in their own way, without trying to be the best, while still using the best-quality ingredients and some pretty great *tortillas*.

Of all these young Alta California chefs, the one whose restaurant I had yet to try was Carlos Salgado. I had sampled Carlos's squid and peanut taco on a black tortilla at the L.A. Taco Festival in June 2015. The memory of this unique dish stayed with me and I yearned to make the trek to Orange County to eat at Tacos María, a restaurant Carlos opened in 2013 after running an upscale food truck for two years. Carlos, who worked at some of the Bay Area's best restaurants, returned home in 2011 to his native Orange County, where his family runs a traditional Mexican restaurant, La Siesta. After so many years away, he wanted to be closer to his family and support his parents, who had decided to expand their business by opening a food truck. They launched a food truck called Tacos María, but this was no run-of-the-mill *tacos*-and-burrito truck; instead, as the *Orange County Weekly* noted, you can find unexpected "*alta cocina* dishes such as bone marrow" coming from Carlos's truck.[37] As Carlos told me in an interview, "We ended up putting all our resources into the truck and it was very successful early on. The truck's success emboldened us to take the next step to opening a physical restaurant."

Carlos and I spoke on the phone while he was stuck in traffic driving to Santa Monica to buy produce at the Wednesday farmers' market. While I could never have maneuvered through Southern California traffic and discuss my culinary philosophy simultaneously, Carlos did so quite eloquently, sharing with me his family background, his thoughts on Orange County's uniqueness, and his desire to always source the highest-quality ingredients. Carlos makes this weekly trek in order to procure the best-quality produce for his restaurant. At the same time, he develops a relationship with the individual farmers and has the opportunity to purchase the produce as it comes into season. As a chef in the Bay Area, Carlos learned to have great respect for ingredients and agriculture. As he explained, "I know that a pot of *frijoles de la olla* or a *tortilla* will taste better if grown by people with good intentions for the transformative effect that good agriculture will have on the flavor of an ingredient from seed to harvest to final presentation." Carlos believes that higher-quality ingredients make for better food experiences and, as a result, supports local farmers' markets, purveyors of natural and humanely raised meats, and sustainable seafood.

Carlos's interest in ethical agricultural practices extend to the corn he uses for his *tortillas*, a food integral to the identity of Mexico's indigenous population, but one that in the United States has not been highly valued. As he explained in a 2016 *LA Times* article, "It's a working-class ingredient and here in the U.S. we haven't typically assigned a lot of value to it."[38] Carlos, on the other hand, wanted to serve his customers high-quality *tortillas* by making his own *masa*. When he opened the Taco María truck, he started out pressing his own *tortillas* using commodity *masa* from a local *tortillería*, but he was not satisfied. So, when Carlos met Jorge Gaviria in 2014, the founder and CEO of Masienda, a brand-new New York-based company that purveys non-GMO maize, beans, and chilies, he described it as "serendipitous." Gaviria "was developing relationships with small maize farmers in rural Mexico" and Carlos was on a quest to produce superior *tortillas*.[39] A 2016 *New York Times* article on U.S. chefs embracing "Oaxaca's native maize" reported that Masienda is working with a growing cadre of chefs in the United States.[40] Carlos was one of his earliest and largest customers. His maize comes from a small family farm in the state of Mexico that has been growing corn for five generations.

Chef Carlos Salgado Shopping at the Santa Monica Wednesday farmers' market.
Photo courtesy of Sarah Portnoy.

Carlos takes the corn he receives from Masienda and puts it through nixtamalization, a process in which the grain is soaked in limewater and cooked for twelve hours at his family's Mexican restaurant, where they have a custom-built grinder. Carlos says that this process happens every day and produces 200 pounds of *masa* each time. In order to make it more cost-effective, Carlos wholesales his *masa* to Broken Spanish and other Southern California restaurants. He explained to me that it would be cost prohibitive to produce *masa* only for their restaurant. Regardless, it is still a very expensive, time-consuming process, but one that is a source of pride for him. He told me that when older Mexicans taste his *tortillas*, they are moved by the flavors and aroma. It creates a sense of nostalgia for them. On the other hand, when younger Latinos who have only eaten commodity *tortillas* try his fresh, flavorful version, they connect with them because Carlos believes they have a "genetic memory" of what a tortilla should taste like.

Despite Carlos's great pride in his cuisine and culture, he had a complex and difficult relationship with Mexican cuisine and identity when he was growing up. His father crossed the border from Mexico to the United States at the age of seventeen and began working in a restaurant kitchen. He met Carlos's mother when they were both working at a restaurant. Both were undocumented immigrants. Despite their status, they bought a house, took out a car loan, and eventually owned their own restaurant in Orange County. Carlos shared with me how he had struggled with his identity as a teenager, "I thought we were poor and rebelled against the humble work my parents did. As a book smart kid, I had a very different idea of what culture was. I was also subjected to subtle racism growing up in a white community." After high school, he moved to San Francisco to work in the technology industry and make it on his own. After a while, he gained a greater respect for the work his parents do. "My parents are the hardest working people I know," Carlos told me. "I am grateful for what they taught me, but when I was growing up I had a complex relationship with their work." Carlos told me that it took moving away to the Bay Area to gain a different perspective. He explained,

Living in the San Francisco Mission, I began to see all the challenges Latino businesses faced and became aware of how they were perceived by non-Latinos. Overnight I realized that my parents had been subjected to institutional racism. The food at their restaurant was seen as lowly because of the perception of Mexican food and the commodification of Mexican food as fast food.

Carlos talked about Mexican fast food's strong roots in Orange County. He believes that his parents were working in a system that did not value Mexican food and thought it should always be cheap. As a result, they struggled to make a profit selling dollar or fifty-cent *tacos*. Over time, Carlos began to embrace his heritage and the food of his culture and decided to go to culinary school. For a decade, he worked in some of San Francisco's most prestigious restaurants until he reached the point where he was eager to return to his roots.

Carlos's roots as a Mexican-American are very important to him, he told me when I asked why he labels his cuisine on his website as Chicano, a word that has been highly politicized and when applied to cuisine connotes burritos and nachos. Carlos told me that his grandfather came to Southern California from Mexico as part of the bracero program. He worked as a migrant worker not far from where the restaurant is located today in what were at the time abundant orange fields. Given the multigenerational struggle of his Mexican family and his upbringing as an American kid in white, affluent Orange County, the label Chicano for his cuisine was a way to acknowledge his belated pride in his heritage and a way to make people question their perceptions—or misconceptions—about Mexican food. Carlos took a similar approach to naming his restaurant. He called it "Tacos María," a name that suggests a casual *taquería* and contrasts with the very high-end presentation of the food. He acknowledges that he took a risk with the name. "Maybe when someone walks by he or she will think they can have lunch for $5, but if they walk in and if their minds are open and we upset their expectations, maybe that's ok." He went on to say that the response has been largely very positive, but some people still get upset by his menu. Their "worldview doesn't allow them to think they can pay this much money for Mexican food." "But Carlos," I replied, "what you are serving at Tacos María is not exactly Mexican food." "You are right," he answered. Carlos explained that Tacos María is not a strictly "anthropological" restaurant; instead, "we are well versed in the traditional language of dishes such as *mole* and *pozole* and evoke those dishes without being entirely traditional or authentic in the classic sense." Carlos also discussed some of the unique challenges of being located in Orange County, as opposed to cities such as Los Angeles or San Francisco. "O.C. is an interesting place," he told me, before adding,

> We have our own sort of complex cultural and socio-political environment here. There is a strong foodie culture, but a lot of Latinos as well. Many O.C. cities are majority Latino. Despite that, Mexican restaurants have been a little slower than Los Angeles to evolve from the stereotypical faux fine-dining places that serve margaritas and chips and salsa. That's still where a lot of the dollars in our community go.

Tacos María has helped change that image by sharing a different, more complex Mexican cuisine, a point of enormous pride for Carlos and one that has earned him a loyal following with Latinos and non-Latinos alike.

Tacos María is located inside the OC Mix, an attractive open warehouse-like space that is part of an upscale, outdoor shopping center dedicated to specialty foods, such as high-end chocolates, oysters, and juices. It was a surprising location for such an acclaimed restaurant that gave the space a casual atmosphere. It has a small open kitchen and outdoor patio and fewer than fifteen tables. The informal space contrasts with the very high-end presentation of the food, the impeccable service, fixed-menu dinner service, and carefully curated wine pairings. The food Carlos serves creatively reinvents traditional Mexican flavors and ingredients. When I had the opportunity to dine there in early 2016, my dinner included *aguachile de zanahoria*, a recreation of the traditional *aguachile*, a type of Mexican ceviche usually made with fresh, raw shrimp, cucumber, red onion, lime juice, and chilies pulverized with some water, thus the name. Carlos's *aguachile* adhered to the classic dish in technique. He substituted raw shrimp for carrots, honeydew radish, and citrus, but kept the spiciness with a Serrano pepper. Unlike a traditional *chile relleno* that has been dipped in egg, fried, and stuffed with cheese and other ingredients, this one was stuffed with crab, potato, and served with a wonderful *salsa veracruzana*. The dessert was a recreation of *atole*, a classic Mexican winter-weather, thick cornmeal drink, served with banana, making it sweeter than classic *atole*. The servers carefully explained the ingredients in each dish to us and Carlos himself came over to meet me and chat on a busy Saturday night. My husband and I were very impressed by the rich and unique flavors of each dish and the quality of ingredients Carlos sources. Many critics have been impressed as well. In 2015, Carlos was named one of *Food & Wine Magazine*'s best new chefs and he has also been selected as a semifinalist for a James Beard award for best chef in the West. Jonathan Gold placed Tacos María in the number 2 spot on his list of Los Angeles' 101 Best Restaurants, a high honor since the restaurant is not even located in Los Angeles. Carlos says that in the future he plans to expand and open more restaurants with the same philosophy, but with a more casual format since "you can't put children through college with a forty-person restaurant." I look forward to following his future endeavors and to many more trips to Orange County to eat his complex dishes and flavorful *tortillas*.

Carlos not only uses *tortillas* of a quality I have rarely tasted in my life, but also supports the legal battle of chefs, scientists, farmers, and environmentalists to keep transgenic (GMO) corn from contaminating other Mexican varieties. Mexican environmental activists have been battling in court to maintain their status as a genetically modified–free territory and, until 2015, they preserved this status through lawsuits. In August, 2015, however, a judge repealed a two-year-old ban on genetically modified (GM) maize. Opponents quickly lodged an appeal that stopped the repeal.[41] Together, they wrote a letter to the Mexican government expressing their concern for the preservation of nongenetically modified corn. "The cultivation of transgenics is an attack on the diversity of our native maize," they wrote. "And puts in danger their very existence."[42] Mexico has fifty-eight different varieties of maize, each with its own unique flavor. The statement Carlos makes by going the extra mile to source his own maize, putting it through the process of nixtamalization, and grinding the *masa* himself, shows his great pride in his Mexican heritage and in serving the highest-quality food.

Restaurants such as Tacos Punta Cabra, Broken Spanish, Tacos María, and the Guerrilla Tacos food truck are elevating the public's understanding of Mexican cuisine in Los Angeles—and hopefully beyond. They have proven that high-end "Mexican" cuisine does not need to be served at a white tablecloth restaurant—or even in a restaurant for that matter. It can be served from a dazzling blue truck decorated with graffiti art to eager customers waiting on the sidewalk, as is the case with Guerrillas Tacos. Wes Avila's modern dishes show just how far Mexican cuisine has come from a time when *señoritas* in flowery dresses served food labeled as "Spanish" to a time when "Mexican" cuisine defies expectations and transcends labels. This group of innovative, young Alta California chefs is only at the beginning of their careers. It will be exciting to see how they evolve over the next few years and where the future lies for Alta California cuisine in Los Angeles. At the same time that these chefs have defied culinary boundaries, racial ones have also faded in recent years. Millennials are not afraid to leave their middle-class neighborhoods to eat in and explore non-Anglo neighborhoods. Instead, many young hipsters or foodies delight in the culinary tourism of East L.A., Boyle Heights, or other Latino *barrios* as they pursue unique edible experiences at *loncheras* (stationary food trucks) or from street vendors and write about them on Yelp, Chowhound, or their personal blogs. Food is a powerful way to transmit social status and power. For the Alta California chefs, their innovative contributions not only elevate the cuisine, but also empower them to make their own decisions and fearlessly transgress culinary boundaries.

Chapter 3

Loncheras and Luxe-Loncheras

The Evolution of L.A.'s Mobile Street Food

As discussed in the first chapter, since California became part of the United States with the signing of the Treaty of Guadalupe Hidalgo, the city of Los Angeles has had a long history of racial tension between its Mexican and Anglo residents. Originally, a small Mexican *pueblo* established in 1781, over a period of decades during the late nineteenth and early twentieth centuries, Los Angeles went from being a small town with a Mexican majority to a booming city with an Anglo majority. It was a city that historian William Deverell describes as coming "of age amidst (and in part because of) specific responses to Mexican ethnicity and Mexican spaces."[1] Conflicts over Mexican street food, therefore, are much more than simply conflicts about food. After all, food is central to who we are, to our identity; it is "a language accessible to all."[2] Attempts by those in power to control or obliterate Mexican street food reflect larger issues of discrimination toward Mexicans and Mexican-Americans that are deeply rooted in California's past. Conflicts over food and who controls public space began with the tamale wagons in the late nineteenth and early twentieth centuries and continue to this day with a 2008 city ordinance designed to restrict Mexican taco trucks as well as the ongoing imprisonment, fines, and confiscation of property of illegal street vendors, discussed in the next chapter.

Mexican street food first became popular in Los Angeles in the latter decades of the twentieth century with the tamale wagons that sprang up around the former *pueblo* of Los Angeles in the nascent downtown. At the dawn of the twentieth century, over a hundred of these tamale wagons wandered the streets selling food.[3] In Gustavo Arellano's description of Los Angeles' early tamale vendors in *Taco USA*, he cites an article from the *LA Times* from 1901:

Strangers coming to Los Angeles remark at the presence of so many outdoor restaurants, and marvel at the system which permits men … to set up places of business in the public streets … and competing with businessmen who pay high rents for rooms in which to serve the public with food.[4]

Even though the vendors had city business licenses, city officials looked upon them unfavorably and tried to outlaw them. As Arellano explains, "By 1897, the City Council proposed to not allow the tamale wagons to open until nine at night, at the behest of restaurant owners who didn't like the crowds the *tamaleros* attracted." The vendors were clustered around downtown, near modern-day Olvera Street. Eventually, the density of vendors became a nuisance for the city and by 1910, "a hundred downtown businessmen signed a letter asking the council to prohibit tamale wagons because they didn't reflect well on the district."[5] Despite these measures, the city never managed to outlaw the tamale wagons completely since they were just too popular. Instead, they faded into history as the city grew far beyond the original *pueblo* of Los Angeles, the automobile came into vogue, and new street-food trends emerged to take their place.

The tamale wagons returned in the 1970s in the form of *loncheras*, Mexican taco trucks that were created to provide a quick lunch for Mexican and Mexican-American construction workers. Just as the tamale men had done a century earlier, Mexican immigrants arriving toward the end of the twentieth century used their traditional foods to navigate and negotiate their outsider status and to create their own microenterprises. Since their original purpose was to provide lunch to construction workers, they were given the name *loncheras* and their owners were called *loncheros*. Nowadays, a staple of street corners in Latino neighborhoods and other major intersections throughout the city, *loncheras* form a vital part of the city's identity, contribute to its economy, and create income and employment for small-business owners.

Originally, the *loncheras* were designed to be completely mobile. They went to and from construction sites selling food where it was not readily available. While trucks like these continue to cater to construction workers, as construction waned during the economic recession of the late 1970s and early 1980s, many of the trucks began to operate on a mostly stationary basis and would park in the same location for long periods of time.[6] These stationary food trucks were owned and operated by Latino families and typically located in underserved Latino neighborhoods such as East L.A. and Boyle Heights. In *Taco USA*, Gustavo Arellano claims that until Raul Martinez, founder of the King Taco chain, began selling *tacos* from a converted ice cream truck in East L.A. in 1974 stationary taco trucks did not exist.[7] Although when his friends heard about his new business, they thought Martinez had "lost his mind," in a short time he was earning $150 an evening selling *tacos*. He was so successful that after six months he expanded to a brick-and-mortar restaurant and eventually opened over twenty King Taco locations.[8]

Today, thousands of *loncheras* operate around the city. Some have a Twitter account or a Facebook page, but most do not use social media. They just stick to their routine and a known parking spot and serve a regular, local clientele. In *Los Angeles Street Food*, Farley Elliot calls these trucks "the most recognizable face of today's street food movement."[9] Some of the trucks operate all day long, but many open only at night and serve young people hungry after a night of drinking or workers ending an evening shift. Most serve the standard *tacos*, burritos, *quesadillas*, and tortas, while others serve specialties. I have taken my students to eat at Cemitas Tepeaca in Boyle Heights, a truck serving *cemitas*, sandwiches originally from Puebla that are made with an egg bread topped with sesame seeds and usually filled with meat, Oaxacan cheese, and avocado. While the food was good and my students were amused by the roosters wandering around on the sidewalk in front of the truck, there are hundreds of others just like it serving *cemitas poblanas* throughout Los Angeles. A few of these trucks have become well-known because they attracted the attention of Anthony Bourdain's television cameras or were reviewed by Jonathan Gold, but most, as Farley put it, "are destined not for fame but for consistency." Farley calls them "the real workhorses of Los Angeles' street food game."[10] Other cities have copied the *lonchera* model or, as is the case with Portland, Oregon, developed their own version of mobile food vendors, but nowhere are they as pervasive as Los Angeles where they permeate the urban landscape.

Despite the *lonchera*'s vital role in the formation of modern-day Los Angeles' "foodscape," opponents, primarily city officials and restaurant owners, have criticized them with much the same language they used about the tamale vendors nearly a century before. They have accused the taco trucks of having unfair advantages over brick-and-mortar restaurants, endangering public health, and contributing to crime and blight, but the reality does not seem to back up their complaints. Just like brick-and-mortar restaurant owners, an estimated 6,000 *lonchera* owners contribute to the city's economy. They pay taxes to the city, pay fees to park their trucks overnight in commissaries, and contribute to the local economy by purchasing ingredients and other merchandise. Unlike the newer breed of high-end food trucks that often park in front of, or very close to, restaurants, *loncheras* are not generally known for competing with brick-and-mortar restaurants. Instead, they mostly serve low- and moderate-income areas where adequate dining options are not always available. As law professor Ernesto Hernández-López observes in his study "LA's Taco Truck Wars," the assumption that customers would go to a restaurant if food trucks were not available is false. Taco truck customers and diners at restaurants are seeking different experiences. The first wants a quick, cheap meal; prices at trucks are lower since there are no amenities and the menu is much more limited. Restaurant diners, on the other hand, are looking for the comfort of a wait staff, a place to sit and park the car, and a wider food selection. They go to a restaurant because they are willing to pay more for these services.

The argument that the trucks endanger public health also can easily be refuted. They are held to the same level of oversight by the Department of Public Health as brick-and-mortar restaurants and, unlike fast-food restaurants, they use fresh ingredients. As Jesús Hermosillo argues in his study of stationary food trucks, the perception that the *loncheras* "contribute to crime and blight may be linked to biases against their customers' ethnic or class backgrounds (after all, 'Twitter trucks' and their relatively upscale fans have not been frequently said to promote crime or blight)."[11] In fact, as Hermosillo points out, greater pedestrian density is linked to increased safety. These accusations are nothing new. Like the earlier ban on the tamale vendors, they often stem from discrimination and anti-immigrant sentiment toward Mexicans and, in turn, fears that the food they peddle is unsanitary and unsightly. In his legal study of *loncheras,* Ernesto Hernández-López labels these factors—the concerns for what is foreign or immigrant with its racist undertones "food culture contests."[12] Criticisms of the trucks reflect larger conflicts about "neighborhood identity, local economies, and public space."[13] In an effort to improve a neighborhood's image and attract businesses to the area, some city officials have worked to get rid of the "unsightly" *loncheras.* In the 1990s some residents complained that they attracted gangs and lowered property values. In response, some Los Angeles County cities, such as the city of Pico Rivera, a city that is predominantly Latino, banned the trucks. Other cities, such as Beverly Hills, have not changed their regulations despite changing attitudes toward street food among younger generations. The city requires mandatory police background checks of anyone working on a truck.[14]

In 2008, the "food culture contests" reached a boiling point when L.A. county supervisor Gloria Molina, who represents East L.A., proposed changes to a city ordinance that would require the *loncheras* to constantly move their location. The proposed ordinance would have effectively ended the *loncheras'* business in East L.A., an area closely identified with Mexican culture. For years, county law had required that the *loncheras* move after thirty minutes, but the law had rarely been enforced. Molina explained that she needed to crack down and create a stricter law after she began to receive complaints from local restaurant owners. On April 15, 2008, the city passed an ordinance that stated that the *loncheras* could only park in the same location for thirty minutes in a residential zone or sixty minutes in a nonresidential zone. Afterward, they had to move at least a half-mile away and could only return to their original location after three hours. If they did not comply they would be fined up to $1,000 and could spend up to six months in jail. Molina's spokesperson claimed the ordinance was a result of residents' complaints that the trucks were dirty, an eyesore, and parked all day in the same spot, but the *loncheros* believe Molina's effort was created to eliminate competition with East L.A. restaurants who complained that the trucks have an unfair advantage since their overhead costs are lower and they do not pay rent. As Molina explained in a 2008 *LA Times* article, there is "a turf war that goes on between the vendors and the merchants."[15] In a *Time* magazine Molina stated that the businesses don't like the trucks nearby and some residents "consider it annoying to have the trucks out until midnight or two in the morning." Molina defended the ordinance by saying, "We're trying to create a better and more livable community."[16] While Molina's explanation sounds convincing, it seems an unlikely coincidence that the conflict with the restaurant owners came at the height of the recession, the same time restaurant owners' sales were hurting because low-wage workers had less disposable income, but perhaps still a few extra dollars for a cheap taco.

Molina tried to paint the conflict as black and white: one between *loncheros* and restaurants, but, as Erin Glenn, former CEO of the Asociación de Loncheros L.A. Familia Unida de California, and Hernández-López point out in their research on the conflict, it is not that simple. Opponents of the "mobile food industry" saw food trucks as the cause of urban blight and blamed food trucks for keeping out potential investors. The "real" issue, Glenn argued, "had more to do with stigma and anti-immigrant sentiment" and how they played a role in developing and passing the ordinance.[17] It is not surprising that while Molina and other city officials were cracking down on the trucks, downtown Los Angeles was simultaneously undergoing a process of gentrification. Boyle Heights and East L.A., the Mexican neighborhoods where the trucks predominate, are a short distance from downtown. The gentrification process was, and still is, flowing over into these neighboring areas, particularly Boyle Heights. The ordinance's unstated purpose was to "clean up" the area in order to attract more corporate investment. As Hernández-López explains, developers worried that "unsightly" trucks parked on the street with Latinos congregating outside "would not fit with the sale demographics of more expensive stores, restaurants, or condominium and home prices." The developers' fears, Hernández-López explains, reflect stereotypes of the *loncheros* as "lower socio-economic class, immigrant, and foreign," fears that echo those of the campaigns against the tamale vendors a hundred years earlier.[18] As Jeffrey Pilcher points out in *Planet Taco*, the taco truck battle "revealed diverse racial and communal fault lines in contemporary Los Angeles." After so many anti-immigrant campaigns, many Latinos "considered this ordinance to be yet another form of discrimination against their livelihoods and culture."[19]

Gentrification, however, has also brought economic benefit to the *loncheros*. As formerly Latino neighborhoods such as Echo Park and Highland Park gentrified, the trucks became the "it" way of dining for a population of young Anglo-American hipsters who had migrated to these more affordable "up-and-coming" areas.[20] Since the population who ate at the *loncheras* changed, Glenn explains, "What was once a symbol of poverty and blight was now seen as chic and novel. What was once passively legislated became spotlighted."[21] As a result, the ordinance not only incensed the truck owners and their Latino clientele, but also angered the young, white professionals who ate regularly at the trucks in or close to their neighborhoods. They organized and rallied on behalf of the trucks. Two recent Occidental College graduates launched a website, http://saveourtacotrucks.org/ with the battle cry "Carne asada is not a crime." They gathered more than 8,000 signatures and sold T-shirts in support of the cause. Signers of the petition wrote comments such as, "The revolution will be served on a paper plate." Concurrently, the *loncheros* began to organize to defend themselves as well. Out of their initial grassroots effort, they formed a union, Asociación de Loncheros La Familia Unida de California, in 2008 that began to meet on their own, biweekly, to discuss their challenges with the city and county and with community organizers to learn the skills for an organizing campaign. In her study, "Taco Trucks on the streets: where food and social justice meet," Erin Glenn, the original organizer of the collective and later its CEO, recounts how the two groups, the *loncheros* and the Anglo customers, finally merged in an effort to advocate social justice and preserve the food truck industry. Each group used the tools at their disposal—immigrant social networks and social media, respectively—to "bring awareness to a cause that eventually transformed into a movement."[22] The local and national media seized on the controversy and labeled the time period between the passing of the ordinance and the start of its enforcement the "Taco Truck War." Headlines in the *New York Times* declared "In Taco Truck Battle, Mild Angelenos Turn Hot" and *Time* magazine featured a story titled "The Great Taco Truck War."

The *loncheros* hired a lawyer to challenge the citations against Margarita García, one of the first truck owners to receive a ticket after the ordinance passed.[23] A few months later, on August 27, 2008, they had cause for celebration. In *People v. Margarita Garcia*, Judge Dennis A. Aichroth of the California Superior Court for the County of Los Angeles found the ordinance "unconstitutional" because its language was "too ambiguous to enforce" and therefore "unenforceable as written."[24] Judge Aichroth explained that his decision was based on the law of the California Legislature that does not allow local governments "to enact ordinances that 'regulate' versus 'prohibit' sales from vehicles" and because it was in conflict with California state law "which only permits local regulation for public safety."[25] The judge said that the county supervisors had not proven that the law was written "in the interest of public safety."[26] Los Angeles County was not alone in its rejection of the ordinance. About a year later, the city of Los Angeles also reversed a decision upholding $1,000 in parking tickets issued by the Los Angeles Police Department (LAPD) against Francisco Gonzalez. Gonzalez had been receiving up to two tickets a day under the ordinance. In *Gonzalez v. City of Los Angeles Department of Transportation* Judge Barry D. Kohn ruled on the side of the vendor, repealed the tickets, and returned the fines charged to the vendor.[27]

Since the ordinance was overturned in 2009, the *loncheros'* situation has been more secure. They have increasingly become a destination of culinary tourism for young Angeleno foodies. This shift occurred in Los Angeles at roughly same time that Chef Roy Choi was serving his first kimchi *quesadilla* at Kogi and other new wave food trucks were gaining notoriety and attracting long lines and media attention across the country. The popularity of Kogi and its offspring caused the once reputed "roach coaches" to become a popular dining destination for Anglos seeking "ethnic exoticism."[28] Food shows, food writers, and bloggers increasingly profiled their favorite trucks. Newspapers such as the *LA Weekly* published articles with headlines that featured the "10 Best Taco Trucks in Los Angeles." While most *loncheros* toil on in anonymity, certain trucks have acquired a degree of fame. Mariscos Jalisco, Ricky's Fish Tacos, and Leo's Tacos are among the most famous *loncheras* operating in Los Angeles in 2016. Mariscos Jalisco and Ricky's have been around for well over a decade, while Leo's Tacos is a newcomer to the scene. Mariscos Jalisco was one of the first to receive national attention, appearing on food shows and receiving a spot annually on Jonathan Gold's list of "101 Best Restaurants."

Customers frequently drive great distances to eat at one of the city's most popular *loncheras*, Mariscos Jalisco, a *lonchera* parked on Olympic Boulevard, a major street in Boyle Heights across from a vibrantly painted housing project. Raul Ortega, one of the most successful and well-known *loncheros* in the city, has owned it since 2001. Raul has been parked in the same spot for fourteen years across the street from the apartment he has shared with his family since coming to the United States from his native Jalisco twenty-eight years ago. He attributes his original success to a sense of community. In the 1980s, his neighbors were all from Jalisco, his home state in Mexico, and they formed a tight-knit enclave. His long-term success, however, stems from the unforgettable experience of eating one of his shrimp *tacos*: crunchy and fried, yet fresh, a unique flavor profile that draws customers not only from the immediate area but from all over the city and around the world. Mariscos Jalisco has been profiled in international magazines and has won multiple awards for the best taco. As Jonathan Gold put it in an article in the *LA Times*,

In some circles, admitting that you live in Los Angeles but haven't visited Mariscos Jalisco is like confessing that you've never been to Dodger Stadium, or driven through the four-level freeway interchange, or eaten a corn dog on Muscle Beach—inexcusable, really.

Mariscos Jalisco is so popular that there have been several copycats that have tried to duplicate his shrimp *tacos*. In fact, Raul told me that his fame is so widespread that someone tried to sell *tacos al estilo de la calle Olympic* (*tacos* in the style of Olympic Street), but none have succeeded because Raul carefully protects his secret recipe.

I frequently take my students and friends and relatives from out of town to visit Mariscos Jalisco because of the delicious, fresh flavor of the spicy, shrimp cocktail called *aguachile*, his ceviche, and especially his *tacos dorados de camarón* (fried shrimp *tacos*), not to mention the affable personality of the *lonchero*. Visitors always enjoy the environment on busy weekend afternoons: families sitting around eating *tacos* and chatting, musicians strolling, and an adjacent cart selling Mexican pastries. Raul's secret recipe for his *tacos dorados de camarón* comes from the family of a friend from his hometown, San Juan de los Lagos, Mexico, a town in the northeast corner of the state of Jalisco. It is its hyperregionality that makes his shrimp *tacos* so unique.

Shrimp taco at Mariscos Jalisco. Photo courtesy of Ebony Bailey.

Mariscos Jalisco is a family-run business, Raul's children work at the *lonchera* and many of his customers have been coming since the truck first opened. When I first started visiting Mariscos Jalisco in 2010, there was no formal seating, so people would eat over their cars or sit on the window ledge of a building in front of the truck. In 2013, Raul rented the room in front of his truck and filled it with long tables and chairs, so now when I take groups of students to visit, Raul can tell them his story without the din of passing traffic. In 2012, Raul expanded to a second location in the Fashion District to attract local workers. This location has struggled since Raul lost his parking place with better foot traffic. Since then, he parks on a nondescript street in a spot that is harder to locate. A truck with food this good and this popular deserves to have a successful brick-and-mortar restaurant. It will be interesting to see what the future holds for Mariscos Jalisco.

Leo's Tacos, a truck that only opened in 2010 and now has four trucks spread around the city, sells $1 *al pastor tacos* in Mid-City L.A., an area less populated with *loncheras* than East L.A. and Boyle Heights. *Eater LA* calls Leo's Tacos "the breakout star of LA taco trucks" and lists it among Los Angeles' eighteen essential food trucks.[29] L.A. taco expert Bill Esparza included it on his list of the top 25 *tacos* for *LA Magazine* and says it dominates Los Angeles' "al pastor scene."[30] Esparza pointed out to me that what makes Leo's Tacos unique is the expertise of the spitmasters, many of whom

Spit for Tacos Al Pastor. Photo courtesy of Ebony Bailey.

used to work at some of the best *taquerías* in Mexico. Their job is to cut thin slices of meat from the massive chunk wrapped around the revolving giant *trompo* (a vertical rotating spit). For these *taqueros*, shaving the meat is an art form.

This style of cooking comes from the Christian Lebanese immigrants to Mexico who arrived primarily between 1880 and 1910 escaping religious persecution from the Islamic Ottoman Empire. The name *al pastor* literally means in the style of the shepherd; in this case it refers to the Middle Eastern shepherds who watched over the lambs. Lebanese immigrants brought their *shawarma* (roasted meat cooked on a revolving spit) style of cooking with them, although in Mexico pork is used instead of lamb. *Shawarma* can be found "everywhere in the Middle East where the Ottoman Empire once reigned," but with different names in other countries such as gyros and doner kebab.[31] In a 2015 radio interview, Jeffrey Pilcher explained that by the 1930s there were restaurants that served *shawarma* in Mexico. While some Lebanese, such as the family of Mexican tycoon Carlos Slim, eventually made their way to Mexico City, the largest group of Mexicans of Lebanese descent still lives in Mérida, Yucatán, where dishes such as *fattoush* (a salad made with stale pita bread) and *kibbeh* remain part of the region's cuisine. Pilcher said that during the 1960s, the cuisine "morphed" when "the Mexican-born children of these Lebanese migrants ... start[ed] opening up their own restaurants, and they start[ed] to create a kind of a hybrid cuisine."[32] He added that the Lebanese created *al pastor* by using the technology of the vertical rotisserie and marinating the meat in a red chili sauce, known as *achiote*, which gives it "its distinctive color."[33] Even the name *al pastor* refers to the original lamb version, Pilcher said. With Mexican immigration, *al pastor* eventually made its way to the United States, where it thrives on the streets of Los Angeles, sold at taco trucks and in restaurants.

On a recent weekday afternoon I studied the truck and the crowd eating at Leos's Tacos as I enjoyed my $1 *al pastor tacos* while crouched over the hood of my car in the parking lot of a gas station at a major intersection in Mid-City. While I do not claim to be a great connoisseur of *al pastor*, I have eaten a fair amount on the streets of Mexico City and these were among the best, sweet with just the right texture and a few small chunks of pineapple and all the red or green salsa you could want to complement the delicious *al pastor* flavor. Unlike the traditional *lonchera*, Leos's is a wrapped truck with eye-catching graphics. The back of the truck is decorated with two men with long, dark mustaches, dark baseball caps, a banner of red, white, and green— the colors of the Mexican flag—draped across their chests, and holding a taco in their right hand while giving the thumbs up with the other. Underneath them is written "Good Food. Good Times. Authentic Mexican Cuisine." The image of the happy, stereotypical Mexican is meant to show the taco's authenticity, but also appeal to a younger generation. Gone is the sombrero wearing *mexicano* of yore found on restaurant signs across the United States; instead, we see baseball-cap wearing Mexicans, likely Los Angeles Dodgers fans. This evolution beyond previous stock images of Mexican-Americans or Mexicans seems to reflect a playful attitude on the part of the *lonchero*, as well as a shift in identity. Unlike Mariscos Jalisco, this truck is not tied to a region or village in Mexico, but instead is its own creation, one that is both Mexican and Angeleno at the same time. Leo's Tacos is a newer addition to the taco truck scene and its self-representation reflects that shift.

There were around twenty customers eating or waiting for their order at 2 in the afternoon, probably a paltry sum compared to the numbers that line up late into the evening. What struck me was the diversity of the clientele. There were two slender hipsters in their late 20s. One of them expressed

Leo's Tacos Truck. Photo courtesy of Ebony Bailey.

Leo's Al Pastor Tacos. Photo courtesy of Ebony Bailey.

concern that he shouldn't be eating this kind of food because it would affect his six-pack. There was a group of young African-Americans eating their *al pastor* in a Prius while a few Anglo and Asian women in their sixties waited to place their order. A group of Latino men dressed in gas station attendant uniforms, probably employees of the station where the truck parks, were eating their *tacos* and drinking bottles of Sangria Señorial, a nonalcoholic sangria-flavored Mexican soda, at a small folding table nearby.

Another *lonchera* that attracts a diverse clientele is Ricky's Fish Tacos. Ricky Piña began with a stand in a Hollywood parking lot serving Ensenada-style fish and shrimp *tacos*, then moved to Chinatown, and finally, in 2013, migrated to an actual food truck. The new truck displays the Los Angeles skyline with palm trees and Ricky's Fish Tacos painted in bright yellow letters. Above, Piña lists all the publications that have given him awards, including Jonathan Gold's acclaimed "101 Best" list in the *LA Times* and the *LA Weekly*'s "99 Essential Restaurants." Food writer and blogger Bill Esparza calls Ricky's "one of the pioneers of the new L.A. street food scene" and says that truck owner "Piña remains one of the most successful traditional Mexican street vendors who crossed over into a mainstream audience." These days, Piña uses Twitter to let his customers know his hours, showing that his clientele has become primarily young, middle-class, tech-savvy consumers. On a recent Friday afternoon visit to Ricky's, there was a long line to order. The crowd I surveyed was mostly twenty-somethings and coworkers on lunch

Ricky Piña inside his truck Ricky's Fish Tacos. Photo courtesy of Ebony Bailey.

breaks. Despite abnormal the heat in mid–February and the wait, the *tacos* were well worth it, crunchy yet tender with just the right amount of cream sauce. Ricky's *tacos* are typical Baja-style made with a secret batter recipe used for frying the fish, plenty of sliced cabbage, red and green *salsas*, and *crema mexicana*.

Trucks such as Mariscos Jalisco, Ricky's, and Leo's Tacos are examples of *loncheras* that have benefited from the explosive popularity of their culinary cousins, the *luxe-loncheras*, a term Gustavo Arellano gave to the gourmet food trucks that began operating on the streets of Los Angeles in 2009. These nouveau trucks were modeled in large part on their Mexican counterparts, but they operate with a different business model. They do not park in the same location for hours with regular customers, but instead change locations after a period of a few hours. Part of their original appeal to a young, urban middle class was their use of social media. They would alert followers of their location by tweeting it, so that only those in the know could find it. As food writers and bloggers profiled the craze over the new trucks, they generated greater awareness of the mobile food industry and influenced the idea that *loncheras* are actually beneficial and an integral part of the city. With the increased coverage from food bloggers and writers, a select few *loncheras* acquired new fame. In 2011, for example, when I attended a program on Global Street Food hosted by the radio station KCRW's program Good Food, Mariscos Jalisco was the only *lonchera* featured, demonstrating that it is much easier for the new-style trucks, often backed up by professional chefs and the infrastructure of the restaurant industry to gain notoriety than the traditional *lonchero*, who rarely uses social media to advertise.

The new-style food trucks contributed to a street-food renaissance that began in Los Angeles in 2008 with the Kogi truck and quickly spread across the country. The Kogi truck is a phenomenon that changed the way young Americans think of eating out—first in Los Angeles and eventually in cities throughout the United States—and changed the way they think of culinary borders. Kogi was the invention of Roy Choi, a Korean-American chef who was born in Seoul and grew up in Los Angeles. Unemployed after the financial crash and desperate to do something exciting, he combined his Korean heritage and knowledge of Mexican street food, thereby gentrifying the working-class Mexican *lonchera*. Kogi grew from Choi's childhood in the culinary and social borderlands of Los Angeles. Choi arrived as a toddler in the early 1970s as part of the boom in Asian migration following the 1965 Immigration Reform Act. His parents struggled to make a living for many years, opening a Korean restaurant in Garden Grove that did not succeed along with a series of other unsuccessful business ventures. During his childhood, Choi ate his way through Koreatown's barbecue restaurants, Jewish delis, Salvadorian *pupuserías*, and Mexican *taquerías*. Choi's taste buds were informed by these years of walking the streets of Los Angeles, where Mexican food blends seamlessly with American fare through cross-cultural marketing and intermarriage. Neon signs advertise historic institutions such as "Lucy's Mexican-American Food" selling hamburgers and *tacos*, or the Kosher Burrito, a downtown food stand opened by a Jewish man married to a Sonoran woman. In this way, a Korean boy would have easily understood Mexican food as part of the mosaic that makes up American food.[34]

The crash of 2008 provided Choi with the opportunity—and the need—to fuse the diverse street foods of his youth with his years of professional training. Having just been laid off from a high-end restaurant, he got together with a former colleague who suggested the idea of a Korean barbecue taco truck. Kogi hit the streets in late 2008, featuring a menu of short rib *tacos*, kimchi *quesadillas*, and Kogi sliders, menu items Jonathan Gold calls "edible symbols of L.A.'s famous cross-cultural inclusiveness, dripping plates of food drawn straight from the city's recombinant DNA."[35] Hip young people used their cellphones to follow the seemingly random tweets of the Kogi truck, and then waited in impossibly long lines to eat. The Kogi trucks thus became a beacon for a generation that could no longer afford the fancy restaurants that had defined status in the precrash era but yearned for a similar form of distinction. It also represented the shifting world of social media in which food trends are not discovered by food critics, but via Twitter, Instagram, and Yelp. In this way, the Kogi truck paved the way for a national trend of mobile dining tracked through social media. By 2009, four Kogi trucks were cruising the streets of Los Angeles as the Korean barbecue taco went viral across the country. Within a year, Kogi copycats were popping up around Los Angeles and major cities across the United States.

Was Kogi "authentic" Mexican food? Not at all, but that was never its intention. Instead, it represents a fusion of two cultures that exist side by side in Los Angeles, a gentrification of once humble street food and a particular moment in American culture that produced Barack Obama as president. As their website proclaims, Kogi would become "an icon of LA street food" that changed how a younger generation of Americans conceived of street food in general and Mexican staples such as the taco or the *quesadilla*. A taco no longer had to be filled with traditional ingredients such as *al pastor*, *carne asada* (grilled beef), or chicken, but instead could serve as a vehicle for creativity. Kogi's success put street food on the minds of the "everyday diner," making it a national trend and a model for the future of fast food. A new generation of truck owners sprang up, inspired by Kogi's success and the freedom of owning their own truck. Many served knock-off Korean *tacos*, burritos, and *quesadillas*. On the east coast, Korilla in New York opened in 2010 selling *tacos*, burritos, and rice bowls, TaKorean in DC, and further south, Chi'Lantro in Austin. Closer to home, trucks such as Bool Koreano Americano play with Korean-Latin cultural fusion with its very name and its menu that includes short rib burritos and "boolitos."

Kogi truck in Venice, California. Photo courtesy of Ebony Bailey.

Guerrilla Tacos, a more recent gourmet food truck, defies easy categorization. It is neither a traditional *lonchera* nor a fusion truck like Kogi and its disciples. Jonathan Gold explains that you can visit Guerilla "as you would any other taco truck" or you can approach it the way you would a "tasting-menu restaurant whose dishes happen to be composed on *tortillas* instead of on fancy plates."[36] I have experienced it as a little of both categories, a place to taste different courses served on a tortilla while sitting on a bench on the sidewalk in downtown or Culver City. In 2012, L.A. native Wes Avila started Guerilla Tacos as a two-person street cart, with the mission of making *tacos* with high-quality, seasonal ingredients. After training under renowned French chef Alain Ducasse and working in high-end restaurants, Avila wanted to strike out on his own and return to his roots, while also moving beyond the same dishes with which Angelenos were already familiar. Tacos were what this Pico-Rivera native grew up eating on visits to family in Baja, Mexico, and on the streets of Los Angeles. He saw them as an accessible platform "to make the taco I'd like to eat with the best ingredients I can find."[37] Avila uses ingredients he sources from the Santa Monica and Altadena farmers' markets, fishmongers, and meat distributors, filling his *tacos* with everything from roasted artichoke hearts, broccolini, scallops, oysters, and ostrich eggs. The combination of taco and local and seasonal ingredients has been magical for Chef Avila. The *LA Times* wrote that Avila "serves compelling dishes that are equal in complexity to those at many fine-dining restaurants, even though they're served on warm *tortillas* and eaten standing up."[38]

Avila's dishes are not Mexican-American, but, as he put it, uniquely Angeleno because of his ability to use local, fresh ingredients; source seafood from nearby; and draw on his Mexican heritage and multicultural surroundings. Mexican food expert Bill Esparza considers Avila to be a leader of the new Alta California cuisine movement, a group of classically trained Mexican-American chefs who are transforming Mexican cuisine and creating something unique to Southern California. When I asked Avila what he thought Alta California cuisine meant, he explained that for him it was not really about serving authentic Mexican food; instead, "it is about being true to myself and my surroundings." Avila's surroundings are the city's cultural and culinary cornucopia of Japanese, French, Middle Eastern, and Armenian foods. Avila lives in Glendale, where there is a large Armenian population, and rattled off a list of Armenian spices and ingredients he has integrated into some of his dishes: sumac, Aleppo peppers, and Armenian cheese. According to Esparza, when Chef Enrique Olvera of Pujol (the highest-ranking restaurant in Mexico) visited Guerrilla, he was so impressed he invited Avila to speak at a gastronomic conference in Monterey, Mexico; in one fell swoop elevating the food prepared by a Mexican-American chef out of a truck in Los Angeles to the level of the elite chefs of modern Mexican cuisine.

Guerrilla's menu is more in line with high-end California cuisine restaurants that pride themselves on sourcing the best-quality ingredients than a traditional taco truck. A recent menu listed *tacos* with "Kurobota sausage," a brand of heritage pork from Japan, and Castelvetrano olives with green cauliflower. When I visited the truck in Culver City, I ate a yellowfin tuna poke tostada with *chile de* árbol, gooseberries, lemon, and cilantro—a mix of ingredients that reflects Avila's many influences, current culinary trends, and ability to use ingredients in unexpected ways. Poke, a raw fish dish originating in Hawaii, is the new sushi of the moment. In fact, the young women who were eating next to me on the sidewalk beside the truck were discussing their favorite spots around Los Angeles for late-night poke. I had only heard of gooseberries in pie before, a tart berry usually used in pies and other desserts. Instead, Avila uses it on a tostada with a small and potent Mexican chili pepper, *chile de* árbol, playing not only with how we conceive a taco but even with how traditional ingredients are used.

The "Guerrilla" truck is painted a vibrant blue and is emblazoned with graffiti artwork. It features a skull wearing an L.A. Dodgers cap with a banner that reads "Guerrilla." Its gritty East L.A. barrio design embodies the image of the tattooed, tough Avila himself, often seen wearing an L.A. Dodgers cap in photos, and stands out against the trendy, hip locations where he chooses to park his truck. Guerrilla changes location on a daily basis, moving between

Guerrilla Tacos truck in Venice, California. Photo courtesy of Ben Singer.

downtown's Arts District, an artsy section of Culver City, Beverly Hills, and trendy Abbot Kinney in Venice. On Wednesdays, the truck parks in front of a high-end coffee shop and an art gallery called Glamour in Culver City. There is always a line of customers waiting to order and others congregating outside enjoying their food. Unlike the socioeconomic diversity I found at a truck like Leo's Tacos, Avila's customers seemed to be primarily upper-middle-class foodies. His food was worth every bite, but who else could afford a $9 tostada and a tiny $4 sweet potato taco? In our conversation, Avila shared that he will be opening a few brick-and-mortar restaurants in 2016. It will be exciting to follow the future of this up-and-coming leader of the Alta California movement.

While chefs like Wes Avila and Roy Choi redefine mobile street food and bring it to an upper-middle-class demographic, thousands of other *loncheras* continue to toil away, serving traditional fare to working-class Latinos—and non-Latinos—throughout Los Angeles. Their traditional foods allow them to become entry-level entrepreneurs and empower themselves in a society in which they have historically been marginalized and suffered discrimination. The *loncheras* operate on the city's streets—urban public spaces whose rules and regulations they have had to negotiate when confronted with an unrelenting city ordinance intended to shut them down. By organizing and forming their own union, the *loncheros* defended their rights and protected their businesses. Another type of Latino microenterprise—the street-food vendors—operates on the city's sidewalks. The Latino street-food vendors are similar to the *loncheras*, but are not as well respected and are illegal in the city of Los Angeles. Despite their outsider status, the street-food vendors' microbusinesses allow them to participate in the public sphere and give undocumented immigrants a way to earn a living. The many challenges the *vendedores ambulantes* (street-food vendors) have faced and their ongoing battle for legalization will be the focus on the next chapter.

Chapter 4

Street-Food Vendors in Los Angeles

The Epic Fight for Legalization

In pre-Hispanic times, people from all over Mesoamerica converged on the market of Tlatelolco, located on the site of a present-day neighborhood in Mexico City. Markets have always been a focal point of Mesoamerican trade and gastronomic abundance, as Bernal Díaz del Castillo, a soldier in the army of Hernán Cortés, observed when he visited present-day Mexico City in 1519. Díaz found all manner of basic and luxury goods being sold on the streets of Teotihuacan, such as cacao, vanilla, pre-Columbian herbs like *epazote* and *hierba santa*, dried shrimp, insect eggs, and even iguana meat. Today, *tianguis*—markets in Mexico—as well as in Latino neighborhoods of Los Angeles—sell a vast array of ceramic cookware, household goods, textiles, fruits, vegetables, *paletas* (popsicles), and prepared foods. These foods are not only sold at markets, but are also found on thousands of street corners throughout Mexico and Central America. The *vendedores ambulantes*, or street vendors, are a vital part of the countries' informal economies. According to a 2012 article in the Mexican newspaper *La Jornada*, 60% of Mexicans participate in the country's informal economy, and in Mexico City alone at least 200,000 street vendors try to make a living on the city's sidewalks every day.[1]

Every Mexican has his or her favorite neighborhood vendor. When I visit Mexico City, I love to buy *tacos de canasta* for less than a quarter on the side streets near the Zócalo: the city's main square; little hotcakes with *cajeta*, or goat milk caramel, on the cobblestone streets of San Ángel; and *esquites*, boiled corn kernels seasoned with salt, *epazote*, butter, and lime in Coyoacán. My nephew, a Mexico City native and connoisseur of the city's street food, is a big fan of *tlacoyos* (oval-shaped, fried or baked masa cakes stuffed with beans, cheese, and other ingredients) and *sopes* (small, fried masa cakes topped with beans, crumbled cheese, lettuce, onions, and other ingredients). He also likes to buy seafood cocktails at La Nueva Viga Market, the second largest seafood market in the world and the largest seafood market in Mexico. While some of the vendors at these markets work illegally, this is not the case with all the vendors. Many have permission from the Mexican government and are members of official vendor organizations, even if they don't have an approved stand in a marketplace. As scenes from Diego Rivera's famous mural at the National Palace in Mexico City demonstrates, street vending in contemporary Mexico has significant pre-Columbian roots that reflect the rich traditions and resourcefulness of Latino communities on both sides of the border.

The tradition of street vending is one that has traveled with migrants from Mexico and Central America to Los Angeles, as well as other cities throughout the United States. On sidewalks throughout Los Angeles, street vendors sell sliced fruit, *tacos*, *paletas*, as well as other merchandise, such as clothing and seasonal holiday items, adding to the city's vibrancy, economy, and culinary tapestry. Los Angeles stands out among other American cities because of its sheer number of Latino migrants and because, as of 2016, it remains the only one of ten major U.S. cities where street vending is illegal. This chapter explores the history of discrimination toward Latino vendors in Los Angeles, the ongoing battle for legalization and street vendor rights, and the vendors' significant contribution to Los Angeles' Latino food culture and economy.

The previous chapter discussed the history of the tamale vendors in Los Angeles, revealing that Latino immigrants have been bringing street food to Southern California for far more than a century. The late nineteenth and early twentieth century witnessed the rise of the tamale wagons selling tamales on the streets of Los Angeles, San Francisco, Chicago, and other U.S. cities. As Jeffrey Pilcher observes in *Planet Taco*, these vendors were often reputed to have "deviant sexuality" and were associated with alcoholism, simply because they often clustered around bars, catering to late-night drinkers.[2] Although street vending was allowed, vendors had to comply with many regulations and their position was always precarious. When the automobile took over city streets in the 1920s, pedestrian traffic and mobile vendors were pushed onto the alleys and sidewalks. In these public spaces, according to popular culture and newspaper reports of the time, vendors were often accused of perversity, criminality, and unsanitary practices.[3] According to Mark Vallianatos, policy director of the Urban & Environmental Policy Institute at Occidental College, in the mid-1930s Los Angeles "banned vending on sidewalks downtown, and then in other major business districts."[4] These actions restricted sidewalk activity and made sidewalk vending more challenging. As the city grew and expanded, Los Angeles became a car-oriented city—a city of enormous freeways, major boulevards that cross from downtown to the ocean, a poor system of public transportation, and pedestrians struggling in an inhospitable environment. During the course of the twentieth century, as pedestrians and vendors were pushed off sidewalks, streets lost their former vibrancy and commerce. In *Incomplete Streets: Processes, Practices, and Possibilities*, Steve Zavestoski explains that in "in a self-fulfilling prophecy, Los Angeles created a car culture by taking away the rights of citizens to practice other cultures on the streets."[5] This hostility to vendors grew and persisted in the ensuing decades.

In 1974, the Los Angeles City Council voted to ban sidewalk vending throughout the city for the first time, but then mayor Tom Bradley vetoed the ordinance because he feared that it would harm poor people. Just as proponents of street vending legalization argue today, the mayor believed that it was important to "encourage, not discourage, the creation of new small-business enterprises, without which upward mobility on the socioeconomic ladder would become that much more difficult."[6] Despite Mayor Bradley's veto, a ban was successfully instituted in 1980 and sidewalk vending was made officially illegal. At the same time that street food was banned in Los Angeles, Mexican, Guatemalan, and Salvadorian immigrants began to pour into the city looking for employment opportunities following an economic recession during the early 1980s in Mexico and Central America. The spike in migration caused an increased demand for street food from new immigrants for whom it was culturally familiar.

This ban on the underground economy, long a part of the city's public landscape, caused vendors to be seen as criminals and violators of a city ordinance. Many vendors were arrested, some were beaten, and others served jail time. In "Struggles, Urban Citizenship, and Belonging: The Experience of Undocumented Street Vendors and Food Truck Owners in Los Angeles," Fazila Bhimji writes that their actions were considered misdemeanors and, at the time, they could serve up to 180 days jail time if convicted of vending, despite earning as little as $20 a day.[7] The harsh treatment of the vendors did not go unnoticed. The *LA Times* ran articles on street vendor conditions and local groups worked to defend street vendors' rights.[8] The ban turned vending into a political issue and motivated vendors to organize themselves. In 1987, they began meeting to discuss targeting by the LAPD and by 1988 they established the Asociación de Vendedores Ambulantes (Association of Street Vendors, known as the AVA). The association discussed immigration, police harassment, and other human rights issues, as well as legalizing vending. Five years later, by 1993, as many as 100 vendors packed a city council committee meeting to ask the council to set a date for legalization.

In January 1994, the Special Sidewalk Vending District Ordinance was enacted to allow selling in eight predesignated areas of Los Angeles as part of a two-year pilot program. Several hundred vendors celebrated their newly legal status, but, despite these efforts, six months later, Robert Lopez of the *LA Times* reported that no vending licenses had been issued and that vendors continued to complain of harassment by the LAPD. Lopez reported that vendors were protesting police harassment outside a police station, waving signs that read "Somos vendedores, no criminales" ("We are vendors, not criminals").[9] In many ways, the city's attempt to impose geographic limits on the practice of vending was a failure. Only one zone was established and none remain today. The process of zone creation, a city report found, is far too cumbersome and costly to work. A 2015 Salon.com article on the rise of street vending in Los Angeles compared its zoning ordinance with a 1993 effort in Mexico City, which attempted to coerce vendors into newly established, designated markets. Of these designated sites in Mexico City, only two remain popular today.[10] Oftentimes, restricting vendors to designated zones hurts the vendors: entrepreneurs who know their customers and the best locations to sell to them.

Nearly thirty years later, street vending remains a contentious—and illegal—activity in Los Angeles. Police harassment and ticketing remain occupational hazards for street vendors. In 2013, the police made 1,200 arrests for sidewalk vending. Yet, an estimated ten to twelve thousand street-food vendors sell bacon-wrapped hot dogs, *tacos* and *quesadillas*, fruit, sodas, and *raspados* (Mexican snow cones) at the beaches, parks, and sidewalks all over Los Angeles.[11] Why do vendors continue to hit the pavement despite the risk of fines, police harassment, and even imprisonment? Typically, vendors have limited education and most of them are undocumented; therefore, they have few employment alternatives. They need to provide for their families. For vendors, street vending offers a vital form of economic mobility and entrepreneurship. Given the undocumented status of many vendors, they also have limited political clout with politicians, creating another obstacle in the fight for legalization. Even though the vendors work outside the formal economy and usually lack legal status, Bhimji argues that street vending gives them agency and empowers them with a "sense of citizenship and belonging through their varied experiences and struggles."[12] Street vending allows the vendors to participate in the public sphere, while the fight for legalization has given them a sense that they have a voice in their community.

Why is street vending still illegal in the city with the highest number of vendors of any city in the United States? There are numerous reasons politicians and business owners have been opposed to vending. Some brick-and-mortar businesses oppose the vendors because they say they create congestion on busy sidewalks, interfere with strollers and wheelchairs, leave trash behind, and create unfair competition since vendors do not pay taxes or rent and can park their carts just outside their restaurants. Yet, as Professor Vallianatos pointed out at a 2015 Boyle Heights town hall meeting on street vending, some businesses benefit from the increased foot traffic. Furthermore, restaurants attract a different clientele than street vendors. People who are looking for a comfortable experience where they can sit down and eat with others go to restaurants, while people who want to grab a quick meal for a few dollars will stop at a street vendor. Others criticize street vendors because they see them as "a manifestation of disorder," believing them to be unsanitary and creating sidewalk congestion in already densely populated areas, particularly in downtown Los Angeles. Still others fear they attract gang activity and violence. However, supporters of the vendors argue that the presence of vendors and their clients in dangerous neighborhoods acts as a deterrent for crime and gang activity.

While these concerns do need to be addressed in the discussion about legalization, the contributions vendors make to the city financially and culturally also need to be recognized. The Sidewalk Stimulus Report estimates that street-food vendors generate over $100 million annually in income for the L.A. economy and vendor spending "sustains 5,234 jobs in Los Angeles."[13] A 2010 study by the USC School of Policy, Planning and Development titled "Street Vending in Boyle Heights: Examining the Challenges and Opportunities" recognized the concerns of community members and local business owners as well as those of the vendors themselves, while also looking at the positive impact of vending in the area. Questions asked in the survey included, "What adaptations, if any, can be made under current political feasibility to address the issue of street vending in Boyle Heights?" The study conducted a pedestrian survey that found that community members ate frequently from

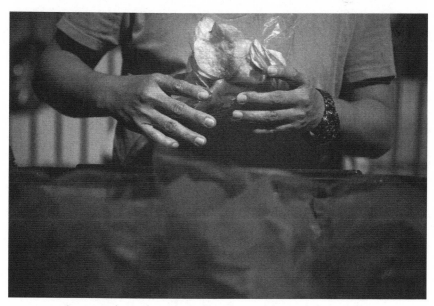

Street vendor in downtown alley. Photo courtesy of Ebony Bailey.

the vendors: 16% as often as once a week, 16% a few times a week, and 20% at least once a month. These numbers show the integral role of the vendors in the Boyle Heights area, an area that is 94% Latino, according to the *LA Times*.

Advocates for legalization say that it would not only prove beneficial for vendors, but also for the public and the city by bringing vendors out of the shadows and allowing them to play an important role as a source of economic activity.[14] Legalization would allow vendors to participate on a greater scale with a proper system of taxation and registration, while also ensuring that their food met the city's health standards. "We need to use all of our tools to promote the local economy," ninth district city council representative Curren Price said. "We shouldn't overlook these micro-businesses, and we need to find a way to formalize this entrepreneurship, because it's been going on for a long time in this city."[15]

Legalization would also improve food safety, as the Public Health Department would be required to review the carts regularly. Yet, Matt Geller, the CEO of the Southern California Mobile Food Vendors Association, explains that most street food will still violate state health laws. According to the Los Angeles County Public Health website on the street vending compliance program, unless a vendor is selling hot dogs or tamales, they must have access to water to wash their hands and utensils—a nearly impossible feat when selling on a city sidewalk.[16] The website claims that street vendors put the city at risk because there is no "portable water for handlers to wash their hands, the food comes from unapproved sources, there are no restrooms for customers, and food is stored at potentially hazardous temperatures" that increase the likelihood of bacterial growth in the food products.[17] Despite these public health challenges, working with the city to find solutions agreeable to all and creating laws to regulate the vendors will give them a way to legally make a living, while better protecting residents and business owners.

Along with the economic and public health incentives for legalization, the city is gradually beginning to embrace pedestrianism and leave behind its car culture. What does this have to do with vendors selling food and other goods on the city's urban sidewalks? In a city designed around the automobile, street vendors create a more vibrant street culture that "promotes cultural diversity and social connections."[18] In a car-centered landscape such as Los Angeles, the value of people congregating around a cart on a sidewalk while stopping to buy fruit or a taco as they walk home from work or an errand can be easily overlooked, but in low-income Latino neighborhoods these scenes are a vital part of everyday life. In the United States today, street vendors are actively reviving urban public life by cultivating traditional practices of street vending. The Latino community, for many years, has been at the forefront of this revitalization of public spaces. Mike Davis, author of *Magical Urbanism,* notes that street vendors are transforming "dead urban spaces into convivial social places," "blending traditions from the *mestijaze* of the Spanish plaza and the Meso-American *mercado*."[19] Public spaces, such as sidewalks, lead to social interactions and the construction of relationships within communities.

Street vending also has the potential to allow easier access to healthy food and fruits and vegetables in urban food deserts: As I discuss in later chapters, low-income Latino neighborhoods do not have enough supermarkets stocked with fresh fruits and vegetables, but instead overflow with corner stores and liquor stores selling chips and soda to schoolchildren. Low-income areas of Los Angeles such as East L.A., Boyle Heights, and South L.A. are considered food deserts. South L.A. has only one grocery store per 22,156 people, according to research from Occidental College's Urban & Environmental Policy

Caridad Vásquez making quesadillas. Photo courtesy of Fernando Abaraca (ELACC).

Institute, while affluent West L.A. has a supermarket for half as many shoppers. It is expensive and difficult to bring in new supermarkets and established chains are either not interested given the risks or the neighborhoods do not have large enough lots with adequate parking. Currently, more than 70% of South L.A.'s food is available at liquor and convenience stores, places that often have dismal looking produce.[20] As Kettles and Morales, professors of law and urban and regional planning, observe in their study of sidewalk fruit vendors, our view of streets has become one-dimensional and, as a result, we often neglect the potential of the street to be our access to food in its own right. Kettles and Morales argue that returning "streets to multiple uses will help improve public health," providing a strong justification for "allowing private buyers and sellers of food to meet and trade in the public street."[21] It is estimated that 25% of street carts already sell whole and/or cut fruits and vegetables. Often, vendors selling sliced fruit at major intersections are the easiest way for low-income residents to access healthy and culturally appropriate produce.

Proponents of legalization argue that a permit process would further the selling of healthy food by providing incentives to vendors who sell this food. In order to improve nutrition and expand access within these communities, the city could offer incentives for healthy food vendors such as expediting the permit process for them, offering them discounted permits, and allowing them to sell near schools and other restricted areas. Vallianatos' map of heavily vended areas in the city of Los Angeles shows that areas with high rates of vendor arrests correspond to areas with high rates of diabetes and obesity, supporting the idea that vendors are selling in food deserts. While all vendors certainly do not sell healthy foods, those that do make a valuable contribution to bringing healthy food into underserved areas. Legalization has the potential to make it easier for these vendors to create an essential service in their communities. It could also prohibit other vendors that do not offer nutritious food from selling within a certain distance of a school by regulating where the vendors sell.

Ironically, even though many vendors offer healthy food in food deserts, they are routinely given fines, have their carts and merchandise taken away, and are occasionally arrested. Others are forced to pay gangs if they sell on their turf, as was pointed out to me by a vendor when I took my students on a tour of street vendors in McArthur Park, an area adjacent to downtown Los Angeles teeming with sidewalk vendors selling everything from used clothes and knock-off watches to *quesadillas* and fruit. The vendor approached me and asked what we were doing, since a group of college students and their professor clearly stood out in this environment. When I explained we were interested in learning about the challenges facing the vendors, he said he thought it was important that we knew that he and his fellow vendors are routinely harassed and forced to pay local gangs.

Over the past few years, community-based organizations have begun to recognize the need for creative solutions to support the unlicensed vendors. In 2008, the vendors' cause was taken up by the East Los Angeles Community Corporation (ELACC), a community organization that works on behalf of the 95% Latino residents of East L.A. to support "a productive, healthy, and fulfilling life." ELACC started working with vendor members who were being harassed, discriminated against, and criminalized by the police. Over the next two years, ELACC tried to create a farmers' market space for the vendors. They worked with the police department to find a space that they would approve, but the vendors needed a larger area to be able to include all interested community members. In 2009, the Leadership for Urban Renewal Network (LURN), a nonprofit working to make the historically marginalized communities of Boyle Heights and East L.A. more sustainable and vibrant, began to investigate alternatives that would best meet the community's needs. The following year LURN teamed up with a group of students in the master's program at the USC Sol Price School of Public Policy to investigate the challenges and opportunities of street vending in Boyle Heights. The USC faculty told the students to "think creatively about alternatives that might support unlicensed vendors as a one-size-fits-all approach may not work." As part of their practicum, the USC students conducted an in-depth literature review using sources from the *LA Times* to Twitter, holding interviews with government and community stakeholders, and reviewing case studies to identify the best policies. They also surveyed over sixty vendors in Boyle Heights. The survey of business owners determined that only 18% had filed a complaint against vendors, 53% had had little or no interaction with vendors, and 35% reported good experiences with vendors. A majority of vendors (55%) reported good interactions with business owners and other vendors and an even greater majority (59%) expressed an interest in legalization with government assistance. These numbers demonstrated that the best approach was to work toward legalization. Soon afterward, the organizations began to work actively toward this goal.

In 2010, the first vendor community forum to discuss legalization was held. After that, the movement began to build momentum. In 2011, the nonprofit ELACC decided to push the city toward legalization. During 2012, ELACC organized several town hall meetings with thousands of vendors around Los Angeles County to listen to their concerns, better understand their needs, and see how the vendors themselves envisioned the legalization process. Many of the street vendors became activists, working to defend their rights. Interestingly, the campaign for legalization has been waged from the bottom up. ELACC and LURN have made a point of going to the vendors first to see how the process can best meet their needs.

In 2012, ELACC and LURN teamed up with a working group from the Los Angeles Food Policy Council to draft an ordinance for legalization.

The information from the town hall meetings, along with additional research, informed the ordinance. In 2013, the working group drafted a formal version of the ordinance. This general framework was proposed to the major's office and, in November 2013, 14th District city councilman José Huizar and Ninth District rep Curren Price authored a motion to look at legalizing the practice. In May 2014, the chief legislative analyst's office issued a seven-page preliminary report recommending that Los Angeles adopt a citywide street vending program. Since then, over sixty organizations from different sectors have been working tirelessly with vendors throughout Los Angeles to make legalization a reality. At a 2015 Los Angeles Food Policy Council Food Day event, the street-food working group stated that the current goals are "to create a permit system that gives micro-entrepreneurs an opportunity to make an honest living, encourages healthy eating, and supports existing small businesses communities all around Los Angeles." Since the ordinance was submitted to the city in 2013, the leaders of the movement have held demonstrations at city hall and engaged in a social media campaign, *#legalizestreetvending* on Twitter and https://www.facebook.com/LAStreetVendorCampaign on Facebook. They have gone so far as to bring cards and stuffed animals to city councilmembers for Valentine's Day in 2014 in an attempt to elicit sympathy for the vendors' stories of hardship and arrest. Yet, the proposal has been delayed time and time again as different city departments weigh in.

During the vendors' Valentine's Day visit to city hall, Spanish-language media captured their stories, such as the plight of Rosa Calderón, a seventy-nine-year-old vendor who has no family in the United States and has faced constant arrest and harassment by police.[22] Among other citations, Calderón was last arrested for selling Christmas tree ornaments. Calderón's story was so moving that University of California, Los Angeles (UCLA) law school students from the Criminal Defense Clinic chose to represent her at her trial at Los Angeles' Metropolitan Courthouse after she accumulated seven tickets for violating the ban on street vending. Calderón estimates she earns $15 a day and had no means to pay the hundreds of dollars she was charged in tickets. Under their professor's supervision, the law students stood with Calderón in court and grilled the police officer who cited her. This sort of representation is unusual in cases such as these and was intended to be a form of "overkill"; to show that properly enforcing the ban on street vending is extremely onerous and a waste of law enforcement's time. Attorney Cynthia Anderson-Baker, a lawyer who helped represent Calderón, explained that to properly enforce the law the police have to take hours out of their busy workdays to document the items they are confiscating. Still, weeks after the court date where the majority of her tickets were dismissed, Rosa Calderón was cited again.[23]

With the media attention and interest from the Los Angeles City Hall, the movement in support of the vendors has growing support. In February 2015, a packed town hall meeting was held at Casa del Mexicano, a beautiful, historic building in Boyle Heights, to generate public awareness on the topic. Leaders from different community organizations and the Los Angeles Food Policy Council spoke along with the vendors themselves. Boyle Heights street vendor Caridad Vásquez and San Gabriel Valley vendor Alfonso García told their stories. They described the hardships of battling police and gangs and explained that they worked as vendors because they had no other choice. As Vásquez voiced with tremendous passion, "nuestras familias dependen de nosotros" (our families depend on us).

In March 2015, Caridad Vásquez visited my class on Latino food culture at the University of Southern California along with Fernando Abarca, senior associate with the nonprofit ELACC, to inform the students about the ongoing battle for legalization. After serving delicious, fresh *tacos* and *quesadillas* to the students, Caridad shared her story with them. While some of the students had interviewed vendors for a class assignment, many of the vendors they had encountered were afraid to give them their names or to even talk to the students. Caridad, on the other hand, told her story with great pride in her voice. Caridad Vásquez is a dynamic fifty-five-year-old woman originally from Colima, Mexico. As a child she sold tamales on the streets to help her family meet ends. After marrying her husband in Michoacán, her mother-in-law taught her how to prepare different traditional *salsas, nopales* (prickly pear cactus), and other recipes. With the knowledge she gleaned from her mother-in-law, Caridad prepared and sold food to support her family. In 1995, she came with her husband to the United States. As she tells it, when she arrived she realized she "didn't know how to do anything ... not sew, cut hair, nothing. All she knew how to do was be a street vendor," so she kept this occupation despite the hazards. She shared with the students that she had a limited education, but that selling on the street had taught her other skills. Caridad wasn't at all embarrassed by her lack of education; instead, she was very proud of her work and passionate about what she does. As she told the class, she prepares and serves food "con mucho cariño" (with much affection). Clearly, Caridad has a strong entrepreneurial spirit given that, despite many obstacles, she has been selling food on the streets of Boyle Heights for twenty years. Soon after arriving in the United States, she set up a little stand with enchiladas, but the police stopped her. Later, she reinvented herself as a nighttime vendor of *pozole*, a traditional Mexican stew, and began to frequent the Breed Street area of Boyle Heights, a Big Lots parking lot that became a nighttime market filled with vendors during the peak of the recession.

In 2008–2009 when the recession began, many Latinos lost their jobs or had their incomes cut drastically. As a result, Caridad and hundreds of other vendors began to sell food—or anything else—to survive. Foodies, bloggers, and journalists from the *LA Times* soon discovered the nocturnal Breed Street vendors and the space became something of an "institution" for a short period of time. Jonathan Gold, the Pulitzer Prize–winning food critic, wrote an article about the Breed Street phenomenon for the *LA Weekly*, "Fried in East L.A.: Antojito's Carmen and the Breed Street Band of Mexican Vendors," describing the street's panoply of culinary offerings:

> sticky, sizzling, crunchy meaty snacks from all over Mexico; *salsas* hot enough to burn small, butterfly-shaped patches into the leather of your shoes; and quart-size foam cups of homemade orange drink. Over here were *huaraches;* over there Mexico City-style *quesadillas*; crunchy flautas; sugary churros; gooey *tacos al vapor.*[24]

In a piece for *Saveur,* Gold mused that in Los Angeles he was "just as likely to find bliss on a folding table in a dicey parking lot as [he] was in a Michelin-starred restaurant."[25] Along with Gold and other journalists, the illegal night-time market also attracted the attention of area residents who were upset by the noise, trash, and crowded sidewalks it created. Residents complained to their city councilman José Huizar and, in response, he worked to shut it down. Residents of Boyle Heights were not the only ones unhappy with the popular night market. The economic recession had hurt local businesses; and business owners saw the vendors as unfair competition and asked the police for help in addressing unlicensed vending.[26]

Studies, however, show a far different reality when business owners and street vendors coexist. According to a the 2015 Sidewalk Stimulus Report, vending does not hurt local businesses, and vendors "avoid selling in places in close proximity to retailers who offer similar products or services."[27] Instead, the report stated that vendors play a complementary role to brick-and-mortar establishments in the "retail ecosystem" and, rather than hurting local businesses, brick and mortars suffer when vendors leave the neighborhood. The study provided the example of Chicago's Maxwell Street Market, a large historic open-air market that had been forced to close in 1994 to allow for the expansion of a university and whose closure caused nearly $50 million in total losses, including to local brick-and-mortar establishments, many of which went out of business. The report goes on to discuss three case study locations in Los Angeles, Boyle Heights, downtown, and Hollywood, where they found that "retail stores and restaurants operating in geographic proximity to street vendors (who typically sold different products than the businesses they were near) enjoyed firm expansion and job growth."[28]

Despite the evidence that brick-and-mortar businesses and vendors not only coexist but also benefit each other, the city responded to business owners' complaints and the LAPD began enforcing state food safety laws and the ban on street vending. Soon, the city shut the Breed Street market down for good. As a result, Caridad Vásquez (as well as many others) lost her cart and her livelihood. She had to save money to begin vending once again. After that, she sold *quesadillas* in front of a local school, but was not able to earn much money in this new location. Since then, she has been selling in a better location in Boyle Heights and her business is doing well. Caridad has been in the United States for two decades and says she could probably find work as a housekeeper or janitor, but she finds great pleasure in what she does and has no desire to do anything else. In her own words, "I make this food with great care and pride, but I also know how to defend what I want, to send a message. This food is healthy, fresh, prepared daily, and not processed."

In 2008, Caridad joined the Los Angeles Street Vendor Campaign and has been working very hard to legalize vending in Los Angeles ever since. In 2012, she was received in city hall along with other vendors and members of the nonprofits ELACC and LURN. Since then, members of these organizations have been working closely with the city to determine what exactly is needed to meet the city's public health codes and have street carts finally approved. While there have been numerous campaigns for legalization in the past, Caridad and others believe that this one is different because this time their voices are being heard by the politicians at city hall.

Caridad was a passionate speaker as well as charming and warm with my students, calling the women *mamita* (little lady), encouraging them to try the food, and taking care the vegetarians. She brought a selection of *tacos*, *quesadillas*, *salsas*, and other toppings for the students. She insisted everything had been prepared that day—warm *tortillas*, four fresh *salsas*, lettuce, radish, *nopales* or cactus pads, *flor de calabaza* or squash flower, meat, chicken—and that she only used ingredients of the highest quality. In doing so, she acknowledged a public safety concern that critics often raise, one that had also been voiced by many of my students as they ventured out to interview street vendors for their weekly blog and sample street food on their own. The food was handled with great attention to cleanliness. She even brought hand sanitizer and served all the food with tongs. Caridad's food spoke for itself. My corn tortilla with squash flower, lettuce, and salsa was fresh and delicious. My students devoured the chicken *tacos*. I found the *nopales*, a pre-Hispanic ingredient that has been consumed for its legendary healing qualities (and more recently for its valuable nutritional qualities) to be tasty and tender. Recipes, such as Caridad's, typically come from oral tradition, handed down by word of mouth from one generation to the next. Caridad's cooking preserves her cultural tradition and passes it on to her customers.

The food Caridad served my students showed how street food can be an affordable means to access healthier food options, particularly in low-income areas such as Boyle Heights where street food is a better option than fast food or junk food. Many of the street vendors sell sliced fruits, such as mango and pineapple, along with whole fruit, a cultural norm in Mexico and Central American countries. Fruit carts with vibrant rainbow-colored umbrellas dot Los Angeles' urban and residential landscape. At the end of my residential street in Los Angeles, I can buy a two-pound container of sliced fruit for five dollars and another half-mile down my street I often buy big bags of oranges for seven dollars. It is easy to pull up alongside the street vendor's stand, pay him, and receive juicy oranges, cherries, or mangoes. These street vendors make up an integral part of the fabric of L.A. life.

Community meetings held throughout Los Angeles County have demonstrated wide support for the vendors. Yet, despite the strong community and media support, vendors continue to be harassed and victimized. On March 16, 2015, the Los Angeles Department of Public Health held a Sunday raid on street vendors in popular McArthur Park, a predominantly Latino area and one of the most densely populated of Los Angeles. The police confiscated carts, supplies, utensils, and food and threw everything into trash bags. Since they must pay fines, it becomes so expensive for vendors to reclaim confiscated items that it's cheaper for them to buy completely new vending equipment. Many street vendors believe the police harassment is intended to stop the vendor's activity. An activist filmed the incident and the local news channel reported it in the evening news in a sympathetic tone. The local news station (CBS Los Angeles) did not depict the vendors as criminals and reported that many say it is time for street vending to become legal in Los Angeles. The reporter interviewed Carlos Marroquín, a local activist who filmed the incident, who stated that "these are people who are not stealing or selling drugs, these are people who are trying to provide for their families."[29] The reporter stated that the Department of Public Health had not answered e-mails or phone calls, portraying it as the villain in this situation. Nevertheless, the piece did repeat the usual criticisms of vendors: "Some neighborhood groups express concern that the vendors could increase noise, trash, and draw customers away from existing businesses."

In April, 2015, UCLA law school students issued a report with five recommendations to reduce the overcriminalization of sidewalk vendors in Los Angeles. The key recommendations were: "cease all sidewalk vending prosecutions, dismiss pending sidewalk vending cases, offer a special four-hour-per-conviction community service program for vendors with criminal justice debt," "work with the Los Angeles Police Department to draft and implement a property seizure protocol for sidewalk vendors that complies with the Fourth Amendment and Due Process," and finally, "collaborate with community stakeholders to develop a city-wide range regime for legal and regulated sidewalk vending."[30] The law school students' report discussed the high fines for low-income vendors. For example, seventy-nine-year-old Rosa Calderón's fine of $50 escalated to $306 when she reported to the cashier's window at the courthouse because of fees and late penalties. To pay off the debt, the elderly Calderón will have to do thirty-eight hours of labor, an amount of time that seems excessive and "untenable" given her age. In these cases, the law school report proposes that sentences be commuted to four hours per conviction.[31]

The law school students' report demonstrates a growing momentum for change. At the same time they issued their report, local news media outlets were also covering the police's increasingly harsh treatment and intimidation of vendors. ABC News coverage showed vendors and activists handing a citizen citation to LAPD Chief Charlie Beck and asking for a moratorium on citations to vendors, which reached nearly 900 in 2014 alone with fines of up to $1,000 each. The piece depicted the vendors not as nuisances, but as victims of unfair harassment and intimidation. In another local television news story, Police Chief Beck took the time to respond to vendors' accusations, saying that "the real answer to this is working with city council on new ordinances, and that's what the vendors are doing, and we support them in doing that, but the department (LAPD) has to enforce the existing laws."[32] Nevertheless, the recent rash of arrests and seizures of vendors' property undermines Police Chief Beck's words of support for the vendors. When will the city decide to finally stop intimidating and arresting the most vulnerable members of society and instead find ways to allow their entrepreneurial spirit to flourish? Yes, health codes need to be maintained, sidewalks need to be passable for strollers and wheelchairs, and fair business practices need to be upheld, but the UCLA report shows that the accusations that support criminalizing vendors have no rational basis and ignore the economic and cultural contributions the vendors make to the city. "The result is that Los Angeles' poor—and, more specifically, a population that is almost exclusively people of color—is subjected to constant policing, stops and seizures, mounting criminal justice debt, and even arrest and incarceration."[33]

Despite the mounting support for vendors from nonprofits, the media, and L.A. residents, the vendors face new obstacles from the city council. On June 17, 2015, the city council voted 13–2 to ban vending in city parks and at beaches. The supporters of the ban argue that unpermitted vending— everything from selling *paletas* to yoga classes at the beach—can bring lawsuits if someone falls sick, and they argue that the ordinance defends the city from such suits. Other city councilmembers contend that green spaces should provide an "urban sanctuary free from commercial vending."[34] The new ban forms part of the larger debate on legalizing vending. Local activists and organizations argue that it doesn't make sense to prohibit vending in parks and at beaches while the city council determines whether or not to approve sidewalk vending. Rather than seeing the decision as a sign of defeat, Janet Favela, leader of the East L.A. Community Corporation, sees it as a minor hurdle since "in some ways it creates some urgency for us to push for parks to be incorporated into the legalization process."[35] The headline in the *LA Weekly*'s article points out the irony of the new ban: "Kids Can Buy Coca-Cola at the Park, but Selling Fresh Fruit Is Illegal." The headline of the Spanish-language newspaper *La Opinión* "Los Angeles Turns Its Back on Street Vendors" calls the action a slap in the face to the 50,000 vendors that contribute over half a million dollars to the city's economy.[36] From what I witnessed as a L.A. resident who spent many hot summer days at the beach in 2015, enforcing the ban was not a high priority. Over the summer, I saw far more vendors than in previous years at the beach. They walked up and down the sand selling boogie boards, umbrellas, cold drinks, ice cream, and fruit, often with a child or two in tow. I never once saw law enforcement.

The summer of 2015 was a busy period for the Los Angeles Street Vendor Campaign. Favela of ELACC and leaders of LURN held community meetings in Boyle Heights, South L.A., downtown, West L.A., and the San Gabriel Valley. Large numbers of community members attended these hearings; many came to show their support for legalization, while some expressed concerns over unfair competition with rent-paying businesses. At a hearing I attended in August, 2015, roughly sixty people came, ranging from local residents and college students to the vendors themselves. Most were vocal supporters of vendors, but not all. A handful of small-business owners spoke out against legalization, fearing it would hurt their businesses. A September 2015 *LA Times* article titled "Shopkeepers not sold on legalizing street vending" highlighted the business owners' concerns about vendors being able to undercut their business by not paying taxes, rent, and other costs.[37] The article quotes César Jimenez, owner of a fish taco stand at farmers' markets, as saying, "I have to pay liability insurance. I have to pay for health department permits. It's a lot of overhead. … And they can just set up a cart on the corner?" The measure proposed by the Los Angeles Street Vendor Campaign, however, would require street vendors to comply with the same rules the small-business owners follow, such as paying business taxes, getting liability insurance, and "ensuring that sidewalks have at least 5 feet clear for pedestrian traffic."[38] If the proposed law would impose the same regulations on vendors as on the small-business owners, some business owners say they would welcome it. José Corona told the *LA Times*, "If they pay taxes, if they're supervised by the city, that's less of a disadvantage for me."[39] To be successful the proposal may need to define what is a vendor in order to differentiate between "vendors" who dress as Spider Man on the Hollywood Walk of Fame and food vendors who sell fruit with chili on Los Angeles' street corners, parks, and beaches.

At the city hearings during the summer of 2015, the moderator from city hall presented the three models under consideration: maintaining the status quo (keeping vending illegal citywide), legalizing it citywide, or allowing individual communities to decide. He brought up issues under consideration such as: How many vendors should be permitted on a block? What are affordable fees for permits? How many hours/days should permit holders be allowed to vend? Should the number of officers regulating enforcement be increased or decreased? How many permits are going to be allowed? Vocal supporters included a seventy-seven-year-old lawyer; the daughter of a street vendor; a UCLA professor who stated that legalization will benefit the entire city and that Los Angeles has lessons to learn from other city models such as Oakland and Philadelphia; and street vendor Caridad Vásquez, who stated passionately in Spanish, "Nosotros defendemos la economía, que nos den permisos adecuados" ("We defend the economy, may they give us adequate work permits"). A UCLA law school student said that it was time for the prosecution of vendors to cease and that there should be a moratorium on enforcement. An immigration lawyer pointed out the irony of prosecuting vendors for selling healthy food where it's not available. While most people spoke in favor, some spoke against legalization. An Iranian business owner spoke about how hard he had worked as an immigrant to grow a successful business and that he did not want his business to be at risk from non-rent-paying vendors. I had never realized until sitting through the long, tedious hearing just how complicated the issue was, that there were people who didn't share my point of view, and that legalizing vending was not as easy as waving a magic wand. Yet, we also have a chance to come together and find a solution that, given the proper regulation of permits, will benefit everyone.

After months of community meetings, it seemed that the Los Angeles City Council was closer to making an informed decision and creating a permit system. On October 27th 2015, the Los Angeles City Council Economic Development Committee held a hearing on street vending. The Los Angeles Street Vendor Campaign organized a rally with live music. Hopes were high that this would finally be the day that the city would make some sort of decision. During the hearing, the committee considered legalizing it citywide, setting up special vending districts, and a third "hybrid" option that would legalize it citywide, "but allow some areas to opt out."[40] Rather than coming to a decision, city councilmembers asked for more information on the hybrid model, a model that was used unsuccessfully in the past in Los Angeles. In response, Mike Dennis, the campaign's spokesman, said ideas such as the cap or setting up "opt-in" special districts would create a "black market" of rogue vendors who compete with the legal vendors.[41] Members of the Los Angeles Street Vendor Campaign have resisted efforts to place restrictions on the proposal to legalize street vending. This meeting was part of a procedure in which the city

Caridad Vásquez speaking at a rally for street vendor legalization. Photo courtesy of Fernando Abarca, East Los Angeles Community Corporation.

weighs the three options and sends them to different departments to determine cost, enforcement mechanisms, etc. When asked why the city is taking so long to reach a decision, Frank Aguirre, business development specialist for the city, said that the opposition is vocal. Business owners in the downtown Fashion District brought photos of the trash and crowding that already exists in their area to the hearing. Also, some affluent districts don't want vending at all and other districts support the vending for some areas but not others.

We are now entering the third year of the debate about whether or not to legalize street vendors. As the years pass, the vendors and their supporters have grown increasingly frustrated with the city's leaders' inability to move forward. A 2015 *LA Times* op-ed piece refers to the "glacial pace" at which the city is moving to regulate this "not-very-underground economy." The reporter notes that the ban is widely ignored and "enforcement is spotty" since "the police turn a blind eye ... until there is a crackdown."[42] During police raids, the police confiscate vendors' carts and merchandise. They are destroyed and never returned to them. This time, the vendors are taking extreme legal measures. On October 30, 2015, the vendors filed a lawsuit alleging that their constitutional rights have been violated. The vendors and their powerful lawyers, the American Civil Liberties Union (ACLU) and other legal groups, held a news conference outside of the Los Angeles Police Headquarters announcing that they are suing the city of Los Angeles and a local business improvement district in federal court. They claim that their carts and belongings have been improperly seized. "This is a clear violation of the street vendors' constitutional rights—both their fourth amendment right against unreasonable seizures, and their right to due process," said Michael Kaufman, a staff attorney with the ACLU of Southern California.[43] When the police or the Fashion District's private security officers confiscate the property of street vendors, they throw it in the trash without providing them a receipt or giving them any opportunity to reclaim it. The lawsuit alleges that the LAPD along with the Business Improvement District officers "threaten vendors with citation or arrest if they do not allow the property to be confiscated."[44] The current nonregulated system creates a legal limbo and breeds these sorts of violations of constitutional rights.

Regulated permit systems can provide a model for what works—and what doesn't—in other cities. As opening brick-and-mortar restaurants has become prohibitively expensive, the numbers of food trucks and street vendors have grown in many U.S. cities. While New York City's street vendor regulatory system has many problems, it has been operating for well over a century and supervises over 10,000 legal vendors. There are four different types of permitted vendors and the permits they receive depend on the type of business they operate. They include First Amendment vendors (vendors who sell books, magazines, art, etc., and can operate without a license under the First Amendment), food vendors, vendors who are veterans, general vendors (selling T-shirts, watches, etc.), and unlicensed vendors. Disabled veteran vendors do not need a license under a nineteenth-century New York State law that was created to protect physically disabled Civil War veterans. Even though there are so many categories of vendors, there is a huge shortage of permits. The waiting list to become a licensed vendor in New York City is ten to twenty years, creating a black market of illegal permits that sell for $6,000 to $8,000 instead of the city's fee of $200. It takes so long to receive a permit legally because the city only gives out 3,000 permits, a number created in 1981 when business interests convinced the city to put a cap on permits. Since then, the number has not increased, despite population growth in the intervening thirty-four years.[45] The vending permit system in New York is so cumbersome that a nonprofit, The Street Vendor Project, works with vendors to explain it to them. The Street Vendor Project teaches vendors about their legal rights and helps them understand the laws they must follow. They also elevate the profession by giving out annual awards for the best street food, known as the Vendy Awards, which their website considers to be the "Oscars of street food for real New Yorkers."[46] The Street Vendor Project's website calls attention to the challenges for New York City's vendors: high fines that reach $1,000, denial of licenses, waiting lists of up to twenty years for a license, and lack of access to certain areas. In October 2015, the vendors held a protest rally to ask the city for more street vending permits.

San Antonio, on the other hand, the seventh biggest city and one with a majority Latino population, has a clear, commendable system for street vendors. In "The Good, The Bad, and the Ugly State of Street Food in America," food writer Lucas Petersen lists New York City under "The Bad," but San Antonio is headlined "The Good." On the city's mobile vending section of their website, there are different rules depending on what you are selling, be it *elotes* (corn on the cob), fish, or snow cones.[47] The city has created incentives for vendors to sell healthy food by not requiring a permit for "foot peddlers." According to San Antonio's website, those vendors selling "whole, farm fresh products" are no longer required to obtain a permit. The city of San Antonio has certainly made it easy for vendors to follow and understand its regulations.

Like San Antonio, Los Angeles is a spread out city with a majority Latino population. Why is street vending legal in San Antonio as well as San Francisco, Chicago, New York, and all other major cities and not in Los Angeles? It seems ironic that in a country where entrepreneurial spirit is praised from a young age and a strong Protestant work ethic has historically been an integral part of "American" culture, vending would be illegal anywhere. We support "American" children who sell Girl Scout cookies in parking lots, lemonade on the sidewalks of our suburbs, and advertise their school teams' car washes, but we arrest the minority vendor peddling fresh, sliced fruit. This inconsistency points to the not-so-subtle racial discrimination embedded in American culture. In his seminal article "The Pushcart Evil," historian Daniel Bluestone describes early efforts in New York City to "conquer the pushcart evil" as part of a larger question of how different social classes use public spaces. Bluestone sees the resistance to the pushcart, the early twentieth-century *carrito* used by Jewish and Italian immigrant street vendors in Manhattan, as a symbol of upper-class residents trying to create distance from the lower classes in the most public of spaces, the streets and sidewalks. Historically, street vendors, along with public markets, dominated food distribution into the early twentieth century. In fact, at one point, street vendors were so numerous that they had their own census category.[48] Yet, over the course of the twentieth century, American streets and sidewalks became spaces that privileged cars over leisure and economic activity and the sidewalk vendors slowly got pushed out.

Discrimination toward street vendors has historically not been based only on social class, but also on racial and anti-immigrant sentiment in the United States. It is impossible to discuss the topic of street vending without considering the racial stereotypes of Latino immigrants. As Lorena Muñoz points out in "Latino/a Immigrant Street Vendors in Los Angeles: Photo-Documenting Sidewalks from Back-Home," "the space in which these immigrant vendors practice their trade is 'racialized,'" meaning ethnic or racial identities are ascribed to a minority group by the dominant one. In the case of Latino street vendors, "their racialized status" is informed by "a combination of anti-immigrant laws, policies and public discourse that seek to impose meanings of belonging, citizenship, otherness and race."[49] In Los Angeles, Latino street vendors are typically regarded as undocumented regardless of their actual citizenship status.[50] These stereotypical representations place vendors into a larger discourse of national and state immigration policies and attitudes that are informed by race. As the early history shows, vendors have been racialized since they first sold tamales on the streets of downtown Los Angeles over a century ago. Would the police have shut down the carts and taken the goods of the vendors in McArthur Park, an area where dozens of immigrant vendors sell on a daily basis, had they been young, white hipsters instead of darker skinned Latinos? It seems unlikely.

Stereotypes about race and vending also take place in the other direction. When Anglo food blogger Lucas Peterson wrote an article for Eater.com about the *elotero* or corn peddler of Lincoln Heights titled "Meet the Man Who's Peddled LA's Best Street Corn for 27 Years," he revealed the whereabouts of Timoteo, the subject of the article. *Elote* is a staple street food in Mexico served with chili, salt, Mexican sour cream, and Cotija cheese. In his article, along with describing Timoteo's delicious sweet corn and his regular corn on the cob "on which to put mountains of unhealthy toppings," Peterson gave the vendor's name and mentioned exactly where he could be found, creating instant, overnight publicity for Timoteo. In response, food writers and bloggers accused the writer of "columbusing," a term Peterson defines as "the act of reckless and thoughtless appropriation (typically by rich white people) of a thing that has been around for years or decades (a thing that usually belongs to non-white people)."[51] The local public radio station KPCC covered the controversy and asked the question, "Can you cover a neighbor-hood if you are not from there?"[52] The question brings up issues of race and gentrification, while the term "columbusing" conjures up centuries of white upper-class appropriation of Latino culture. Peterson responded to his critics by saying the vendor was not naive, he knew exactly what he was doing when he gave permission to Peterson to write the story. He quoted the corn man's response as, "Yeah, great. I get to go home earlier. We sold out."[53] Clearly, the vendor benefited from his outing with the media.

Mexican-American food writers Gustavo Arellano and Bill Esparza jumped into the controversy to defend Peterson, saying food is food, irrespective of issues of race or gentrification. Arellano, the editor of the *Orange County Weekly*, and Esparza, Mexican food contributor to *Los Angeles Magazine*, have been covering street vendors for quite a while and have always sup-ported non-Latinos documenting street vending. Arellano cleverly named the controversy "Elotegate" and wrote about the hypocrisy of the situation in the blog post of the *OC Weekly*. Arellano's blog on January 20, 2015, describes how he, Esparza, and food blogger Javier Cabral have been writing about illegal vendors for years without being accused of exploitation because they fit the "right *raza* profile." While Arellano criticizes Peterson in his blog for apologizing for his story and for resorting to revealing his own ethnic back-ground—saying he is half Chinese on his mother's side—as a way to justify his article, he points out that the real story here is the policy against street vendors that the government has pursued for over a century in an "eternal war" waged by "stupid politicians" and "*pendejo* (idiot or explicative) health inspectors."[54]

Elotegate stirred up controversy in food blogging circles in early 2015. Every well-known blogger/journalist had a position. In Zócalo Public Square, a website that blends live events and humanities journalism, the young Latino food blogger and writer Javier Cabral disagreed with Arellano's position in a provocative article titled "Why This Food Writer Refuses to review Street Vendors: If I Tell You Where to Find the Best Goat Stew in L.A., I'd Be Put-ting People—and Their Livelihoods—at Risk."[55] Cabral's piece was intended to generate discussion about where food writers and bloggers should draw the line in an era in which every food item and food memory is photographed, documented, and blogged about ad infinitum. Cabral starts off piquing our interest by describing the "best *birria*" (goat stew originally from Jalisco, sold in Mexico at *birrerías*) he ate in his life on a sidewalk in Los Angeles. He writes about the wonders of the flavorful *birria*: "locally raised, slaughtered within the past 24 hours, simmered overnight." Cabral explains that attention by the press will generate more business for the vendor, but revealing his whereabouts also puts him at risk as he would be "on the radar" of the health department and the local police. Not only does Cabral's piece entice us to seek out vendors of *birria* and other regional Mexican dishes on the streets of Los Angeles, but it also elevates the vendor to the level of an artisan, a fine craftsman who has perfected, in this case, the art of street *birria*. Cabral contends that the street vending experience is "vital to the Los Angeles way of life," creating jobs (a 2014 study by the Economic Roundtable showed that street vendors in Los Angeles County created 5,234 jobs), culinary delights (such as sidewalk *birria*), and vibrancy on the streets of a car-centered city.

The street vendor's way of life is part of what makes Los Angeles such a Latino city, a Mexican and Central American immigrant city dotted with rainbow-colored umbrellas and carts selling sliced fruit, *raspados*, or *tacos*, where undocumented workers can be small-business owners who support their families, even if they do so at constant risk of police harassment and fines. The stories of Rosa Calderón and Caridad Vásquez are not only ones of illegal street vending; they are part of a larger story of a disenfranchised group trying to use their cultural heritage to make a living. These stories show that, despite their outsider status, the vendors find empowerment through vending and that the city needs to work with them, not against them, to find a solution agreeable to all. Vendors, such as Caridad and Rosa, show how the sidewalks of Los Angeles are overlooked spaces that serve a key function in the informal economy, employing over ten thousand people and creating rich urban cultural landscapes for migrants and residents alike. Clearly, street vending remains a complex problem that requires a holistic approach when considering solutions.

Chapter 5

Where Is Trader Joe's?

Food Deserts in Latino Los Angeles

This chapter tells the story of inequities in the food system in areas like South L.A.: a vast, low-income, Latino and African-American neighborhood near downtown Los Angeles, through the life of one fictionalized resident, Marina Gutierrez. Even though Marina is not a real person, her life resembles those of thousands of other low-income Latina immigrant mothers. On a daily basis, she struggles to provide fresh, healthy, culturally appropriate food for her family. Marina's story reveals the challenges in our industrial food system, one in which processed foods are heavily subsidized by the government, while fresh fruit and vegetables are less affordable. In this chapter, I examine the challenges of the lack of access to fresh fruits and vegetables and its consequences: the dramatic rise in food-related diseases, particularly diabetes and obesity, which plague many low-income neighborhoods in Los Angeles. In addition, I look at why diabetes afflicts the Latino communities in particular, examine the effects of acculturation on Latino immigrant families, and explore the reasons why processed foods are more affordable than fresh fruits and vegetables for those on a limited budget. Finally, I describe how, during the second half of the twentieth century, as a result of racial discrimination, poverty, and white flight, many of today's low-income Latino neighborhoods have become food deserts. During the later decades of the twentieth century, in neighborhoods such as Marina's, grocery stores closed down and, over time, became dominated by liquor stores, vacant lots, and fast-food restaurants.

The United States Department of Agriculture (USDA) defines food deserts as rural or low-income inner city areas lacking access to affordable or good quality fresh fruit, vegetables, and other healthful whole foods. While Marina's story explores the lack of access to fresh, healthy food in low-income Latino neighborhoods in Los Angeles, it could be the story of many impoverished areas around the country, both rural and urban, where residents have lower levels of education, incomes, and higher rates of unemployment. These are areas that lack supermarkets, but abound in fast-food restaurants and liquor stores. To make matters worse, such neighborhoods also have fewer parks and green spaces, while the ones that do exist are often underused because of a fear of violence, thus making it more challenging for children and families to exercise. Not to be overlooked is the reality that for parents who work multiple jobs to pay the bills, taking their children to the playground is probably not a top priority. As a result, these children have fewer opportunities to play outside.

Let's examine the life of Marina Gutierrez, an overweight Latina with type 2 diabetes living in South L.A. Marina is in her mid-40s and is from Mitla, a town about 30 miles from the capital of Oaxaca, whose name in the local indigenous language Zapotec means "Place of the Dead." Marina, her husband Ricardo, and eldest daughter Tania arrived in Los Angeles in 2007. Tania was born in Mexico, while her younger siblings were born in the United States. Marina and her family live in the Exposition Park area of South Central L.A, in a small 2-bedroom apartment. In Marina's neighborhood, liquor stores and corner markets are far more prevalent than grocery stores and safe, clean parks. Increasingly, Marina and her family live in fear of gang violence. During the summer of 2015, there was a spike in shootings near her home as part of a social media campaign that threatened 100 killings in 100 days in South L.A. When a child was shot in a drive-by shooting outside a birthday party, incensed community members met and declared, "We have to go out by the thousands and take our community back."[1] Living in this tense environment, Marina is afraid to allow her children to play outside their apartment when she is not home, but she works long hours, and sometimes they are left watching television unsupervised until she or her husband return from work.

In Mexico, Marina's extended family grew some of the produce that they ate or bought it weekly at a market where bags of avocados were only 10 pesos—less than a dollar. Squash, corn, and beans were abundant and affordable at the outdoor market or from a family member's backyard garden. In Mexico, however, Marina's husband could not make a decent living and they wanted to provide a better future for their children. Marina and her husband had very limited education. She stopped school by age 11 to help her mother and never really got a good education at the school in her village. Marina and Ricardo wanted to live in a place where their children could have a good education, go to college, and one day work as professionals—opportunities that were much harder to come by in their hometown in Mexico.

Despite their high hopes, when Marina and Ricardo arrived in Los Angeles, not everything was as they had imagined. Instead of the television fantasy of a suburban house with a grass lawn, Marina's family found that they could only afford a 2-bedroom apartment in a low-income area surrounded by apartment buildings, liquor stores, vacant lots, and fast-food outlets. Marina works cleaning houses and as a nanny, while her husband washes dishes at a restaurant six days a week, sixty–eighty hours a week at $9/hour, wages far below the poverty level. She takes two buses to get to work on the affluent Westside of Los Angeles, a commute that can take up to an hour each way to go only 9 or 10 miles. Once a week, she takes a bus to Superior, the Hispanic supermarket, where she loads up on as much food as she and her children can carry. Since the supermarket is over a mile from her home and the grocery bags are heavy, she must take the bus, but it costs $2 each way, eating up her limited income. A few corner stores sell a very limited supply of produce, but typically it is not fresh or of good quality and the price of a banana or an apple can reach upward of $1. Marina needs to feed a family of five, so she tries to avoid shopping at the corner stores unless she is out of a household staple or she has extra money to give her children for a bag of chips or a liter of soda. In her village in Mexico, on the other hand, fresh produce was readily available and she had more time to prepare nutritious, home-cooked meals for her family. Her sisters and mother lived nearby and there was always a pot of beans cooking on a stove. She relied much less on grocery stores for her shopping than she does in the United States.

Why are there so few supermarkets in Marina's neighborhood, an urban area very close to downtown Los Angeles? Why do liquor stores and convenience stores dot this urban landscape with three of four at every major intersection? Why is it so much easier for her children to find—and afford—Flamin' Hot Cheetos than fresh broccoli? A 2010 study by researchers Mark Vallianatos, Andrea Misako Azuma, and Susan Gilliland from the Center for Food & Justice at the Urban & Environmental Policy Institute at Occidental College emphasizes the lack of healthy options available to low-income Latino residents of Southern California. They performed a community-based study of three distinct communities in South and Central L.A. and surveyed the populations on their opinion of access to different food resources in the community. The areas surveyed were largely Latino—82% of one of the community's residents were Latino, 61% were born outside of the United States, 85% spoke a language other than English at home, and nearly one-third of families in this area had an annual household income below the poverty threshold.[2] The researchers found that among these three communities, there were a total of 1,273 retail food outlets of which 30% were fast-food restaurants and 22% were convenience or liquor stores—more than half of the retail food options available—while less than 2% were supermarkets. One of the three communities didn't even have one supermarket within its boundaries, and, at the time of the survey, there were no farmers' markets, although a few have opened in the intervening years since the study.

Liquor store near McArthur Park. Photo courtesy of Ebony Bailey.

After surveying residents, the researchers asked the community members to survey their supermarkets, convenience stores, and specialty food stores to see which had certain items such as carrots and broccoli, which had them for the most affordable prices, and which stores had poor-quality products or products that were past their expiration dates. Not surprisingly, the community members reported that supermarkets had the highest quality and most affordable healthy options, and convenience and liquor stores had the fewest options, with available healthy options at higher prices. For example, 85% of the convenience or liquor stores that were surveyed sold Flamin' Hot Cheetos and 89% sold Pepsi, but only 32% sold carrots and 17% broccoli. All of the retail options sold products that were past their expiration dates, but supermarkets sold the fewest.[3] These statistics provide a compelling argument for these community members to shop at supermarkets; however, as stated above, only a small fraction of the food establishments in these communities are supermarkets. It is for these reasons that South L.A. is considered "the very definition of a food desert."[4] In fact, photos of South L.A. are among the first images that appear when doing a Google search of food deserts.

This bird's eye view of a low-income neighborhood demonstrates the link between food justice and environmental issues, and how they have contributed to the inexorable rise in diabetes and obesity. Type 2 diabetes is commonly referred to as adult-onset diabetes, and usually occurs in people over the age of forty.[5] Despite this tendency, type 2 diabetes is growing increasingly common among children and has become much more prevalent than its other form (type 1 or "juvenile" diabetes), accounting for 90–95% of all diabetes cases today.[6] This disease is marked by the body's insulin resistance, meaning that the body's fat, liver, and muscle cells do not respond properly to insulin. Additionally, the body itself is unable to properly make or use insulin, a hormone needed to move glucose (blood sugar) into cells for later energy use.[7] Because sugar cannot move into the cells, it begins to accumulate in the blood, causing hyperglycemia, or elevated blood sugar. Excessive eating exacerbates this situation. Type 2 diabetes frequently goes hand in hand with weight issues, particularly obesity, and the connection between weight and diabetes can cause a vicious, yet preventable, cycle.

Obesity is the single most important risk factor for type 2 diabetes and is prevalent among low-income minority communities. In California, Latino citizens are disproportionately affected by both diabetes and obesity. According to the Latino Coalition for a Healthy California, nearly seven out of ten California Latino adults are overweight or obese. Among California adolescents ages 12 to 17, Latinos are the most likely to be overweight or at risk of being overweight.[8] In Los Angeles County, obesity levels among Latinos and African-Americans are among the highest (over 25%). In some communities, 35% of Latino children are obese.[9] As a result, Latinos are at an even higher risk for heart disease, cancer, stroke, and diabetes, all of which account for nearly 60% of all deaths among Latinos.[10] In 2011, a survey by the County of Los Angeles Public Health Department noted that the rate of diabetes among Latinos and African-Americans was more than double that of whites. Latinos have the highest prevalence of diabetes of any ethnic group in Los Angeles County (13.5%) and the percentage of the population diagnosed is gradually increasing every year. As of November 2012, the County of Los Angeles Public Health Department reported on its website that among pregnant Latinas, the number diagnosed with gestational diabetes has grown from 10.5 to 13.1 in a time span of only five years (2005 to 2010).[11]

Some data suggests that Latinos have a greater genetic predisposition to type 2 diabetes than non-Hispanic Caucasians. In *Making the Mexican Diabetic*, professor of medical anthropology Michael Montoya explains that geneticists, epidemiologists, analysts, and journalists frame diabetes as an "ethnoracial disease."[12] Despite their genetic predisposition to diabetes, experts point out that "genetics should not ... be confused with destiny."[13] Researchers have observed the complex interplay of genetics with environment, lifestyle, and our food abundance. How much of the spike in the diagnoses of diabetes among Latinos is due to socioeconomic status and environmental factors and how much is genetics? Since the percentage of the population with diabetes was significantly lower a decade ago, the environment in which they live must be playing a major role.

Along with genetics, access to healthy food and exercise are also determining factors in these remarkable disparities. Another key factor is acculturation, a long-term process during which individuals simultaneously learn and modify certain aspects of their values, norms, and behavior—including diet and lifestyle. It has been discovered that within one generation of moving to the United States from Mexico, the influence of the Mexican diet is almost entirely lost.[14] In fact, first-generation immigrants consume significantly less fat and more fiber and have a lower prevalence of obesity than do immigrants of subsequent generations.[15] The longer a Latino immigrant spends in the United States the more their rate of obesity tends to increase. Contrary to popular belief, a study of food acculturation among Mexicans born in Mexico, Mexicans born in the United States, and non-Hispanic white Americans observed few significant differences among the U.S.-born subpopulations. The study's findings showed that, compared to Mexicans, subpopulations of white children within the United States have greater intakes of saturated fat, sugar, and processed foods, such as salty snacks, pizza, and French fries, than Mexican immigrant children.[16] Mexican children are influenced by the habits of their non-Latino neighbors in Los Angeles, especially within the school setting, where cafeteria food caters to the tastes of the white subpopulations. A correlation has been found between acculturation and food insufficiency within Mexican households in the United States; household food insecurity and poor diet increase with acculturation.[17] From this data, it would appear that maintaining a traditional Mexican diet would be more beneficial than adopting the typical "white" diet of processed foods popular in the United States—so why the disparity in rates of obesity between Mexican-Americans and Anglo-Americans if acculturation exists and equalizes these groups' diets? The answer is—money.

In addition to food acculturation, the diets of Mexican children in Los Angeles are affected by the socioeconomic status of their parents. On average, the median household income for Hispanics is much lower than for whites, and nearly one in 4 (24%) of Latino households are classified as food insecure, as opposed to 1 in 10 of Caucasian households.[18] Mexican immigrants often come to the United States with a low level of education and little English-language ability. As a result, they are forced to work in low-paying, blue-collar, minimum-wage jobs. Many immigrants are undocumented and, therefore, have few employment alternatives. Their status gives them little recourse if exploited by an employer or injured on the job. They are among the most vulnerable and exploited workers in the United States. Farm workers are another underpaid, exploited sector dominated by Latino immigrants. U.S.-born Latinos fare much better economically, with higher levels of employment and greater job security. As a result, first-generation Latino immigrants have little money available to make healthy choices for their families.

Along with socioeconomic status, one must also consider the food products that have been made affordable to low-income families across the United States since the Farm Bill's inception during the Great Depression as part of Franklin D. Roosevelt's New Deal. Since then, the U.S. government's Farm Policy has heavily subsidized ingredients in processed foods (wheat, corn, rice, and soy) at a rate of 84% while fruits and vegetables only receive 1% of the available funding.[19] Fortunately, the situation is beginning to change. A shift in the government's approach to subsidies in the 2014 version of the Farm Bill is meant to promote healthier eating. It increased funding for fruits, vegetables, and organic programs by more than 50% over ten years to about $3 billion, while it cut the funding for traditional commodity crops by more than 30% over ten years.[20]

Since the 1980s, when the obesity epidemic first exploded in the United States, the price of processed foods has dropped by 40% while the price of fruits and vegetables has risen 40%.[21]Accordingly, people with limited funds end up spending the most on the cheapest calories available: the ones found in processed foods. Unfortunately, many low-income Latino residents and other minorities live in neighborhoods where processed foods provide not only the cheapest, but also the most accessible calories. In South L.A., for example, Taco Bell and Burger King line the main avenues, displaying "We Accept EBT" signs in the windows. Hot Cheetos are visible on racks from the open entryways of corner and liquor stores, and city parks are often dangerous and dirty. A 2007 study of the food environment of East L.A., an area almost exclusively Latino, found that 49% of all food outlets were fast-food restaurants and 63% were within walking distance of a school. Of the existing grocery stores, only 18% sold fresh fruits and vegetables of good quality.[22] For a family with limited time and resources in East L.A., or Marina's family in South L.A., eating fast food is the most readily available option.

How did Marina's neighborhood of South L.A. and other predominantly low-income Latino neighborhoods, such as Boyle Heights and East L.A., become food deserts? The story behind these impoverished landscapes of vacant lots and liquor stores is one of racial discrimination and poverty; a historic, centuries-old struggle in the United States that cannot be separated from a discussion of what Ron Finley, revolutionary guerrilla gardener of South L.A. calls "food prisons."[23] While this history is not unique to Los Angeles, it is integral to the history of a city that has been "built around racial exclusion.

Racial exclusion emerged in the 1880s as the Anglo population boomed when the city was first connected to the rest of the state and country by the railroad. During the first three decades of the twentieth century, Los Angeles went from being a small town made up, in large part, of Native Americans and Spanish speakers of Mexican descent known as *Californios,* to the fifth largest city in the United States. The population of Anglos boomed as Midwestern, middle-class farmers flocked to the West Coast for opportunities in agriculture and for the chance to live on land with a favorable climate.[24]

With the growth in farming came an increased demand for agricultural workers. As a result, the Mexican population of Southern California grew rapidly. Between 1900 and 1930, approximately 1.5 million Mexicans migrated to the United States, a loss of about 10% of the population of Mexico by 1930.[25] By 1928, Los Angeles had the largest Mexican population of any city in the United States.[26] Some of these immigrants lived in isolated areas, while others lived in the multicultural neighborhood of Boyle Heights alongside Jewish and Japanese immigrants. Over successive decades the Jewish immigrants left Boyle Heights and moved west of downtown to areas such as the Fairfax District, the Hollywood Hills, Santa Monica, and beyond to the San Fernando Valley. The Japanese immigrants, on the other hand, were removed from their homes and sent to internment camps during World War II. After the war, they returned to their homes in Boyle Heights, but eventually the Japanese community relocated to other parts of the city, including West L.A. and Torrance.

By the late 1940s Boyle Heights had become largely Mexican and Mexican-American. In later decades, immigrants, particularly Central Americans, began to settle in other enclaves, particularly South L.A., a once majority African-American area of the city. During the Depression and World War II, large numbers of African-Americans came to Los Angeles seeking economic opportunity, a period known as "The Great Migration." The black population of the city leaped from 63,700 in 1940 to 763,000 in 1970 with two-thirds in the South L.A. area, making the once small community more visible.[27] When the Supreme Court struck down race-oriented restrictive covenants in 1948, contracts that prohibited the purchase or lease of a piece of property by a particular group, many African-American newcomers began to settle in other neighborhoods of South L.A. from which they had been excluded. Originally an area that included wealthy white neighborhoods with stately mansions, it became a predominantly African-American area in the 1950s when freeways were built and many white residents moved to the suburbs. Over time, the area once known as South Central Los Angeles became the largest black community in the Western United States.[28] It had thriving dance halls, theaters, and a commercial area, but by the 1970s and 1980s, rising property values and gang violence caused many African-American residents to leave the inner-city area for more affordable, mid-sized suburban cities east of Los Angeles. As African-Americans left, more Latino immigrants, particularly Central American immigrants, settled in the area. As a result, South L.A. became one of the fastest growing Latino neighborhoods in the city.[29]

Between 1970 and 1990 it went from 80% African-American and 9% Latino to 50.3% African-American and 44% Latino.[30] Latinos, particularly Central Americans, were drawn by the low rents and, ironically, by the opportunity to escape the drug-related violence in other parts of the city. In 2004, the area was renamed South Los Angeles in an effort to halt the stigmatization of the fifty-one-square-mile area west of downtown known for gangs, shootings, and urban poverty.

During the second half of the twentieth century, as Los Angeles grew, people began to leave the confines of the city and move further away to places where they could afford a nice house in a quiet neighborhood among a similar racial demographic. Suburbanization expanded during the 1950s and 1960s as whites began to abandon cities nationwide. This population shift took place at the same time that major social movements were occurring across the country. Schools were being desegregated as a result of the 1954 Supreme Court case, *Brown v. Board of Education*, and the 1960s' Civil Rights Movement emerged and gained traction. The movement fought to end racial segregation and discrimination against African-Americans by staging acts of civil resistance, including marches, sit-ins, and boycotts. By the mid-1960s through 1970, alternative voices, particularly the Black Power movement, disagreed with Martin Luther King's philosophy of nonviolence and cooperation. During this period, a wave of inner-city riots undercut support from the white community and led to an increase in "white flight" to the suburbs.

The Watts riots of 1965 and the Rodney King riots thirty years later shed light on how South L.A. transformed from an area with supermarkets, cinemas, and shops to one dotted with vacant lots and convenience and liquor stores. On August 11, 1965, Marquette Frye, a young African-American was pulled over in the predominantly black neighborhood of Watts, suspected of drunk driving. Resentment over Frye's arrest, racism, and police brutality led to six days of massive rioting that left 34 people dead and over 1,000 people injured. The riots spread over a fifty-square-mile area of South L.A.; rioters looted stores, torched buildings, and beat whites. Historians have noted that black residents, feeling under siege from an overwhelmingly white police force, rioted in part "against powerlessness."[31] Looters and arsonists destroyed the heart of the historic Central Avenue. Business owners, many of them Jewish immigrants, survivors of the Holocaust, watched as their stores and dreams went up in smoke. Patrice Fisher recalls her grandfather trying to carry furniture out of his store as it—along with his other businesses—was torched. "Everything was ruined. We never rebuilt."[32] This was the worst and most costly urban riot in twenty years and foreshadowed riots in other American cities. It contributed to grocery stores and other businesses leaving the area, never to return.

By the early 1990s few of the promises of the civil rights era had been fulfilled. There was staggering unemployment among young African-Americans and Latinos, violence and drug addiction plagued inner cities, and Los Angeles was no exception. Then, in March 1991, the videotaped footage of the brutal beating of an African-American man, Rodney King, by five LAPD officers was broadcast around the world, raising concern about police treatment of minorities and sparking a debate about police brutality and racial injustice. A year later, on April 29, 1992, a jury in the white suburbs of Simi Valley acquitted four LAPD officers for the beating of Rodney King. The verdict stunned residents of Los Angeles. The news sparked massive riots in areas throughout the city, but particularly in South L.A., the largest riots since the Watts riots decades earlier. National Guard troops were deployed and a citywide curfew was ordered. The four-day riot destroyed more than 1,000 buildings, killed 58 people, and resulted in one billion dollars in damages.[33] Korean merchants in South Central and Koreatown formed vigilante groups arming themselves against the looting and burning of their businesses. During the riots, they received little if any aid from police authorities. Along with increased awareness of the state of black-white relations, the visibility of Koreans as well as Latinos in the riots forced Americans to acknowledge the complexity of race relations. Surprisingly, the *LA Times* reported at the time that the majority of the people charged with crimes in the riots were Latino young men (51%). The high numbers reflect various possibilities: Latino involvement in the looting, their failure to flee or resist arrest, or the LAPD's avoidance of arresting black men out of fear of confrontation. As criminologist Joan Petersilia noted at the time in an *LA Times* article, "This was clearly not a black riot. It was a minority riot."[34]

Twenty-four years later, the United States is presided over by its first African-American president and African-Americans have risen to many other important positions in the country. Nevertheless, history continues to repeat itself with the same cycle of violence and rioting nationwide from Ferguson, Missouri, to Baltimore to Staten Island. The media commented during the Baltimore riots in 2015 that they couldn't believe these things were happening in the United States and called the rioters "thugs" and "animals." While violence and destruction of property can never be justified, as long as inner-city neighborhoods lack resources such as basic access to food, housing, and protection from the police, rather than abuse and mistreatment,—anger will continue to fester in these communities. Low-income neighborhoods in Los Angeles are no exception. South L.A. still suffers from many of the same problems of poverty, inequality, and violence that plagued it fifty years earlier, only now the makeup of the population has changed with Latinos outnumbering African-Americans. While African-Americans remain, Latinos arrived in record numbers during the later decades of the twentieth century, transforming a historically African-American area into one with a Latino majority. As the *Huffington Post* reported in 2015, in the twenty-first century, "The idea of South Central as a black community is out of date."[35] Instead, there are many areas where African-Americans and Latinos live together or in close proximity. In fact, in the year 2000, "Latinos represented 58.5% of the population of South LA; by 2010, 66.3% and in this same year the 'black district' of South Los Angeles was only 31.8% black."[36] While the racial makeup of South L.A. has changed, the factors contributing to health inequality among its residents have not. According to the Health Atlas for the city of Los Angeles, children born in South L.A. live ten years less, on average, than children born in the wealthy neighborhoods on the west side of the city, such as Pacific Palisades or Beverly Hills.[37] Given these striking health disparities, one can see why the argument has been made that diabetes is not necessarily the "genetic destiny" of Latino residents and that environmental factors play a major role.

Racial discrimination, and resulting inner-city riots, is just one of the factors that explain why grocery chains fled urban centers in the last decades of the twentieth century. In the 1960s and 1970s when white middle-class families left urban centers for the suburbs, so did the grocery store chains. They took jobs and tax revenues with them. As Mark Winne, expert on community food systems, explains in his book *Closing the Food Gap*, the operating expenses of inner-city supermarkets, including rent, insurance, and security are higher than those of non-inner-city stores.[38] As a result, dense urban areas often cannot accommodate larger, new stores as easily. The Community Health Council, a health-focused nonprofit based in South L.A., identified other barriers to grocery store development in the area, such as difficulty identifying viable sites, costly infrastructure requirements, a lack of skilled workers, corporations' reluctance to spend money in the area, and negative perceptions of the neighborhood. Given these barriers, new stores open far less frequently in low-income urban areas.

The history of grocery stores abandoning inner cities is also the story of a change in the landscape in the United States that began in the mid-twentieth century as the freeway system developed nationwide, making it easier to travel further away to the suburbs. Freeway construction reinforced traditional segregation lines. White, middle-class families left crowded city centers, and supermarkets followed, beginning a long-term migration to the suburbs. The grocery store exodus started during the 1960s and continued through the 1980s as big-box stores sprung up to serve affluent suburban areas. The change in demographics led banks to reduce lending in inner-city neighborhoods. This phenomenon, known as supermarket redlining, has disproportionately affected communities like South L.A. and left food deserts in its wake. As a result, urban areas were left with far fewer supermarkets per resident than wealthier ones and access to healthy food became a growing issue. To make matters worse, in 1981, during the Reagan administration, the food stamp program experienced severe budget cuts, leading to a rise in hunger in the United States, a crisis that has only worsened in the intervening decades, as the 2013 documentary *A Place at the Table* demonstrates through very moving stories of food insecurity in homes around the country.[39] Food stamps, officially known as the Supplemental Nutrition Assistance Program (SNAP), suffered deep cuts during the welfare reform of the 1990s, but the numbers of SNAP recipients doubled under President Bush and again under President Obama as the country suffered a recession. As of October 2014, 46 million Americans relied on SNAP benefits to feed their families, 14% of the U.S. population.[40]

Sadly, many of the promises made to low-income, minority Angelenos since the 1992 Rodney King riots have not been fulfilled. Corporate super-markets come to South L.A., take tax credits and public dollars, but then leave when stores are not profitable enough. Over the past few years, two Ralphs in South L.A. have closed and in 2015 residents faced the imminent closure of the British newcomer Fresh and Easy in and around South L.A., a chain that arrived in 2007 offering organic, quality produce in low-income areas, but declared bankruptcy by 2013. As South L.A. shoppers learned of the chain's closing, they lamented the distances they would now have to travel to find quality, affordable produce. When Loretta Jackson learned the news, she exclaimed, "I'll have to go way across town to shop. That takes me seven to eight miles away. We have all this fast food around here."[41] In the case of Loretta Jackson and so many other residents of Los Angeles, access to healthy, affordable food is about so much more than just access. As Angela Glover Blackwell, founder and CEO of PolicyLink, explained at a 2015 speech for Food Equity Day I attended "It's about feeling respected and included, it's about helping people start small businesses in the community, and giving young people in the community jobs." In her speech, Blackwell talked about growing up in an African-American neighborhood of St. Louis where she shopped with her family at local supermarkets. She remembers returning to her neighborhood years later as an adult and being astonished to see that all the supermarkets were gone and her parents were driving out to the white, affluent suburbs to do their shopping.

How can the environment be modified and improved so that L.A. residents like Marina and her family can easily buy fresh broccoli and lettuce instead of Hot Cheetos? How can responsibility be shifted from the individual to all of us—the communities and their residents, the government, and corpora-tions—to decrease health inequities and increase affordable, healthy food choices in low-income, minority communities? As the following chapter demonstrates, the answers are multifaceted. Simply opening a new grocery store in a low-income area has not been proven to fix the issue. It will take governmental programs and funding, the work of grass roots organizations, nutrition education, and the efforts of individuals to change the situation in these communities.

Chapter 6

Grassroots Solutions

Improving Food Equity in Latino L.A.

In recent years, a food justice movement that works to ensure equal access to healthy food regardless of race, culture, or socioeconomic class has grown globally. At the same time, a food movement has swept the United States, thanks in large part to the work of journalists and intellectuals who have championed the cause in newspapers, documentaries, books, and increasingly popular university courses. Journalist and writer Michael Pollan is the most influential and well-known of these figures. Food policy experts suggest making changes by "voting with your fork," yet Michael Pollan—and the mainstream food movement—fails to recognize that this choice is not available to everyone. Eating local, sustainable, and organic food is central to the food movement and vital to rethinking our industrial food system, yet it does not consider the relationship of race and class to food. "Voting with your fork" is a privilege that most low-income urban Latinos, and other minorities, cannot afford, given that they often lack access to these food choices. Furthermore, often, healthy food in low-income areas is priced even higher than it would be in a wealthier area. As Alison Alkon points out in *Cultivating Food Justice: Race, Class, and Sustainability*, minorities and low-income communities are the ones who suffer most under the current food system; their stories, however, often remain absent from the dominant food system narrative. In order to create change, U.S. food policy needs to recognize the influence of race and class on the production, distribution, and consumption of food and support alternatives that meet community need.[1]

Increasingly, there is hope through the work of local grassroots organizations. This chapter explores their efforts to combat obesity, diabetes, and create access to healthy food. It looks at how in Latino neighborhoods of Los Angeles, in particular Boyle Heights and South L.A., grassroots organizations have worked with the community to improve residents' food sovereignty through farmers' markets, new community markets, corner store conversion programs, a moratorium on new fast-food restaurants, and innovative nutrition programs. It examines programs that have been effective at creating change, while also recognizing those that have met with resistance and have been less successful.

FAST-FOOD MORATORIUM

Activist groups in Los Angeles such as the Community Health Council have taken steps to convert South L.A.'s food desert into a "food oasis." In 2007, Los Angeles city councilwoman Jan Perry proposed an ordinance that temporarily banned the development of new stand-alone fast-food establishments in South L.A., a low-income area where the median household income is $24,000.[2] This moratorium stated that fast-food restaurants were not allowed to open within 1 mile of another fast-food restaurant. The goal of the ordinance was to correct the oversaturation of fast-food restaurants in South L.A. and provide healthy alternatives to the numerous fast-food chains. The ban was followed by a General Plan amendment limiting new stand-alone fast-food restaurants from locating within a half-mile radius of an existing fast-food establishment. The overarching goal of the ordinance was to promote greater commercial diversity by reserving the land for grocery stores, markets, or healthy restaurants. While other cities have passed zoning restrictions for environmental, aesthetic, or economic reasons, Los Angeles is the first city to pass a moratorium on fast-food construction as part of a public health effort.[3] The Los Angeles City Council estimates that there are nearly 1,000 fast-food restaurants in the 30 or so square miles of South L.A. covered by the regulations. Some 30% of the 750,000 residents in the area are obese, twice the rate in wealthier parts of the city, according to the Los Angeles County's Department of Health.[4]

While proponents see it as part of a multipronged process to decrease fast-food availability in South L.A. and reserve available lots for healthy food outlets, the moratorium's critics have argued that these measures are paternalistic, making the same argument for low-income residents of South L.A. that is "normally made for restricting children's food options at school—that they're more dependent and vulnerable than the rest of us" and they claim that the moratorium will not achieve its goals.[5] While the ban will limit openings of new stand-alone fast-food restaurants, it in no way assures that grocery stores and other markets will come to South L.A. and it has no effect on the number of fast-food restaurants already in the area. As Robert Creighton states in "Cheeseburgers, Race, and Paternalism: Los Angeles' Ban on Fast Food Restaurants," "It does nothing to change the reality that fast food is, and will remain, the cheapest and most convenient food option for many Americans."[6]

Public health advocates also argue that other solutions such as labeling calories on menus are far more effective than the moratorium or what critics call "food zoning." Other critics recognize that in areas with a population that is more than 50% Latino, the definition for fast food used by the city allows culinary concepts that are familiar to Latinos to be banned. In the ordinance, the city prohibits establishments that sell food with the following characteristics: "a limited menu, items prepared in advanced or prepared or heated quickly, no table orders, and food service in disposable wrapping or containers." This sweeping definition includes *pupusas*, a thick corn tortilla filled with a variety of fillings such as meat, cheese, or refried beans, a culinary staple for the local Salvadoran community, or the *tamal*, a pan-Latino staple. Although *pupusas* and *tamales* can definitely expand your waistline if eaten in excess, they are healthier options than Big Macs and fries. *Pupusas*, depending on what they are filled with, have about 200 calories. They are always accompanied with a healthy *curtido*, a slaw of cabbage, carrots, and onions. On the other hand, a McDonald's Big Mac has 563 calories and their medium-sized French fries have another 378 calories. Even if you eat two *pupusas* for lunch, you are still consuming far fewer calories than if you eat a cheeseburger.

Seven years after the moratorium was put into effect, public health experts remain ambivalent about its success. A 2015 study by the RAND Corporation says that since the ban was put into effect in 2008 the percentage of South L.A. residents who are overweight or obese has only increased from 63% to 75%.[7] City leaders who helped initiate the moratorium dispute the RAND Corporation's findings. Former councilwoman Jan Perry, one of its original backers, defends the moratorium not as a way to "cure" obesity, but rather as a way to set aside more land for grocery stores and healthy dining.[8] Other critics see public education as a more effective tool for improving community health. William McCarthy, a UCLA School of Public Health professor, believes "the jury is still out over whether the ban has had a positive impact on the community's health."[9] Despite the criticism, since the moratorium began, stand-alone fast-food development has slowed in the area; only one such business has been established in a regulated area. A study of the issue by a local nonprofit, "The South LA Fast Food Impact Assessment" shows that between 2007 and 2009, there has been a 2.2% decrease in the number of adults eating fast food 4–5 times weekly and that between 2007 and 2011 there was a 3% decrease in obesity rates.[10] While these numbers indicate some progress, fast food is only one of the causes of obesity in the area. As Gwendolyn Flynn, the policy director for nutrition resources at Community Health Councils, said, "These are behaviors that have taken a lifetime to build up. It takes longer than five to seven years to turn around a lifetime of operating in a certain way."[11] Along with the moratorium, other policy measures, including expanding farmers' markets and community gardens, have been put into place to improve access to healthy food that have met with varying degrees of success. With the support of government programs that help lure new markets, grocery stores, and other healthy food venues to the area, in the future, hopefully, residents will have better options than Pollo Loco, McDonald's, and Taco Bell.

CALIFORNIA FRESH WORKS

California FreshWorks, a public-private partnership loan fund created to finance grocery stores and other forms of fresh food retail distribution in low-income areas, has raised over $272 million to date to help underserved communities. This program is meant not only to improve community health, but also to spur economic development. It has given grants to many wonderful businesses and nonprofit organizations that increase healthy food access and create new jobs. Numero Uno Markets in South L.A. is an eight-store chain that has some junk-food-free checkout aisles. Food Forward L.A. is a local nonprofit that forages fresh, local produce that would otherwise go to waste and distributes it to food banks and food kitchens. Other California Fresh Works funds have gone to start up a year-round farmers' market in Compton, California, a low-income, underserved community. Another recipient is Homeboy Industries, a large non-profit organization that provides job training and other services to former gang members.

Homeboy Industries is the largest and most successful gang intervention, rehabilitation, and reentry program in the world. Father Greg Boyle began the program in 1988 after witnessing too many young men in his community die from gang violence. The services they provide help former gang members and recently incarcerated men and women leave gang life and reenter society through parenting courses, job training, legal services, tattoo removal, domestic violence services, etc. Seventy percent of Homeboy's clients are Latinos, so these services help this population find a path out of gang life and a way to reenter society. Their social enterprises include Homegirl Cafe—a wonderful restaurant just outside downtown Los Angeles—catering, farmers' markets, food trucks, silk screen printing and embroidery, selling products at grocery stores, etc. Homeboy's products, including *salsas*, tortilla chips, bread, and other baked goods, are well established at local grocery stores and farmers' markets. I often buy their multigrain bread and my children are big fans of their croissants. The former gang members work at the café and farmers' market stalls,

Food Justice Class Visits Homeboy Industries with Father Greg Boyle. Photo courtesy of Sarah Portnoy.

providing employment opportunities for a population that often has tattoos on their face, visible markers of a violent past.

In November 2015, I took my USC students on a tour of Homeboy Industries. It was like no other tour I have taken before. Our tour guides, Mario and Jac'queena, began by telling us their life stories. Jac'queena was an African-American woman in her late 20s. She was very petite, maybe 5 feet 2 inches and around 100 pounds, wore big golden hoop earrings and had faint traces of tattoos on her face. She had served four years in jail for armed robbery, kidnapping, and being an accessory to a crime. She had also suffered from addiction. This wisp of a woman had three children with three different fathers; one of whom was dead and another was in prison. When she talked about how her mother never showed her affection, her voice cracked and she dried a tear. She quickly regained her composure and talked about how as a result of Homeboy's eighteen-month training program, she had got her life back together. She now has her own apartment and custody of her three young children. She showed us where she had removed part of a tattoo that was once emblazoned across her face. The other guide, Mario, had never been to prison, but had been involved with gangs since he was thirteen years old. At age 14, Father Greg Boyle had offered him a job, but he wasn't ready. Mario had worked at Homeboy for brief periods when he was younger, but each time had gone back to his gang. He expected that he would die before he turned eighteen. Instead of dying, he had been shot in the head and arm and suffered stroke-like symptoms. He spent a year in a wheelchair and had to learn to walk again. He did walk, but with a limp, and his right arm was paralyzed and hung in a sling. Even with his disability, when he returned to Homeboy, Father Boyle gave him a job opportunity. He participated in the eighteen-month training program and came out a changed person. Homeboy had given Mario and Jac'queena opportunities in life they otherwise wouldn't have had; they had worked in the café and the catering business, while many other employees had trained as bakers in the massive industrial bakery at their headquarters. One of those bread bakers, Javier Medina, went on to work in the kitchen of Chef Thomas Keller's high-end restaurant Bouchon in Beverly Hills after spending decades in a gang and serving time for armed robbery, dealing drugs, and other crimes.[12]

Homeboy's various initiatives show the organization's commitment to food justice on many levels. They compost all of their food waste, use plant-based plastics, grow 30% of the produce they serve in Homegirl Café & Catering, and all of their produce is grown organically. But for Homeboy Industries and Father Boyle, food justice is not just about healthy, local, organic food; it's about using food as a tool to empower former gang members and convicts to redirect their lives and provide them with hope for their future.

CORNER STORE CONVERSION PROGRAMS

As discussed previously, low-income neighborhoods such as South L.A. and East L.A. lack grocery stores, but abound in small corner stores and liquor stores. A survey conducted by the Los Angeles Food Policy Council, a non-profit initiative of the mayor's office, found that South L.A. has twice as many corner stores as the county average, and that there are three times as many corner stores in South L.A. as there are in West L.A. In East L.A., there are 150 locally owned corner stores and only four full-service grocery stores, according to the UCLA-USC Center for Population Health and Health Disparities.[13] These corner stores are typically stocked with snack and junk food that have high calories and low nutrition, along with beer, cigarettes, and lottery tickets, and offer few, if any, fruits and vegetables. Various nonprofit organizations are working to transform some of these corner stores so that they offer more healthy produce and display it in more visible and appealing locations. The Community Market Conversion project, a program under the umbrella of the Los Angeles Food Policy Council, focuses its efforts on South L.A., while the Market Makeovers project, organized by the UCLA-USC Center for Population Health and Disparities and Public Matters, works in East L.A.

The mission of the Community Market Conversion program, which launched in 2011, is to increase healthy food access in underrepresented communities of Los Angeles and shift consumption patterns in these neighborhoods.

The Los Angeles Food Policy Council's Healthy Neighborhood Market Network works with store owners to provide ongoing support "to ensure the sustainability of healthy food retail efforts" and create new market makeover project opportunities. They offer trainings and workshops for business owners to learn how to become successful healthy food retailers. Esther Park, a community outreach coordinator for the Los Angeles Food Policy Council, has worked on corner store conversion programs. One of the markets she touted as a success by the Food Policy Council is Alba Market on Vermont, close to the USC campus. The grand opening was celebrated with a block party for the community. Formerly known as $1 Dollar Warehouse, in March 2014 it was reopened as Alba Snacks & Services. During 2014, the owner Nelson García worked with staff at the Los Angeles Food Policy Council to develop a redesign plan for the store. The new store was designed with a new section of nutritious and affordably priced snacks for the students at the middle and high schools across the street. Healthy products including fruits, trail mix, and protein bars were placed on the vertical racks at the entrance to the store. In October 2014, I began to plan a tour for my USC students of successful converted stores. Esther Park suggested I take them to visit Alba Market, since it is very close to the USC campus. When I visited, however, I found no healthy food offerings. The owner's son told me that the middle- and high school students were not interested in buying healthy food and only wanted chips and other junk food. So, his father had stopped purchasing and stocking healthy food options. The failure of Alba Market to successfully sustain the healthy offerings points to the need for education along with physical transformations and the importance of greater community involvement.

Public Matters is a social enterprise group that has succeeded in transforming local stores by engaging the community and creating a comprehensive approach to healthy food access. In the transformation of Euclid Market in Boyle Heights, for example, Public Matters worked with local Roosevelt High School students to create a grassroots social marketing campaign to promote healthy food consumption. The students became involved at a hands-on and educational level. They took a food justice course, painted the store both inside and out, and created attractive, colorful signs. They were able to succeed in the long term by teaching students how to serve as community advocates on behalf of the project and by involving the owner. Later, the high school students were hired as community liaisons. Shirley Ramirez, one of the students, describes the experience working on two market makeover projects in her community.

Food Justice class visit to Ramirez Meat Market. Photo courtesy of Sarah Portnoy.

We drew out and planned out how Euclid was already laid out and took inventory of all of the random products it had. We then started to visualize what we wanted the store to look like, not only in the floor plan but also on the outside and inside. Then we started working in the store. We started out by taking off the shelves. We cleaned them, sanded them, painted them, and then reinstalled them back into them into longer, more customer-friendly rows. The store already seemed more inviting.[14]

Preliminary data shows that patrons are starting to change their eating behaviors as a result of the store's transformation and the social marketing campaign.

Over the course of five years, Proyecto Mercado FRESCO has been working to "green the food desert" by transforming selected stores into places where people can buy fresh fruits and vegetables and learn about healthy eating and food preparation. The stores were chosen as part of a highly selective process by a UCLA Fielding School of Public Health project. The four chosen stores had to be family-owned and operated and run by people "with an interest in community development" who were willing to take a risk.[15] The goal of the project is to transform the stores both inside and outside from dark places that sell liquor and lottery tickets to "family friendly" and "focal points of community engagement," according to Dr. Deborah Glick, professor of community health sciences at UCLA and a principal investigator on the study.

Andy Alvarez was one of the high school students who worked on the transformation of markets in his community and went on to continue his work with the program. In the fall of 2014, Andy spoke to my students about his work as a community liaison for Public Matters and the efforts of his organization to transform some of the local corner stores. Andy is a junior at Cal State Los Angeles studying nutrition. He grew up in Boyle Heights and his career choice has been inspired by his community work. The first store he helped convert as a high school student was the YASH market in Boyle Heights. Andy talked about how it had taken two months to redo the store. Andy and the other volunteers had stripped the beer advertisements from the windows, painted the outside neon lime green, built a garden in the back to emphasize home-grown produce, and set up organized, clean aisles that featured fruits and vegetables. All the efforts have paid off. Alvarez told the class that after the transformation the YASH market earned 20–25% more than before.

In November 2014, my class visited two converted markets in Boyle Heights, Ranirez Meat Market and Salva Market. Ranirez Meat Market was painted bright blue on the outside and had an ample selection of fruits and vegetables just next to the entrance. The owner proudly showed the students her photo album that documented the store's transformation. Salva Market was smaller and the transformation seemed to still be in the works. Even though the store was not as brightly painted and the selection was much smaller, the owner exuded great pride in the organic fruits placed on a center display. She even sliced up and let the students sample an organic apple. The students spent a few dollars buying the fruit so that they could get an idea what it would take to feed a family on a limited budget. The organic apples and bananas at Salva Market were a dollar apiece, hardly an affordable price in a low-budget community, especially when you can purchase a bag of chips or a soda for the same price. Will the community invest in healthy food at these prices? Clearly, access is only the first step in solving the problem. Demand from community members is the next part, but this can be challenging, as human behavior doesn't change overnight. People are used to routines, including what they buy and where they buy it. However, cooking classes in the stores and nutrition education classes in local schools can make small inroads.

One recent success story proves change is possible with pressure from the community. A South L.A. liquor store recently changed its name from Century Liquor to Century Market and began offering fresh produce. This transformation did not happen overnight. In the late 2000s, local residents picketed the store for being a negative influence in the neighborhood. The store is located across from a park and a library and drug dealers and loiterers used to hang out outside. In 2008, the city declared the store a "public nuisance."[16] After a nearby grocery store closed in 2013, Community Coalition, a local organization, set up a farm stand just a few feet from the store. When the store owner saw customers shopping at the stand, he became aware of the need for fresh produce in the area. A seed was planted and a store was eventually transformed, offering fresh produce—and hope—to the community. The long-term effect of the conversion programs on public health is still unproven, but the examples above demonstrate that, when executed properly, they are very effective at improving food equity in underserved communities. They can only be completely successful, however, if they combine physical renovation and technical assistance with grassroots community engagement and education.

NEW SOCIAL ENTERPRISES IN SOUTH L.A.: GROCERY STORES

Social entrepreneurships are another valuable source of potential change in communities such as South L.A. Currently, there are a few social entrepreneurships working to improve access in the area. As a result, the media is celebrating a "food renaissance" in South L.A. Community Services Unlimited Inc. (CSU) is a social enterprise that provides healthy, quality food to local families, a market for farmers, and a source of income for the organization's youth programs. These programs are funded through the businesses CSU operates, including the weekly produce bags, catering, as well as the distribution of wholesale produce. They are currently working on creating an urban farming enterprise. Unlike many of the newer organizations, CSU has shown a long-term commitment to improving South L.A. that began nearly forty years ago.

CSU was established in 1977 as the nonprofit arm of the Black Panther movement in South L.A. with the mission of creating "justice-driven community-based programs and educational initiatives." Today, as Executive Director Neelam Sharma explained to me, the organization's mission remains tied to a holistic understanding of the right to culturally appropriate, high-quality, affordable, fair food and "emphasizes the need for oppressed communities to organize themselves and build sustainable skills, commerce and jobs." Sharma visited my class in the fall of 2014, and spoke about the organization's early ties to the Black Panther movement. When she moved from London to Los Angeles in the late 1990s, she began to volunteer with the organization when she discovered how difficult it was to feed her own family high-quality, healthy food while living in South L.A. Eventually, Sharma became executive director of CSU and, since then, has worked tirelessly, on behalf of those not served by the current food system to expand CSU's programs that increase access to healthy, culturally appropriate food in South L.A. and create new jobs in the community. As she explained to me, "We have been patiently building a localized food system from the ground up, one that engages community at every level, builds a market for local famers, creates real living jobs for local residents, keeps our dollars local, and makes good food accessible." When I asked Sharma whether, after so many years working to improve the food landscape in her community, she had seen an improvement, she said that despite "the huge amount of talk and media attention to the issue, there has been a net decrease in the number of stores in and around the area selling fresh food. The positive changes I have seen have emerged from within the community."[17]

One of CSU's most successful programs, the Village Marketplace, distributes and sells fresh organic produce from their urban mini farms. This produce is sold through a produce bag subscription program (available at a reduced price for community members). After discovering CSU through my research and realizing that it is based on my own campus, I began to receive a weekly community supported agriculture (CSA) bag from them. The bag comes filled with seasonal produce and exposed my family to fruits, vegetables, and herbs I would not have purchased otherwise: kumquats, mustard greens, *nopal*, fennel, sage, and the most delicious bananas I have ever tasted. The bag costs $14 per week, less than I would pay for the equivalent produce at the farmers' market and time-saves. The other added benefit is that there is a lower price for residents, making healthy, seasonal produce far more affordable for them than otherwise.

In 2015, CSU announced that they had purchased a 10,000-square-foot lot in South L.A. for use as a produce and grocery market, café, on-site commercial kitchen with an urban farm, and community space that will serve the community of South L.A. with fresh produce, healthy prepared food, and an array of classes and programs including wellness services. Given their success growing and distributing organic produce—they distribute over 100,000 pounds of produce in South L.A. through a variety of means—they need a bigger space to pack and prepare food, a space that will allow them to serve many more residents. This organic market will be the first of its kind and will allow money to flow back into the community, giving residents a chance to determine their own health. In an interview with KCET radio station, Sharma explained what makes her organization unique:

> Our bottom line is not profit. ... We have a double bottom line: making money and also the community's well-being. As we've always suspected, you can do both. You don't have to be greedy, but you can make some money and at the same time make really good food accessible to people who want it and have always wanted it, but nobody's ever spoken to that need in a way that makes sense.[18]

Karla Vásquez, director of community programs in the With Love Community Garden.
Photo courtesy of Ebony Bailey.

CSU is not the only grassroots organization contributing to the nascent South L.A. food renaissance. After so many years of neglect of the local food system and a failure to serve those most in need, the situation seems hopeful with new, widespread interest from social entrepreneurs. In March 2015, I attended a fundraising dinner for a nonprofit, Groceryships, where I sat next to Andrew McDowell. He introduced himself as the founder and CEO of "Con amor/With Love Market & Café," a market that opened during early 2016. McDowell spent nearly five years securing loans for the market and redoing the early 20th century brick building that had been used as storage for Hollywood sets. Today, the building is a beautiful airy space with high ceilings, a welcome addition to an area blocks from the freeway surrounded by auto parts shops and resale stores. The café features delicious smoothies, green drinks, specialty coffees, and healthy salads and sandwiches, which can be enjoyed in their lovely out-door patio and garden. The market offers locally sourced organic produce, meats, and dairy at affordable prices. They provide nutrition, cooking, and entrepreneurship classes and internships for local youth through their nonprofit, With Love Community Programs. Karla Vasquez, director of Community Programs, runs these community classes and is excited about the community's interest. On a tour of the brand-new market, Karla showed my students the market's vegetable garden—With Love Community Garden, where the pro-duce they grow is used in the cooking and nutrition classes. The market has locally sourced, organic produce, meats, and dairy at an affordable price. They also provide health/food education, entrepreneurship classes, and internships for local youth.

Since opening in early 2016, the market has become a stakeholder in the local community, since the money it earns stays in the community and since it employs local residents. Social entrepreneurships such as this one have the potential to address food justice issues in urban, low-income neighborhoods, such as South L.A. While they were waiting to secure loans and begin the building process, they are already working with the community at school health fairs, distributing canvas bags with their logo, organizing community clean up days, and even creating a weekly walking club for local Latina women ("Club de caminar"). Since they have opened, many local residents have come to the market. One of my students said he overheard a teenage girl encouraging her mother to go inside one day. The question that remains to be answered is whether local Latinos community will embrace this unfamiliar location that is not a recognized Hispanic chain. Hopefully, their early footwork, both literal and figurative, with the community will lead to a successful venture.

FARMERS' MARKETS

Farmers' markets began popping up across the United States in the mid-1970s as interest grew in the environment and healthy eating. Los Angeles, Santa Fe, and New York City were among the first cities in the country to connect local farmers and urban consumers. In 2015, the USDA estimated that there were over 8,000 farmers' markets nationwide and that between 30,000–50,000 farmers sell at farmers' markets. With the growth of large industrialized farming, farmers' markets also provide opportunities for small farmers and businesses to sell their products, and help meet the increased demand for locally produced food. Over the years, farmers' markets have generated an enormous increase in interest in local food nationwide. Farmers markets' not only provide fresh, local produce, and a personal relationship with the farmers who grow it, but also have the potential to address food security issues and increase access in low-income communities underserved by retail grocery stores and poorly stocked corner stores.

Certified Farmers Markets (CFMs) were established in 1978 in California, when then governor Jerry Brown signed legislation known as the Direct Marketing Act. This enabled California farmers to sell their own produce directly to consumers at locations designated by the Department of Agriculture. According to the website of the city of Santa Monica, in 1979 the Interfaith Hunger Coalition sponsored the first Los Angeles County farmers' market consisting of four farmers in the parking lot of a church in Gardena.

This humble beginning has quickly grown into a vigorous statewide movement of over 700 weekly markets.[19]

In the twenty-first century, farmers' markets dot the Los Angeles landscape. According to the Los Angeles Food Policy Council, there are currently 67 certified farmers' markets in the city. Some are located in low-income areas, providing a valuable source of healthy food, but most are found in wealthier areas where stalls sell fruits and vegetables as well as specialty foods such as kimchi, pastries, and killer ladybugs. The Santa Monica Wednesday Farmers Market, located blocks from the beach, is truly a beautiful spectacle of multicolored peaches, tomatoes, and flowers (depending on the season) that ends in a sweeping view of the ocean. The Wednesday market is recognized as one of the largest and most diverse certified farmers' markets in the country, frequented by over 9,000 weekly shoppers and the city's most elite chefs. This farmers' market is a place I take out-of-town visitors to Los Angeles. We examine unusual produce, get something to eat at one of the stalls selling pastries, and enjoy the view of the nearby Pacific Ocean. The Santa Monica markets accept electronic benefit transfer (EBT) cards, allowing low-income shoppers to take advantage of the produce. All shoppers have to do is slide their cards and they receive money to spend on produce. This market, however, is located in affluent Santa Monica, nowhere close to Boyle Heights, East L.A., and South L.A., low-income, minority areas described in earlier chapters of the book.

Less than 45% of the city's farmers' markets accept CalFresh EBT cards, making farmers' markets largely inaccessible to the 17% of the city population that receives CalFresh benefits, according to data from the Los Angeles Food Policy Council. A map provided by The Ecology Center's Farmers' Market EBT Program, a program that helps market operators and community partners to establish, implement, and promote CalFresh EBT access, show very few markets that accept EBT in low-income areas, while they dot the map in more affluent parts of the city. A current priority of the Los Angeles Food Policy Council is to expand CalFresh access to all farmers' markets, promote CalFresh enrollment at farmers' markets, and support increased funding for the Market Match program, a nongovernmental program that receives money from private donors and foundations and allows users to double the first $10 of their benefits.

As awareness of food deserts has grown in recent years, there has been increased effort to reach the underserved at farmers' markets. One of the first programs to create incentives for shoppers using federal nutrition assistance was the Double Up program that began in 2009 at five farmers' markets in Detroit and has served over 3,000,000 families in Michigan. The successful program matches up to $20 of what shoppers spend on fruits and vegetables with federal SNAP funds. This program has become a model for other programs nationwide. Other farmers' market incentive programs are slowly expanding. In 2002, the Farmers Market Promotion Program was created to establish, expand, and promote farmers' markets and CSAs. According to the USDA website, the 2014 Farm Bill included $100 million dollars over five years to support the Food Insecurity Incentive Nutrition grants program, a USDA program that provides incentives for low-income consumers to increase their produce purchases. While these changes have been slow to take place, they are one way to allow some of the 46.5 million Americans who receive SNAP benefits to access healthy food.

In Los Angeles and throughout California, CalFresh (the federally funded food assistance program for qualifying low-income families and individuals) and WIC (the supplemental nutrition program for women, infants, and children) benefit shoppers who qualify for nutrition assistance programs. CalFresh has undergone a number of changes in recent years and has improved significantly. Unfortunately, the program has had limited success among Latinos in Los Angeles. Many Latinos are eligible to receive benefits, but have not enrolled, while others have been excluded from the program because of their immigration status. California has the lowest participation rate in the nation in the program.[20] In Los Angeles only 59% of residents eligible to receive CalFresh benefits have applied. Many choose not to apply because they have received incorrect information about the program, while others fear receiving CalFresh benefits could negatively impact their chances of obtaining citizenship in the future, or even put undocumented family members at risk of deportation. This underenrollment has significant consequences for low-income families as well as state and local economies. They lose out on around $2 billion in federal aid annually; $1 billion in Los Angeles alone.[21] Improved awareness of the program and its use at local farmers' markets would greatly benefit residents, the local economy, as well as farmers as every CalFresh dollar spent generates $1.79 in economic activity.[22] Local farmers' markets also rely heavily on CalFresh funding. In fact, purchases from customers using benefits make up 40–60% of all sales at a typical farmers' market.[23] According to a February 24, 2015, *LA Times* article CalFresh and WIC aid make up the bulk of business at many markets. In Long Beach, for example, 65% of sales come from customers using benefits. During 2014, the use of benefits at certain markets increased by as much as 50%.[24]

Along with the benefits from CalFresh and WIC, low-income customers can also double the first $10 of benefits through the Market Match program that gives $10 a week to shoppers who receive CalFresh, WIC, or Social Security to shop at participating farmers' markets. The *LA Times* reports that the program reached 38,000 families during 2013 and is quickly expanding.[25] The growth in funding is a critical component of supporting community food security in low-income areas. The program not only improves customers' diets by enabling them to purchase healthier food they would not otherwise be able to afford, but also supports local California farmers who use sustainable methods. Allen Moy, executive director of the Pacific Coast Farmers' Market Association, says that there is no other program that has had a more significant impact on California farmers who struggle to keep price points competitive for healthy food.[26]

In April 2015, Southern California's recipients of the Market Match program received an additional million dollars from the USDA's Food Insecurity Nutrition Program. This grant will increase the number of farmers' markets where the Market Match program is available from 22 to 36.[27] Statewide, an additional 240,000 shoppers will benefit from the additional funds totaling 3.7 million dollars over two years. Frank Tamborello, executive director of Hunger Action L.A., a local organization that will receive a portion of the grant, says the impact is four-way: "It reduces hunger, especially among our senior population. It encourages healthy eating. It boosts the California small farm economy. And it supports environmentally sustainable agriculture."[28] Market Match reports far more low-income shoppers spending money at farmers' markets than they would otherwise. According to the study on Market Match's website, in 2014 79% of customers surveyed reported an increase in fruit and vegetable consumption as a result of the program. One customer who shops at the Adams Vermont Farmers' Market, a low-income market in South L.A., said that the Market Match program helps her family purchase fruits and vegetables that are "vital for our nutritional needs. Not only am I able to bring home whole foods to my family, but I am very happy to support the hard working farmers who help bring these whole foods from the soil to my family's table.[29] Nevertheless, some obstacles for low-income customers remain; shoppers report not being able to complete all of their shopping at the farmers' market, while others report being unaware of the markets' location or hours. Even with such challenges, low-income Latino shoppers at the East L.A. Farmers' Market, Riverside Farmers' Market and many other markets that service these communities will be able to increase their purchases of produce. Thanks to the market match program.

Between 2007–2009, a study was conducted in East L.A. and South L.A. on the role of farmers' markets in the communities. Using anonymous surveys, the researchers found that the shoppers were primarily Latina women earning less than $22,000 annually with less than twelve years of education. These women reported being able to buy more healthy fruits and vegetables within their own communities as a result of the growth in farmers' markets in their neighborhoods. The study also reported a disproportionately high rate in South L.A. of Latino shoppers in comparison to African-Americans:

40% of residents are African-American, but 78% of the shoppers are Latinos, reflecting a cultural norm among Latinos of shopping at outdoor markets for produce in their home countries. The customers surveyed also shared the impact on a personal level: "Now I don't have to go 10 miles for fresh fruits and vegetables. Someone actually cares."[30] This study shows that if markets and public transportation are available, Latino shoppers will take advantage of them.

While farmers' markets have grown rapidly nationwide during the first decades of the twenty-first century, by 2015 the situation in Southern California was changing. In a 2015 editorial in the *LA Times*, Russ Parsons asked, "Has the farmers market movement peaked?" Parsons noted that the growth rate of new markets has slowed from 7% to 5.5% over the past few years and in Southern California total revenue declined from $4.2 million in 2007 to $2.3 million in 2012. Managers of farmers' markets say that there has been a saturation of markets and that at smaller markets there are not enough farmers or shoppers.[31] This news is troubling for organizations that run farmers' markets in low-income areas.

IF YOU BUILD IT, WILL THEY COME?

Increased assistance for low-income shoppers to use at farmers' markets, new organic grocery stores opening in South L.A., corner stores being transformed to offer a selection of healthy foods and look more inviting to shoppers—these are all important solutions that should create change in the shopping and eating habits of low-income shoppers. Despite these advances, studies show that increased access fails to do as much to improve the health of low-income neighborhoods as hoped. Why is that? Study after study has shown that simply placing a grocery store in an underserved area does not solve the problem alone. A recent piece on NPR made this point. In 2015, Walmart celebrated achieving its goal of opening at least 275 stores in food deserts by 2016 as part of the retailer's healthy food initiative launched with the First Lady four years earlier. Despite the possibility for increased access to fruits and vegetables, new research from the *American Journal of Preventative Medicine* suggests that, as a result, Americans junk food calories come increasingly from big-box stores rather than smaller corner stores. According to the NPR piece "Why Walmart and other Retail Chains May Not fix the Food Deserts," "The share of calories from packaged food products purchased at mass merchandisers, convenience stores and warehouse clubs nearly doubled from 2000 to 2012."[32] Not only has the percentage of junk food calories increased, but the piece goes on to say that the products offered at large retailers contained, on average, more sugar, sodium, and saturated fats than the processed foods they had bought previously at corner stores and smaller grocers. Dalia Stern, lead author of the study, explains that the problem "is that big box stores sell plenty of junk along with healthy options —and shoppers don't necessarily go for the latter."[33] Evidently, just placing a grocery store in a food desert is not enough to change people's habits. The study's results point to the importance of education so that people can make more informed choices.

The results also demonstrate that improving access to fresh fruits and vegetables is only one part of a multifaceted approach. The Obama administration's Healthy Food Financing Initiative has spent $500 million since 2010 to provide funding to develop new grocery stores, small retailers and corner stores, and farmers' markets selling healthy food in underserved areas.[34] In New York City, for example, a city tax incentive program to bring healthy food into a high-need area paid 40% of the cost of construction on a new grocery store in the Bronx. A 2015 article in the *New York Times* stated, "The neighborhood welcomed the addition, and perceived access to healthy food improved," but a 2015 study in *Public Health Nutrition* showed that the residents' diets did not show substantial change.[35] The study compared this area with a similar demographic in a nearby neighborhood and found that, within the first year of opening, the new store had little impact on residents' purchasing and consumption. The studies' findings demonstrate that merely opening a store is not enough to change people's diets. According to the study, convenience turns out to be not as important a factor as shopping and cooking habits, and affordability.[36] Shoppers' education level, instead, is a far bigger predictor of people's buying habits. Another study on the public health effects of food deserts by the National Research Council and the Institute of Medicine examined whether lack of access was the main contributing factor to poor diets or entrenched food preferences. The authors found that food preferences were a greater predictor than accessibility.[37]

As the above study shows, just making healthy food cheaper and more accessible does not solve the problem. Access must be accompanied by expanding nutrition education and changing the system of subsidizing processed food while whole foods receive little in the way of subsidies. Another new approach being taken is to apply a "sin tax" to junk food and/or soda. Researchers at the University of Buffalo tested the theory of loss aversion, an economics theory of people's tendency to strongly prefer avoiding losses more than acquiring gains. In their first experiment, the researchers lowered the price of healthy food by 25% and found that participants did buy more of it, but, surprisingly, used the leftover money to buy more junk food. Next, researchers added a "sin tax," charging more for unhealthy food, and found that the participating mothers did buy less junk food.[38] The second experiment proved loss aversion, showing that people respond more to price increases than decreases. Charging more for the unhealthy food, the study shows, could have a positive effect. While it would not change eating habits or people's approach to nutrition overnight, "sin taxes," such as the ones passed on soda in Mexico and Berkeley, California, in 2014, are important first steps. As the above studies demonstrate, building the field of dreams by itself will not change the outlook for the future. It takes organizations and leaders from within the community that know the area's needs and have the cultural competency necessary to incentivize the community to make small changes.

GROCERYSHIPS

Another new nonprofit organization Groceryships, founded in 2014 by Sam Polk, is taking a completely different approach to improving health in the community. Groceryships' staff and volunteers work with small groups of South L.A. residents to improve health and diet through a peer-led education and support program. Polk's road to Groceryships has not been a traditional one. As a college student at Columbia University and later as a young adult, Polk was addicted to drugs and alcohol. Later, Polk climbed the ladder of power and success to become a very high-paid hedge-fund manager on Wall Street. Eventually, Polk realized he was always scrambling to make more money and had become addicted to the wealth it brought. In a *New York Times* op-ed piece Polk confesses, "In my last year on Wall Street my bonus was $3.6 million—and I was angry because it wasn't big enough."[39] After years on Wall Street, Polk tired of his shallow lifestyle and searched for something more meaningful than making money.

In 2010, Polk quit his Wall Street job, got married, began to speak in jails and juvenile detention centers about getting sober, and taught a writing class to foster children. He continued his quest for a meaningful life. Polk and his wife Christine began to watch documentaries as they explored healthier lifestyles and alternative paths. Documentaries about food-related issues, including *Forks over Knives*, a film that explores the claim that rejecting animal-based diets and processed foods can help eliminate or control diseases such as cancer and diabetes, and *A Place at the Table*, a 2014 documentary about hunger in America, really spoke to them and inspired them to change their own diets. Polk's wife, a surgeon-turned-psychiatrist, had suffered from high cholesterol for years. The idea of a plant-based diet was a way to improve her health and eliminate her dependency on medication. Slowly, Sam and Christine began to change their eating habits and her cholesterol level decreased. Not only did they want to improve their own health, they also wanted to do something about the epidemics of hunger and obesity in the United States, but what? Within a month, Polk's idea had turned into the early stages of a nonprofit that he called Groceryships, a program that provides scholarships for groceries and offers support and education to South L.A. community members who are food insecure and suffering from health issues.

In 2014, Polk and his team created their first pilot program with ten participants, all women and low-income African-Americans and Latinos. Months later, they launched a second group with eleven participants. Along with weekly grocery store gift cards, the participants receive a free Vitamix blender, a "wellness toolkit" that includes a food journal, healthy recipes, and exercise strategies, and ongoing medical screenings and tracking of health metrics. The participants also learn how to read labels and distinguish between processed foods and whole foods. To learn these skills firsthand, the participants tour grocery stores together. This is all part of the process of learning healthy ways of navigating their environment.

The participants meet weekly for two hours to share their experiences and learn from one another. Despite initial reluctance on the part of the women to open up to one another, after a few sessions they felt much more comfortable sharing their concerns and fears with each other and their white, upper-middle-class guide, Polk. They began to unite as a cohort. At the end of five months, the members of the first group had all lost weight and were eating a healthier diet. They had begun to open up to one another as well, providing support for each another on emotional and health issues, and, in the process, building a sense of community. As a result, participants began to feel better emotionally, an important change since obesity correlates with stress, depression, and low self-esteem. They also developed a close bond with Polk and deeply appreciated all he had done for them. Evidently, the first two pilot groups had been a great success. Soon, Polk was hiring new employees and fundraising to expand the organization and to reach out to the local Latino community. As of June 2015, two out of three groups were Spanish-speaking. By the end of 2015 they had increased the number of program participants from 20 to 100 families and had launched ten new groups, all of which are Spanish-speaking. The groups are no longer being led by Polk, but instead by former participants and local *promotoras*, Latina community members who are not professional health care workers, but have received training to provide basic health education to the community.

In 2016, Groceryships plans to expand to twenty new groups and is using a crowdfunding site to raise money for their own community center in South L.A., which they plan to be a hub for nutrition education and program meetings, as well as a storefront for their new food enterprise. Polk and his team have begun work on a social enterprise to sell healthy, plant-based meals at SNAP-affordable prices ($2.00–$2.50 per meal). These meals are intended to support the program's families and other families in the area on days they are not able to cook healthy meals for themselves to provide a quick, convenient, cheap, and healthy alternative to McDonald's, and go hand in hand with the educational component of the program.

After reading about Groceryships in August 2014 in the *LA Times* article "South L.A. Women Changed Their Lives, and It Started with Food" and reading Polk's op-ed piece "Yuppies Watching Documentaries," I contacted to Sam Polk to learn more about the organization and to see if any of his students would be interested in visiting my class to speak about their experience with Groceryships.[40] Yoloxochitl Correa and her sixteen-year-old daughter Paola volunteered to speak to my class. Yolo had come to the United States from a town outside Puebla, Mexico, only ten months earlier. She has no family here and did not speak the language well. She felt isolated and depressed. This took a toll on her physical and mental health. Walking around her new neighborhood in South L.A., Yolo found fast-food restaurants everywhere and began to gain weight. Through her daughter's high school, she discovered the Groceryships program, bound to lose weight and improve the health of her family. When I met her, she was only six weeks or so into the program, but had already adopted a vegetarian diet and had lost weight. Her daughter, too, had lost weight and had become very aware of her dietary choices. When she went on a camping trip through a school organization, she opted for the tofu vegetarian option over pepperoni pizza. Choices like this require discipline and are hard to make; coming from a fifteen-year-old, I was impressed!

In December 2014, I visited one of the sessions of Groceryships. A group of twelve African-American and Latina women sat in a circle of chairs along with Polk to begin their weekly check in. One by one they went around and talked about how their week had gone, the challenges they had faced, both in their desire to eat healthier as well as in their personal lives. The group was surprisingly intimate, considering that they had not known each other six weeks earlier and that they were from different backgrounds, some recent Latina immigrants and others lifetime residents of South L.A. When one woman tearfully shared that an aunt was dying of cancer, all the other women offered their heartfelt support. Halfway through the session, the group took a break and went to the kitchen. Karla, a health coach gave them eggplants, onions, and red peppers to chop up and then sautéed the vegetables in some olive oil. She introduced the women to eggplant, a fruit many of them were not culturally familiar with, and showed them how to cube it and serve it in a whole-wheat tortilla to make a healthy wrap. The group chatted as they prepared and ate the healthy snack. This experience of cooking and eating together seemed to give the participants an added connection beyond sharing their challenges and experiences.

Despite the short amount of time the program has been operating and the small number of participants to date, it has been very effective locally and beyond South L.A. Polk says that requests have poured in from 50 cities around the United States for him to duplicate his program, but for the time being he is going to focus his efforts on South L.A. Given his business background, Polk has managed to decrease costs with each group. He started out at $2,800 per family with the first group, then reduced costs to $1,500 per family, and, in the future, he believes he can operate groups for as little as $800 per family since he has received donations from Farm Fresh to You, a farm that delivers boxes of organic fruits and vegetables to people's homes.

Questions about the long-term success of the program remain to be answered. Will these women be able to maintain the same level of healthy food consumption when the support from Groceryships ends? Will they continue to cook and eat healthy meals without the support from coparticipants? How does Polk plan to measure long-term success? In the meantime, the program has received many accolades. According to Groceryships' website, the former CEO of Kaiser Foundation calls it "a unique approach that is already showing impressive results in hard to serve neighborhoods of Los Angeles" and says the program is "simply amazing." Polk believes the program has achieved a high level of success in such a short time because of his unique approach—stressing the importance of a wide social support network to exact change. Polk argues that improving health is not just about improving one's environment but also about changing social norms. In a January 2015 op-ed piece in the *LA Times*, Polk gives an important message about group norms, using smoking as an example. He states: "This is intuitive—if your friends smoke, you are likely to smoke. Less intuitive was the discovery that your friend's friends can affect your health." Change has to come by providing a supportive social network as well as improving the food landscape. So far, this approach is working. Eighty percent of their referrals are word of mouth and many of their graduates stay involved by volunteering with other groups, an effective way to provide ongoing support once they finish the program.

In March 2015, I attended the graduation ceremony for the second cohort of Groceryships. Over a hundred friends, family, and supporters came to the event at Manual Arts High School in South L.A. The eleven women graduates spoke about the impact of the program on their lives. They were very grateful to Polk for the opportunity he had given them, and very emotional. Many graduates were brought to tears, as were some audience members. The women spoke of the friendship and bond they had formed with the others. They talked about the new confidence this program had given them and how their children, slowly, were starting to eat a more nutritious diet. Many had lost weight, some a significant amount. Polk emphasized, however, that the program does not focus on weight loss, but instead on education and support. He believes that the key to the program is pairing the nutrition education with deep emotional support and that there is no teacher-student relationship in the program. Instead, everyone brings something valuable to the table. Tavis Smiley, the renowned radio and television talk show host, was the keynote speaker at the graduation. Smiley talked about the need for "servant leaders" such as Polk to address the acute, intractable problem of overweight and obesity in low-income, minority areas. He told the women that what they have learned from this program is discipline. With discipline, they can do anything. Smiley also made an interesting observation. He apologized on behalf of the media. He pointed out that not a single member of the news media was there to report the event. He remarked that if a shooting or an incident of gang violence had occurred at the high school, media trucks would have been lined up to cover it, but that, sadly, good work doesn't often get the exposure that shootings and violence do. Hopefully, the lessons learned from the Groceryships program will continue to impact its graduates, even without the weekly grocery stipends and the support of their peer group. Yoloxochitl Correa has remained in touch and tells me that the program has had a huge impact on her life. She feels part of a larger community and is serving as a leader for two Spanish-language groups.

Let's return to the life of another Latina immigrant woman, the Oaxacan immigrant Marina Gutierrez, but fast forward ahead a few years. What will her life be like as a Latina, a mother, and low-income worker in the future? Will she be able to buy her produce at one of the new social ventures opening in 2016? How will she get there? Will her children be able to play in safe parks or will gang violence continue to plague the area? Will the food renaissance in South L.A. the media has celebrated make a difference in her life or is it just hype? If the organizations discussed above can make a difference in Marina's life, then her future will be in a world where the corner store sells healthy, delicious produce at an affordable price, produce that is culturally appropriate for the Oaxacan dishes she prepares for her family; a world in which the street vendors in her neighborhood sell sliced mango and pineapple with chili, salt, and lime without fear of the police; a world where she has a plot at a community garden within a short walk of her apartment, a community garden where she grows corn, *epazote* (an strong-tasting herb common in Mexican cooking), beans, squash, *verdolaga* (purslane), and other staples of her homeland; and a world where her children eat healthy, affordable meals and play safely outdoors.

Chapter 7

Urban Agriculture and Latino Roots in Los Angeles

L.A. urban farmer Ron Finley proclaims that "growing your own food is like printing your own money." In his 2013 TED Talk, Finley describes his neighborhood of South L.A. as a food desert, a land of "liquor stores, fast food, vacant lots." In 2010, when Finley got fed up with driving forty-five minutes for an apple "that wasn't impregnated with pesticides" he decided to plant a "food forest" in the parkway in front of his house. This is a strip of land that is owned by the city, but maintained by the individual homeowner. Finley and the organization L.A. Green Grounds planted fruit trees and vegetables in this small 150- by 10- feet strip. The garden was a verdant, beautiful oasis, a source of free fresh fruit and vegetables for Finley and his neighbors until someone complained to the city that Finley had planted on city property. The city issued Finley a citation and then a warrant for growing produce in a food desert. Really? Finley fought back. A Green Grounds member put up a petition on Change.org that got 900 signatures, the *LA Times* covered the story, and support for Finley grew quickly. All of a sudden, Finley's city councilmember was calling to tell him that he supports what he is doing. As Finley puts it, "What's not to like?" Finley considers himself a "guerrilla gardener" and calls his actions a "revolution." His simple action of gardening has generated greater public awareness of the need for increased access to healthy food and of the many benefits of getting your hands dirty and growing your own food in low-income areas such as South L.A.

Finley's revolution led to the creation of the Edible Parkways Ordinance in March 2015, a city ordinance that allows Angelenos to plant fruits and vegetables in their parkways without a permit. Previously, they were fined for growing food without paying for a $400 permit, but under the new ordinance they can plant edible plants in this city-owned space.[1] Finley not only succeeded in getting the law changed, but also changed the structure of his community, South L.A., a notorious food desert, and planted the seeds of an urban agriculture movement.

For residents of low-income communities where parks and playgrounds maybe scarce or dangerous, community gardens, urban farms, and residential parkways offer so much more than a place to grow fruits and vegetables. They provide spaces for healthy outdoor activity and serve as outlets for therapy and expression in marginalized, immigrant communities. Ron Finley's story is one example of the renaissance in urban agriculture that has taken place across the United States since the beginning of the twenty-first century. Other stories of transformation are occurring at farmers' markets and community gardens around the country, but these most visible forms of urban agriculture are not the whole story. Increasingly, vacant lots and other spaces are being used to grow food and transform blighted properties into community assets. Urban agriculture or urban farming, as defined by Jason Mark in *The SAGE Encyclopedia of Food Issues*, refers to "the cultivation or production of food within urban areas, often in underutilized city locales such as vacant lots, community parks, or rooftops."[2]

Numerous studies tout the many benefits of community gardens for low-income areas and their residents. These include improving nutrition, increasing food security and physical activity, improving mental health, and creating stronger community relationships. Interestingly, healthy food is not always the main impulse to participate in a garden. A study conducted in Philadelphia's urban gardens found that recreation (21%) was the most important reason for a participant's involvement followed by health benefits such as mental health (19%).[3] A study by faculty at the School of Public Health at the University of Colorado-Boulder found that "community gardeners eat more vegetables, exercise more, weigh less and feel healthier than non-gardeners." They also feel more protective of their neighborhoods.[4] While community gardens benefit all residents of urban areas, they are especially advantageous to those living in low-income areas where access to healthy, fresh foods and green spaces to exercise and socialize with neighbors are daily challenges. In this way, urban farming is a uniquely accessible tool for change that can be used to reshape communities that lack access to sufficient grocery stores and healthy food markets. As Sarah Rich points out in her 2012 book *Urban Farms*, "It is often easier to plant vegetables than to alter the inventory of mini-marts and liquor stores."[5]

In his captivating TED Talk, Ron Finley calls gardening "the most therapeutic and defiant act you can do," a concept backed up by studies that demonstrate its positive effects on mental health, including a form of therapy known as "horticultural therapy" or "therapeutic horticulture," in which people "suffering or recovering from illness (mental or physical) are engaged in horticultural tasks as a means to ease their clinical suffering or as an aid to promote longer-term recovery or cure."[6] Gardening is not only a therapeutic act for those suffering from mental and physical illness. A 2014 study on the benefits of gardening and food growing for health and well-being discusses benefits like promoting social inclusion for excluded groups such as immigrants.[7] While Latinos are not considered a socially excluded group in the same sense as refugees fleeing war-torn countries, a 2011 dissertation on the importance of studying Mexican immigrants' mental health shows that immigration can be traumatic. In her study, "Acculturative Stress of Mexican Immigrant Women and the Nature and Role of Social Support," Barclay Stone, a psychologist at UCSF School of Medicine, observes, "Many of the realities of their lives in the U.S. put Mexican immigrants at risk for developing psychological problems."[8] Stone also points out that "the 'everyday absence' of familiar smells, foods, and routines can be disorienting and disruptive enough to cause serious psychological disturbance."[9] She explains that as immigrants settle in their new country the adjustment process presents new stressors: "a new language, different values and behaviors, and the disruption of community and social networks." Along with the adjustment to a new culture and language, immigrants are also faced with the stressors of living in poverty, substandard work and living conditions, discrimination, and the fear of deportation for those who are undocumented.[10] Stone observes that immigration often separates people from family and other social support networks. In the face of these multiple mental health stressors, community gardening offers immigrants a sense of community by connecting gardeners to one other and to the traditions and practices of their native lands.

A study of the role gardening and agriculture can play in reducing diabetes on the Navajo nation, a historically socially excluded group, included among the benefits "positive mental outlook through a combined sense of accomplishment at harvest time, bonding with the earth, and spiritual growth."[11] The spiritual value of communal gardening found in Native American communities is an important value in Latino communities as well, a culture in which a garden represents much more than a space to grow organic foods and feed ones' family. For Latino immigrants and their families, the act of gardening has symbolic meaning. It ties them to their roots since a connection to the land is such an important part of Mesoamerican cultures. In an article in the Spanish-language newspaper *La Opinión*, Paulina Ortiz talks about how she feels transported to her native Oaxaca, where she used to help her grandfather grow corn, when she comes with her children to her plot at Mariposa Nabi, a community garden near her home in Koreatown in Los Angeles. The article describes the garden as "un espacio rodeado de edificios en el que decenas de familias se han reencontrado con la tierra y sus nostalgias" (a space surrounded by buildings in which dozens of families have been reunited with the land and their nostalgia).[12] In the case of Paulina Ortiz and many other immigrants, gardening heals them as they adjust to their new lives and allows them to maintain their cultural identity through the cultivation of plants that connect them to their native foodways. Connecting Latino immigrants and their children to their cultural heritage gives them a sense of pride, a pride in themselves, their culture, and their neighborhood.

Many of the Latino immigrants in Los Angeles are indigenous peoples from Mexico or Central America where their families farmed the land either for their own sustenance or for profit. In Latino urban landscapes of the United States such as Los Angeles, Phoenix, Albuquerque, San Antonio, Chicago, and Houston, Latinos continue to play a vital role in community gardens where they typically plant native food crops and medicinal plants. According to anthropologist Devon Peña in "Farmers Feeding Families: Agroecology in South Central Los Angeles," "Mexican-origin gardeners are involved in more than 40% of the total number of urban gardens."[13] Many immigrant families have found that certain ingredients are not as readily, if at all, available in the United States. Through community gardens, people can plant fruits and vegetables from their native countries, particularly in Southern California where the growing season is long and bountiful. In her work, Deborah Barndt emphasizes a dimension of food security that goes beyond the ability of all people, regardless of race, age, or social class to access safe, healthy, and affordable food. "Food security is achieved when people have access to adequate amounts of safe and nutritional foods *that are both personally and culturally acceptable.*"[14] For many Latino immigrants to the United States, access to foods that are personally and culturally acceptable is of great importance, an aspect of nutrition education often overlooked. Many Latino families use the herbs and vegetables in dishes from their native countries that they otherwise would not be able to cook. In this way, community gardens allow immigrants to preserve a culinary connection to their homelands. Not only do Latinos grow food for themselves and their families, but they also cultivate traditional medicinal plants and herbs that are culturally meaningful and useful in traditional culinary practices. Plants such as aloe vera, rue, and peppermint serve a variety of medicinal functions. They are used to treat skin burns, cancer symptoms, digestion problems, diarrhea, and much more. Unlike in Western medicine where patients see a doctor and rely on a prescription only when they are ill, Latino immigrants and their offspring use herbal medicine on a day-to-day basis for general health and well-being.

Along with the importance of a spiritual connection to one's roots, urban agriculture is also a way for low-income Latino families to exert greater control over their economic futures: a benefit backed up by studies that demonstrate the ability of urban farms to strengthen local economies by creating new jobs, keeping consumers' money in the local community, supplementing incomes, and increasing property values.[15] At small urban family farms, residents not only grow food, but also raise chickens for eggs or animals for meat. The food can be sold at local farmers' markets, as in the case of Reis Flores, a third-generation Mexican-American and Angeleno, who raises ducks, turkeys, and quail at a lot near his L.A. home. He sells the eggs he produces for a dollar apiece since they are not genetically modified. At Thanksgiving time he sells turkey and pork from the animals he has raised. For Reies the payoff of raising animals and growing vegetables is not only financial. He told the Spanish-language newspaper *La Opinión* that for him "Producir en la propia casa es una ganancia en todos los sentidos en especial para los latinos, porque nos regresan a nuestras raíces, a nuestros abuelos" ("Growing in one's own home is a win in every sense, especially for Latinos, because it returns us to our roots, to our grandparents").[16]

In San Jose, California, a local nonprofit, La Mesa Verde, provides local Latino families with two raised beds per yard with soil, seedlings, and a drip-irrigation system at the cost of $210 a year. One family with four children said that prior to their garden, they were spending $4 a week on cilantro alone. Another resident, María Alarcon, said the program was saving her family $90 a month in grocery bills, a substantial amount for a low-income family on a limited budget.[17] Programs like La Mesa Verde show that vegetables can be grown in spaces beyond the more recognized community gardens and farms. A study of entrepreneurial agriculture mentions the value of growing food on vacant lots in urban areas as a way to improve the image of "troubled neighborhoods" and increase "neighborhood green space." Transforming vacant lots from blighted spaces to green ones gives inner-city residents "more pride and self-sufficiency" while also "creating food-based employment" for young people in areas where job opportunities are scarce.[18]

Vacant lots are an enormous problem in many parts of the country. In South L.A., there are over 3,000 vacant lots.[19] In May 2015, an organization called LA Open Acres created a database and map of all the city's vacant lots. Their website says that they see the mapping as a way to empower the community to "change blights to public assets." Current legislation would go a step further in supporting urban agriculture. A new state law, known as AB551 or The Urban Agriculture Incentive Zones Act, allows property owners of vacant lots of three acres or fewer who lease their land for agricultural uses for a five year period, to pay reduced property tax rates. This allows farmers a longer time frame to cultivate the site and invest in better irrigation systems. It also incentivizes some property owners to not sell to developers.

San Francisco was the first California city to write the law into local code on August 7, 2014. It has benefited community members and property owners alike. The first San Francisco property owner to be approved under the new law, Dr. Aaron Roland, used to grow fruits and vegetables on a lot he owned in the city for years, but when he moved to a different neighborhood he gave his land to friends to use as an educational garden. When his application was approved for AB551, Roland went from paying $16,000 a year in property taxes on his 5,000-square-foot lot to paying only $16. Roland explained that there is a "huge opportunity cost in letting your property be used for a garden."[20] In other words, he has not gained nearly as much financial benefit as he would have from selling the lot, but it gives him peace of mind to know that the space is not being turned into yet more expensive condominiums. In a speech to the San Francisco Board of Supervisors, Roland said,

> I am hopeful that the passage of this new law will inspire other landowners to step back from the search for a way to squeeze out another dollar from each square foot of land and let them lean in to the possibility that land ownership can benefit the community and enhance the enjoyment of urban space.[21]

Hopefully, Roland and the city of San Francisco will serve as a model for Los Angeles as the city council considers the bill.

As of October 2015, the city and county of Los Angeles had not yet adopted AB551, but it was being championed by two city councilmembers, Curran Price and Felipe Fuentes, as a way to wage war on urban blight. Curran Price represents the Exposition Park area around the USC, a low-income area within the boundaries of South L.A. The Los Angeles County Board of Supervisors has determined that 56,950 parcels in the county could be eligible under AB551.[22] If passed, the law has the potential to increase access to healthy foods, create local jobs, have a positive impact on the environment, and transform vacant spaces into community hubs. A possible challenge to the bill is that it has to pass both the city council and the County Board of Supervisors to be put into effect since the change in property taxes would affect city and county revenues. L.A. supervisor Mark Ridley-Thomas was quoted in an *LA Times* article as saying that the program "'seeks to provide a carrot—literally and figuratively' to property owners and will 'increase the amount of healthy fruits and vegetables grown within urban areas while reducing the number of vacant lots that often become blighted.'"[23] Although the law would create a loss of up to 13.3 million dollars in property tax income for the city, this drawback is offset by the fact that it would raise neighbors' property values.

While AB551 has the opportunity to create more green spaces for residents of Los Angeles, another new law in the city protects one of the planet's most threatened insects—bees. After 136 years as a prohibited activity in the city, beekeeping has finally been legalized in Los Angeles. The new proposal allows beekeeping in single-family residential zones and creates jobs for urban beekeepers. The beekeeping law was first put into place in 1879 by lawmakers who thought that bees were damaging fruit trees and wanted to protect crops, however, as a 2015 op-ed in the *LA Times* explains, bees make a $15 billion contribution to the U.S. economy "in their role as pollinators of more than 100 fruit and vegetable crops."[24] At an event at a community garden in Boyle Heights, I met a Latino beekeeper Amadeo Delgado, who was publicizing his new business installing residential hives and teaching local Latino residents about the benefits of owning their own hive. New proposed legislation such as AB551 and the repeal of the city's 136-year-old ban on urban beekeeping demonstrate the city's growing support for urban agriculture.

URBAN AGRICULTURE IN LOS ANGELES: THE HISTORY OF SCHOOL AND COMMUNITY GARDENS

Since the early nineteenth century, school gardens were an integral part of early childhood education in Europe. Their mention began much earlier with the writings of the eighteenth-century philosopher Rousseau who discusses the importance of nature in the education of young children.[25] By the late nineteenth century, the idea that not all learning had to take place in the classroom had made its way across the Atlantic, and in the United States educators were beginning to combine classroom learning with outdoor experiences. This philosophy made its way to the emerging city of Los Angeles in 1910 with the arrival of Marie Aloysius Larkey, an expert in agricultural economy who brought the first school gardens to Angelenos.[26] The children of L.A. factory workers and other blue-collar workers tilled the first school gardens in Los Angeles. These 70,000 students went on to create gardens out of more than 150 vacant lots around the city during the first decades of the twentieth century.[27] The food they grew fed Los Angeles' residents during World War I.

During World War I, the federal government created the United States School Garden Army (USSGA) in an "an unprecedented governmental effort to make agricultural education a formal part of the public school curriculum throughout the United States."[28] As Rose Hayden-Smith outlines in her work on these early school gardens, the Federal Bureau of Education declared, "Every boy and every girl ... should be a producer. The growing of plants ... should therefore become an integral part of the school program."[29] The USSGA adopted the motif "a garden for every child, every child in a garden" as a way to make school gardens a more integral part of the war effort at a time when the nation's food system was archaic and there was a dire need to increase agricultural production.[30] During World War I, planting gardens and food conservation were considered national priorities. These gardens, first known as "liberty gardens" during World War I and, later, during

World War II renamed "victory gardens" or "war gardens," were created to reduce the shortage in the food supply brought on by the war and encourage civic duties among youth. Nationalistic posters proclaimed, "Sow the seeds of Victory! Plant and raise your own vegetables."[31] By 1943, Americans had planted more than twenty million victory gardens that yielded over 40% of the produce consumed that year.[32] Once World War II ended and soldiers returned home, however, the growing popularity of suburban homes with private backyard lots discouraged community gardening efforts.[33] As Mark Winne observes in *Closing the Food Gap*, "once the culture of scarcity was transformed to one of abundance," as occurred in the booming postwar years, urban gardening was largely abandoned.[34]

During the later decades of the twentieth century, the reemergence of the community garden movement revived the victory gardens that, in some cases, had been planted decades earlier during the world wars.[35] For gardeners during the Civil Rights Movement of the 1960s and 1970s, the urban garden provided a safe place for interactions among different racial and ethnic groups. It was also a period when the term "community garden" first took on a broader meaning. According to Laura Lawson in her history of community gardening in the United States, in the past, a community garden referred to "a large property divided into individual gardens," but with "the resurgence of urban gardens in the 1970s, the community garden was not only a type of garden, but also an expression of grassroots activism."[36] Later, during the economic decline of the 1980s, the community garden movement grew even stronger as people in cities started growing their own food again "in response to the parallel demise of America's urban manufacturing, distribution, and food processing industries and the blight they left behind."[37] In the 1990s, gardening organizations, such as the American Community Garden Association (ACGA), had expanded and grew increasingly sophisticated. The ACGA conducted surveys to better understand the communities they served. They found that the main reasons for the closure of community gardens were the lack of continued interest in maintaining the garden (49%) and the loss of the land to a public agency (20%).[38] In response, garden organizers began to focus on the role of community development and political activism in the gardens' long-term success. Some activists began to expand the movement beyond gardening to social justice, education, and environmentalism.[39] As a result, the gardens' mission became more centered around improving communities than was the case with their earlier counterparts, the victory gardens. As one community garden activist shares in *City Bountiful*, "The community garden movement has to be more about *community* than about gardening."[40] This focus on community and education continues in the twenty-first century as the number of community and school gardens grows around the country. In 2015, there are an estimated 18,000 individual plot-based community gardens in the United States, while Los Angeles County has an estimated 700 school gardens.[41]

The community garden movement has expanded at the same time that awareness of the harmful effects of the industrialized food system has increased and an interest in organic and sustainable food has exploded. Michael Pollan has influenced millions of Americans to be more ethical eaters and to vote with their forks. Younger generations of Americans are much more engaged with their food system. Despite this progress, disparities remain between inner-city minority residents and the upper-middle class in the suburbs. As anthropologist Devon Peña observes, the organic and sustainable agriculture movements "have largely neglected the food sovereignty needs of urban Latina/os."[42] Since their voices are largely left out of the mainstream conversation, migrant and U.S.-born Latinos have created their own "third space," an alternative place for community and sustainability. These spaces include community gardens, urban farms, school gardens, as well as abandoned, vacant lots. The vacant lots that the urban Latinos have appropriated have nurtured a sense of community and a source of culturally appropriate food, but also have become, at times, contested spaces.

One challenge to urban agriculture is the high cost of land in cities such as New York, Los Angeles, and beyond. The value of land in these cities pits the interests of real estate developers against those of community gardeners and urban farmers, leading to conflicts between wealthy developers and community advocates. In a study titled "The Effect of Community Gardens on Neighboring Property Values," the authors discuss how gardens that are originally catalysts for improving a neighborhood can later become a point of contention when private owners or public agencies try to reclaim the land for affordable housing or private development.[43] The study found that community gardens have, on average, significant positive effects on surrounding property values and that there is a "statistically significant impact" on houses that are located within 1,000 feet of the garden, an impact that increases over time.[44] This increase in property value can cause the garden to turn into an area of conflict, as these sites become potentially developable. This conflict is taking place across the United States in urban centers undergoing gentrification where lots once considered of little value, suddenly are coveted properties by developers. In his book *Food Justice*, Robert Gottlieb observes that the "politics and economics of urban real estate" have created enormous barriers to the creation of urban farms and community gardens. Gottlieb bemoans the irony that, in many instances, the same community gardens that caused the value of the property to increase were later uprooted to make way for new property development.[45]

Under former mayor Giuliani of New York City, there was a privatization of many community gardens to make way for low- and middle-income community housing. During the 1970s and 1980s, the city had made many vacant lots city property and granted community groups the right to use them as community gardens. Toward the final years of mayor Giuliani's term in the late 1990s' his administration wanted to use some of these gardens to build more housing. In 1999, the *New York Times* reported that the city was going to auction off 112 community gardens to the highest bidder for real estate development.[46] In response, protesters dressed as ladybugs and insects filed lawsuits and staged acts of civil disobedience; some were arrested in protests at City Hall. The dispute between community gardeners and the city was not resolved until a few years later when the city agreed to preserve 500 of the gardens and use others to build more than 2,000 apartments.[47]

The struggle between development and preserving community gardens has extended to Brooklyn, an area that has undergone extreme gentrification since the final years of the twentieth century. In Crown Heights, Brooklyn, a small community garden known as "Roger That" is under direct threat of development. The garden was built in 2006 on the site of a long-abandoned hardware store. The Crown Heights Youth Collective, a local nonprofit, succeeded in having the dilapidated building torn down since it was considered a public hazard because it was pulling down their neighboring building. In 2011, the Roger That team created the garden as a communal space for residents to come together. In the past decade, the neighborhood where the garden is located has undergone extreme gentrification. In May 2015, the website Curbed.com reported that Steve Billings of TYC Realty had filed plans to build six condominiums on the site of the Roger That Garden Project. The website reported that Billings claims that he now owns the property. Apparently, he had tracked down the hardware store's owner or the owner's daughter in Florida and convinced him or her to sign over the lease for a mere $10 in 2013. The gardeners and residents are fighting to save it from development using social media, fundraising, and the courts.[48] The garden's members are trying to convince the city to invoke eminent domain (a legal way for the government to take control of private property for public use) and buy the property. After months fighting the eviction in court, in November 2015 a judge threw out the case, siding with gardeners who have maintained and planted at the space for the past few years.[49] The campaign to protect Roger That did not end then, however, since garden members wanted to insure long-term protection. In January 2016 a state senator and an assemblywoman introduced bills in the legislature that would use eminent domain to take control of the garden plot and turn it into state parkland "to be managed by neighborhood volunteers through the New York City parks department," according to the bill.[50] Garden members held a letter-writing campaign to state politicians urging them to support the bills. The letters are meant to show the politicians that the community cares more about a garden plot that provides outdoor space and healthy food than luxury condos.

The story of this small garden in Brooklyn highlights the ongoing conflict over valuable land between developers and community members. One of the most famous examples of urban land as a contested space, is the South Central Farm in Los Angeles. In "Of Other Spaces," Michel Foucault is concerned with how we define the spaces in which we live. He wrote that "the garden is the smallest parcel of the world and then it is the totality of the world." Foucault refers to the garden as a heterotopia, a concept from geography used to describe places and spaces that function in nonhegemonic conditions. Gardens, such as Roger That, are heterotopias since they are "other spaces" low-income people occupy when they exist outside a place of power. Urban gardens and farms such as Roger That and the former South Central Farm are excellent examples of modern-day urban heterotopias: contested spaces where the community comes together in opposition to powerful, wealthy forces such as real estate developers or city agencies. The story of the South Central Farm is one of struggle, pain, and loss, but is also one of community bonding, ritual, and defiance in the face of defeat.

THE SOUTH CENTRAL FARM: A STORY OF LOSS AND HOPE FOR LATINO ANGELENOS

The South Central Farm was a 14-acre urban farm that operated in an industrial section of South L.A. between 1994 and 2006, an oasis in the middle of pavement, freeways, and bloody gang violence. With so many acres of open, green space in the middle of urban L.A., it was considered the largest urban farm in the United States. In 1992, former mayor Bradley gave the land to the community in light of the Rodney King that had taken place that year as a way to restore peace in the community after so much violence and unrest. The move to create a farm was spearheaded by the Los Angeles Food Bank as part of their mission to improve food access and nutrition to low-income households.[51] The land for the South Central Farm had been acquired by the city by eminent domain in the mid-1980s. The farm brought together indigenous immigrants of Mixtec, Nahua, May, Seri, Yaqui, and Zapotec origin, people who planted *huertos familiares* (family gardens) like the ones their families had planted back in Mexico or Central America.[52] At first the Los Angeles Food Bank managed the farm, but soon the farmers took over responsibility of operations and created a collective organization they called The South Central Farmers Feeding Families. The collective was modeled on the Mexican *ejido* system, a form of communal governance practiced in Mexico since the early twentieth century as a key strategy for land reform. The *ejido* land was formally owned by the state, but granted to villages to use as collective farm space with different families working different plots.

For the South Central farmers, the *ejido* system consisted of a council and a general assembly, a traditional democratic structure that was culturally familiar to the farmers.[53]

Not only did the farm provide a space that connected the Latino farmers with their agricultural roots, but it also became an integral part of their daily lives. The farmers' children ran and played among its tomato stakes and cactuses, they socialized with each other as they walked between plots, and they formed a strong community. This community and the garden's 14 acres were a safe space in the midst of turmoil. The dangers of urban gang violence and widespread drug use were all around them, but the garden was a beautiful oasis for these immigrant farmers and their families. In her article on the South Central Farm, Laura Lawson describes its value for the Latino farmers and their families who worked its land.

> In an area of the city that lacked recreation facilities and open space, the garden provided food, nutrition, household income savings, recreation, social interaction, and a place to carry on agrarian cultural traditions for 350 families and their social and familial networks.[54]

As time passed, the value of the South Central Farm's land increased and, in 2004, the city sold the land to a developer in a secretive, back-room deal. The developer, Ralph Horowitz, had originally sold the land to the city in the 1980s, when a local activist group, The Concerned Citizens of South Central, blocked construction of a waste plant on the site. Years later, this same group, led by a local resident Juanita Tate allegedly colluded with L.A. city councilwoman Jan Perry to sell the property back to Horowitz for only five million dollars. Tate's indifference to the plight of the farmers, advocacy for a sports field on the property, and purported collusion with Councilwoman Jan Perry are at the center of the Academy Award nominated 2008 documentary, *The Garden*. The documentary depicts the work of the gardeners and the rich community they created as well as their later attempt to mobilize against eviction and save their beautiful farm. It told the stories of Latino farmers such as Tezozomoc who discussed the farm's importance for his family:

> With many families struggling to put food on the table each night, local residents transformed the land into a thriving community garden and popular neighborhood connector. My father, who had recently become disabled and could no longer work, visited the garden often, engaging with community leaders, helping to grow fresh, healthy food for our family, and building a system to help those suffering from some of the worst poverty in the area.

Tezozomoc and Rufina Juarez were two of the key players in the fight to save the garden featured in the documentary. Tezozomoc immigrated to the

United States with his parents from Mexico during the 1970s. He was raised in South Central and East L.A. and earned a degree in electrical engineering. From 1998 to 2006 he tended a plot of land on the South Central Farm. Later, he became actively involved with the community of urban farmers in their work to preserve the farm. Rufina, the daughter of Mexican immigrants, grew up in the Imperial Valley, an area of southeastern California, where she worked on her family's farm. She went on to receive a master's degree in public administration from Bernard M. Baruch College in New York. Later, she moved to Los Angeles when she received a fellowship to study traffic congestion issues. In 2003, after she taught a group of children visiting the South Central Farm where corn comes from, she began to volunteer there regularly. Over time, she became one of the most visible leaders in the battle to preserve the farm.

In 2004, the South Central farmers received an injunction that allowed them to farm for another two years, but in 2006 the city of Los Angeles finally evicted them from their land. In the meantime, they organized and worked with lawyers who defended their case. Rufina Juarez led the effort to organize the farmers. They raised enough money to offer Horowitz his asking price of $16 million dollars for the land, but the developer would not budge and, in the end, the court ruled in his favor. Despite massive protests and support from celebrities such as Darryl Hannah, Martin Sheen, Joan Baez, and Willie Nelson, city workers bulldozed the farm. Would the city have acted differently had the farmers not been Latino largely undocumented immigrants? It's hard to say, but the farmers clearly felt they were the victims of discrimination. As one of the farmers states in the film, "Sólo porque somos latinos no nos quieren."("Just because we are Latinos they don't want us.") Sadly, today the space where the South Central Farm once stood is just an empty lot. In January 2015, nearly a decade later, a report on the South Central Farmers' website showed documentation that the city of Los Angeles was conducting an environmental impact report to decide whether to allow the construction of an industrial park made up of 4 buildings on the site.

Fortunately, the story does not end here. As South Central farmer Tezozomoc explains, "In the politics of impossibility, you win by losing. We won by losing. And we continue to win, planting hope all along the way."[55] After the demolition of the farm, Tezozomoc and several others went on to create a worker-owned, organic farm, the South Central Farmers' Cooperative, on 85 acres near Bakersfield. Using Mesoamerican farming practices, the cooperative "preserves traditions" and "offers quality organic produce," "while providing a voice, dignity and a livelihood" for the farmers and workers.[56] The cooperative transports the produce they grow in Bakersfield to farmers' markets in underserved neighborhoods of Los Angeles and for distribution through CSA programs. Tezozomoc has received numerous awards for his work on food justice and is a frequent speaker at social justice conferences. Over the years, the cooperative has expanded its mission to include assisting farmers with education and services. Tezozomoc is the president of the South Central Farmers Health and Education Fund (SCF-HEF), a nonprofit that provides support for a diverse spectrum of farmer-owned refugee or immigrant cooperatives.

While Tezozomoc and others formed a cooperative, other former members of the South Central Farm joined the Stanford-Avalon community garden in 2006, a garden that was created in Watts as a way to placate the displaced gardeners. Since the garden was not large enough to accommodate the 300 interested families, preference was given to the older gardeners and the remaining plots were distributed in a raffle. Juan Gamboa, the garden's first leader, told the *LA Times* that he was "happy to have the controversies of the past behind him" and hoped that this garden was "for life."[57]

Not only were the lives of the farmers transformed by their involvement with the farm, the relationships protesters formed led to valuable, ongoing collaborations. Lane Gold was one of the protesters who fought to save the South Central Farm. She described to me how she and a group of other chefs met while doing social justice work in soup kitchens and were on the front line fighting to save South Central Farm. Later, they formed the Sol Catering Cooperative that serves vegan food and provides nourishing meals to homeless people on Skid Row in downtown Los Angeles. All the vegetables that they use come from the South Central Farmers' Cooperative and other local organic farms. Despite the unhappy outcome of the South Central Garden, the stories of Rufina, Tezozomoc, Juan Gamboa, and Lane Gold demonstrate the great potential for the possibility of a healthier and greener future in urban megalopolises like Los Angeles.

LATINO COMMUNITY GARDENS TODAY IN LOS ANGELES: PROYECTO JARDÍN

The multiple benefits of community gardening for the Latino community in Los Angeles can be seen in the efforts of a smaller-scale community garden such as Proyecto Jardín in Boyle Heights, a one-acre garden overflowing with plants, cactus, and beautiful tile mosaics and walls hand painted by local children. The garden was started in 1999 when a doctor at the adjacent White Memorial Hospital envisioned it as a community health tool. At the time, Boyle Heights was a dangerous neighborhood, plagued by gangs and shootings. Gunshots and police helicopters flying overhead were a part of daily life. The garden offered an oasis, a refuge in the midst of so much danger, for the residents. Over the fifteen years since it opened, it has grown into a multifaceted space with trees and gardens, exercise classes, and spaces for community events. Member farmers grow medicinal plants, corn, *nopal*, amaranth, and many other plants native to Mexico and other Central American countries. It also has a covered solar-powered exercise area for classes in capoeria, aerobics, and dance. The garden's director Irene Peña says that for many Latino communities in Los Angeles, food is a public health concern and that Proyecto Jardín allows community members to grow food that is delicious and culturally appropriate. Peña believes that Latino food traditions, "everything from what we eat, and how much we eat, to how we prepare it," are supported by community gardens because they increase access to healthy and fresh food, provide nutrition, and organize cooking and exercise classes. Peña emphasizes that the role of community gardens goes way beyond fulfilling the nutritional needs of the Latino community: "Gardening preserves people's wellbeing and fulfills a mental health need because it connects Latinos to the land, and thus, to their culture." She says that these spaces are especially important to Latino immigrant communities because of their cultural roots in agriculture. Peña believes that Proyecto Jardín provides "food for the body and food for the soul," especially given the difficult economic situation of many of the Latino immigrants who garden there.

I have witnessed the magic of Proyecto Jardín and it has become an integral part of my food justice classes. In 2011, after reading about it in the newspaper, I began bringing my USC classes to visit so that they could experience a community garden designed and sustained by a local Latino community. Proyecto Jardín is unique in that it does not have assigned plots of land for individual families like most other community gardens. Instead, the land is farmed communally and individuals volunteer to farm certain crops. This approach reinforces Proyecto Jardín's collective spirit. For years, Irene Peña has led my students on tours where she points out herbs unique to native Mesoamerican cuisine, such as *epazote*, a musky smelling herb often used in *quesadillas* and soups, as well as a variety of herbs with medicinal properties. As discussed earlier, Mexico has a rich, indigenous tradition of herbal medicine, using native herbs and plants as healing agents. The *jardín* maintains this tradition with a medicinal plant garden that includes *sábila* (aloe vera), used to treat diabetes, cancer, and skin burns—peppermint, used as a tea to remedy stomach viruses, bloating, and cramps—and white sage, used to reduce anxiety and promote mental health. My students were fascinated by the *caracol* (snail) medicinal garden, a snail-shaped space filled with a variety of traditional medicinal herbs. During the tour, the students got to chew on and smell a few herbs and learn about their uses.

The traditional arts also enhance the garden's beauty and cultural pride. A beautiful ironwork sign hangs over the entrance to the garden that says "Proyecto Jardín" and displays an idyllic, countryside scene with mountains and majestic cornstalks. As you walk up the brick pathway to the garden, you see beautiful tile work and mosaics along the concrete wall created by local Latino artists and schoolchildren. The mosaics include bright colored pieces of broken plates donated by a local ceramic company. The tiles display images such as a large yellow sun with big eyes, the red, white, and black eagle banner, a symbol of the United Farm Workers that incorporates the Aztec eagle, and the words from "De colores," a Spanish folk song that was sung often by the United Farm Workers during protests in the 1960s, all representations of Mexican-American pride. Another section of tiles written by schoolchildren includes phrases such as "me gusta este jardín" ("I like this garden"). Another tile says in both English and Spanish, "The fruits and vegetables are healthy. I like the strawberries … the cucumbers with salt, chili, and lemon," spices commonly used on top of fruit in Mexican culture. The red bricks on the path leading up to the garden are from an early twentieth-century brick foundry. Once inside the garden, a mural painted by local Chicano artist Jose Ramirez, who incorporated colorful paintings of flowers and plants done by local school children, adorns the retaining wall behind the stage area. Along the fence that separates the garden from the sidewalk outside, a row of *nopales* (cacti) stands, creating a natural, green barrier.

In the summer of 2015, Proyecto Jardín's director Irene Peña and I received a grant from the USC's Good Neighbors Campaign for $52,500 to develop a bicycle-powered farm stand that will go from the garden to a low-income housing project, Ramona Gardens, a mile or so away. The program, known as Youth HEAL, is a ten-month program in which at-risk Latino youth participants learn about growing and planting food, food systems literacy, and community organizing. They also have the opportunity, along with a group of my USC students, to help design the mobile farm stand that they will use to bring produce from the garden to Ramona Gardens. The youth for the program were recruited from local high schools and community organizations. They work in conjunction with a group of adult volunteers and take weekly classes in the garden. Peña and I designed different projects for the USC food justice students that would not only support the mobile farm stand project and the garden but also allow the students to practice Spanish with native speakers, learn more about the local Latino community, and apply their particular skillset to the project. The students chose among projects focused on marketing and media, bicycle design and development, the development of a business plan, and ethnographies of the garden's members. Students spent several weeks of the semester working alongside their volunteer in the garden. At the end of the semester, they wrote ethnographies of their assigned volunteers. The volunteers include Liliana Arellanes, a Mexican vegan chef who has a small catering business, *Vegano Cósmico* (Cosmic Vegan). Liliana uses what she grows in the garden in the recipes she prepares for her family and for events in the garden. Ernestina, another volunteer, described her story of immigrating to Los Angeles hidden in the back of a truck, twenty-three years ago, to one of my students, Laura. Ernestina told Laura that when her husband died in Mexico, leaving her a young widow with two young daughters, she decided to make a better life for them in the United States. Over the past four years of volunteering in the garden, the space has come to mean a lot to Ernestina. Since her family in the Unites States is limited to her daughters and grandchildren, the garden and its members represent an important support network for her. Not only does she grow food there, but she also honors the deceased with photos and food on the altar at *Día de los Muertos* (Day of the Dead) and participates in other events. The time she spent with Ernestina really touched Laura. She said that on the last day she planned to just come by briefly to ask her some questions, but they ended up talking for a few hours instead.

When I brought my students to visit Proyecto Jardín in early fall of 2015 it was in disarray. The garden had been closed for repairs for six months because of funding issues. Weeds had sprung up everywhere, the space was overgrown, and few vegetables were growing. Despite the overgrown conditions, the garden still had a certain charm. My students noticed its beautiful tile work, learned about the native plants and their uses, and saw firsthand how dyes are made from the dried, crushed bodies of the cochineal, the crimson dye-producing insect that look like tiny white fuzz balls, traditionally used by indigenous peoples, that are found on the cactus pads. The students got to squish the dried insects and see how the brilliant red dye stained their fingertips. They learned that a dye that at one time was valued as much as gold by the Aztecs could still be found in a Boyle Heights garden. At the end of our visit, the students weeded and hoed different parts of the garden underneath the sweltering October sun, contributing to the effort to rehabilitate the space. A few weeks later, when I returned for an event in the garden, the space was transformed. Chard, lettuce, beets, onion, and amaranth grew in different plots and young seedlings were just beginning to emerge.

The garden offers so much more to the community than a place to grow food; it is a place for the community to come together. In October 2015, Proyecto Jardín and the *Boyle Heights Beat*, a bilingual community newspaper written by local high school students, held a community meeting in the garden so the young reporters could introduce themselves and invite residents to suggest future story ideas based on their concerns about the neighborhood. The idea for the interactive community meeting emerged after a reporter, high school student Samantha Olmos, wrote an article about the recent trend in community gardens. The garden seemed an ideal spot for residents to discuss issues such as the lack of bicycle lanes, Boyle Heights as a food desert, and trash dumping on sidewalks. Kenneth Sánchez, a high school senior, brought up a concern of his: the lack of healthy food options for residents, demonstrating that youth in this community are aware of the problem and want to find ways to work to fix it. The question, of course, is how to do so in a low-income area infested by gangs, broken sidewalks, and corner stores selling chips and soda. The answer lies, in part, in the solutions offered that day in the demonstrations in the garden. After the discussion, community members were divided into groups to participate in different demonstrations that included a cooking presentation using produce grown in the garden, a composting workshop, and a seedling giveaway. A local beekeeper discussed his work with the community, an important contribution since the ordinance permitting urban beekeeping in Los Angeles was passed only days later.

This year I participated in the garden's *Día de los Muertos* celebration that also marked their fifteen-year anniversary, *Quinceñera con Calavera* (fifteen-year birthday with skull). *Día de los Muertos* is celebrated throughout Mexico, but especially in indigenous communities where traditionally people spend the night at the cemetery with deceased family members and bring them their favorite food and drink. To celebrate the lives of their deceased loved ones, family members create altars with photos and the deceased's favorite food in their homes and in public spaces. Proyecto Jardín's Day of the Dead celebration was unusual in that it is held in a garden, rather than a cemetery or a home. Its beautiful altars, *papel picado* (perforated tissue paper), paper flowers, and *cempazutchil*, the bright gold marigold omnipresent in Mexico on Day of the Dead, were quite representative of the tradition. The altars included one small tombstone to commemorate the millions of bees that have died over the past few decades, and another one made by Marissa Magdalena, a local artist, honoring strong women, including Frida Kahlo, a Chicana actress, and a Boyle Heights street vendor who used to sell *elotes*, Mexican corn on the cob, on a nearby sidewalk. The artist said she did not know the vendor personally, but had always been struck by her dignity and strength. The large, central altar was decorated with paper flowers, photos of deceased family members, and their favorite foods. Various garden members had contributed to the altar, demonstrating Proyecto Jardín's collective spirit. Many of the gardeners come from indigenous Mexican communities where the concept of the circle of life is very prevalent. It is understood that people, just like plants and trees, return to the soil one day.

Programs such as these not only celebrate community and collaboration, but also demonstrate the importance of government and private funding for community garden projects. Proyecto Jardín operates on a shoestring budget. Between late 2014 and early 2015, its budget constraints were so severe it was forced to close for six months while buildings on the property were repaired. At the community event participants were asked to donate anything they could, but these small donations are hardly enough to support the garden's many programs. USC's grant pays part of the director's salary and will launch the bike produce stand, but the organization needs additional long-term funds to thrive.

Funding is only a small part of the current challenges Proyecto Jardín faces. Since December 2015, the garden has been fighting eviction. In August 2015, hospital administrators told the director Irene Peña that they had no intention of renewing the garden's lease after it expired at the end of the year, but they welcomed Proyecto Jardín to try to "change their minds" by addressing their concerns. As a result, Peña held "listening sessions" with the hospital's executive team. In November, Proyecto Jardín submitted a request for a six-month extension of the lease and pointed out the progress they had made, but the hospital firmly refused to extend the lease. By early December, the hospital offered the garden a six-month lease extension contingent upon three key terms: cutting Proyecto Jardín down to a third of its current size—roughly 1/9 of an acre—a size so small it could not possibly serve its current members; requiring the garden members to faithfully comply with the Seventh Day Adventist Policies (these include "faithfully complying with Sabbath Policy and participating in Sabbath education"); transferring garden management to the hospital; and renaming the garden with street signage and new logos as "White Memorial Garden." White Memorial Medical Center is a Seventh Day Adventist Church medical center, but in the past had never imposed religious requirements on the garden. Peña told me that the hospital also wants the entire garden to be organized into individual lots, instead of communal ones, effectively changing the garden's very philosophy of collective farming.

When the garden members received the terms of the lease from the hospital, they met and decided they could not agree to them. In response, they sent the hospital a counteroffer in which they expressed a desire to "address our mutual concerns and explore creative solutions." By early January, the hospital replied with a rejection of all the lease terms Proyecto Jardín had submitted, rescinded their original six month offer, and directed Proyecto Jardín to "surrender the premises" by January 31, 2016. Until this point, Peña had been trying to settle the situation directly with the hospital administration and had hoped for a last-minute offer to negotiate, but the hospital had not had any direct dialogue with the garden since their last listening session in November 2015, showing they were not really interested in trying to resolve the situation. The garden was in dire straits and I feared for the worst.

By the end of January 2016, Proyecto Jardín had announced a call to action to its members, supporters, and community members. I contacted journalists at the *LA Times* and *Univisión*, Irene Peña posted an announcement on the garden's Facebook page for an *encuentro* (gathering), and circulated a moveon.org petition asking to "Stop the Displacement of Proyecto Jardín." The petition asked the hospital to rescind the 30-day notice to surrender the premises by January 31, 2016; to place a six-month moratorium on all eviction actions in order to expand the window of opportunity for "reasonable minds" to come to the table to negotiate a win-win lease agreement; and, pleaded for "new opportunities to heal, rebuild, and sow seeds of hope and promise for a robust and productive partnership between the community of *Proyecto Jardín* and White Memorial Medical Center."[58] The petition gathered over

The author at the press conference to save Proyecto Jardín, January 30, 2016.
Photo courtesy of Salomón Singer-Portnoy.

1,000 signatures in just five days. Former students of mine who had visited the garden with me years earlier signed and circulated it on Facebook.

On Saturday, January 30, I spoke at the a press conference at the garden. It was an exciting, but tense, day. Garden and community members gathered and chanted, "Aquí estamos y no nos vamos!" ("Here we are! We are here, we are not leaving!") Along with garden members and Clare Fox, the director of the Los Angeles Food Policy Council, I spoke about the importance of the space for the community not only as a garden to grow food but also as a gathering space. I discussed the different community events I had been to that had brought together different age groups from the neighborhood. I talked about how the Youth HEAL program taught skills to at-risk youth from the area and gave them a sense of pride in their Mexican heritage, a pride that is of great value considering the history of discrimination Mexican-Americans in Boyle Heights have faced over decades. Clare Fox stated that Proyecto Jardín is "a shining example of how a community can come together and grow food that nourishes the individual and community as a whole." After the press conference, Elena Popp, a lawyer from the Eviction Defense Network, spoke and a group of members, primarily local twenty-something youth, created a plan of action. They decided which city officials they would ask to write letters of support to the hospital and agreed to "occupy" the garden by being there at all times in case hospital officials came to change the locks. They named themselves "guardians of the garden." The guardians ended the afternoon on a bright note with a young woman playing *son jarocho*, a regional folk music style from Veracruz, Mexico, played on a small guitar known as a *jarana jarocho*, a genre that is popular among young mexican-Americans of East L.A. and Boyle Heights. I left the garden after the press conference worried about the future of Proyecto Jardín, hoping that its most recent *quinceñera* won't be its last, but also proud to see a community coming together to fight for something they believe in.

On January 31, 2016, the *LA Times* published an article titled "Group Rallies to Secure Stake in Community Garden after Lease Talks Falter." The article talked about the garden as a "community treasure," but also addressed the hospital's concerns that the garden has not always been well maintained. It quoted hospital vice president of business development Cesar Armendariz as saying, "The state of the garden was concerning, but there was never any intent to kick out Proyecto Jardín."[59] Armendariz's statement left me wondering why, if there was never the intention to remove Proyecto Jardín, did the hospital create a lease with conditions that were extremely difficult to meet? The article went on to say that the hospital was making these changes so that more community members will have access to the space—as a way to increase participation. But, as I repeated in a phone conversation with Armendariz, if the hospital is making these changes to benefit the community, why did they not ask the community members directly what they wanted, instead of making changes from the top down? As the petition stated, the hospital "plans to evict *Proyecto Jardín* in order to impose their own plans without input or participation from the community that's made the

ng space it has become." New garden member Consuelo
ld the *LA Times* that these changes "will push out the
nity that has coalesced around the garden and limit the
dren, such as her son, to contribute to it" and that she
.... happen.[60] On the morning of February 1, a security guard tried
to evict occupants from the premises, but they did not budge.

As I revised this chapter to reflect the garden's current situation, my friends
over at Proyecto Jardín were camped out in the garden on a cold and windy
winter night, hoping to save their precious "life-giving oasis" in the middle
of the urban desert of Boyle Heights. They used the hashtags *#todossomo-*
sproyectojardin and *#aquiestamosynonosvamos* on social media to gather
support and inform people about events held nearly every night for the first
ten days of February. Their events have included a nighttime candlelight
vigil, a run to support the garden, visits from local schoolchildren bringing
letters of support, and a land use meeting at a local public library. As the representative to the garden from USC, I called Armendariz, repeated, to see if
I could convince him to come to the table with the garden's leadership to end
the conflict, but he resisted, saying people were too emotional and it would be
better to wait for everyone to calm down first. Armendariz repeated to me that
the hospital planned to bring in two other unnamed organizations to manage
the other two-thirds of the garden in an effort to increase its productivity, but
refused to disclose which organizations they were. He expressed his frustra-
tion with the garden's leadership for disseminating the CEO's, CFO's, and
board members' phone numbers to their supporters on Facebook. I tried to
reason with Armendariz, but he seemed to lack the authority to make a decision about the garden's future. As the days passed with no resolution in sight,
I began to think that the hospital was just waiting for the garden members
to give up and end the occupation, but when the garden members remained
camped out four months later White Memorial Medical Center hired an eviction attorney of their own. The garden members have also decided that their
only recourse is to take the hospital to court with a defense that includes religious discrimination, misappropriation of a cultural treasure, and fraudulent
misrepresentation in fundraising for a nonprofit.

Proyecto Jardín is just one example of a community garden that has been
threatened with eviction and has fought to defend itself. From Brooklyn to
Santa Cruz to Los Angeles, as formerly low-income neighborhoods gentrify
and their land becomes more valuable, community gardens face the threat
of removal. In the case of Proyecto Jardín, the hospital has never said that it
plans to turn the space into something other than a garden, but their long-term
plan may very well include paving the garden over to expand the hospital.
Protecting the garden represents so much more than fighting for the right to
grow one's own healthy, culturally appropriate food; it is about empowering

a minority community that has been historically oppressed and displaced and allowing them to have a voice in decisions about the long-term future of this Boyle Heights treasure.

GARDEN SCHOOL FOUNDATION: GARDEN-BASED EDUCATION IN A SOUTH L.A. SCHOOL

School gardens are another way to work with the local community, improve children's nutrition, allow them to spend valuable time outdoors, and offer them a chance to have a positive relationship with fruits and vegetables. In the process, children learn that vegetables that they grow and harvest themselves are delicious. In an ideal world, they not only increase fruit and vegetable consumption but also come home with recipes and new foods that they introduce to their families. At a time in which nearly one-third of children are classified as overweight or obese, these public health interventions have an increasingly important effect on students' dietary and academic performances. I have planted small vegetable gardens at my children's elementary school in Santa Monica, Edison Language Academy, a Spanish immersion school where most of the children are low-income Latinos. The children eagerly put their seeds in the dirt, come to water the garden, and return to see the development of their sunflowers, green beans, lettuce, and other treasures. The moment when the seed germinates and emerges from the dirt is miraculous and exciting for them. When the lettuce or broccoli is harvested, the kindergarteners clamor for a piece, vegetables they would likely otherwise reject.

In 1990, after visiting too many schools in Los Angeles with asphalt play yards and little or no green spaces, Rachel Mabie, a former Peace Corps volunteer in Central America who had taught local people how to start a vegetable garden, had a vision to reconnect schoolchildren with their natural environment.[61] At the time, she was the Youth Gardening Coordinator for the L.A. office of the University of California Cooperative Extension Common Ground Garden Program. She initiated the Gardening Angels School Garden Program with the hope that all students—especially inner-city youth—would more completely experience the world around them through the joys of gardening.[62] Fifty gardens were started by 1994 under this program. By 1997, the California State Superintendent set the goal of having a garden in every school. Despite these lofty goals, eighteen years after the garden-in–every-school program was implemented, this goal still hasn't been met. According to the Los Angeles Food Policy Council, only one out of three schools in Los Angeles County have school gardens; the 2013 estimate from the report "Cultivate L.A.: An Assessment of Urban Agriculture in Los Angeles County" is that Los Angeles County has only 700 school gardens.[63]

In 2006, State Assembly bill 1535 was created in order to provide state-wide funding for school gardens and establish and maintain comprehensive and high-quality garden-based learning projects. The bill provided eligible schools one-time three year grants for the "promotion, creation, and support of instructional school gardens."[64] The following year, then governor Schwarzenegger signed legislation that provided $15 million for school gardens for the 2008–2009 school year. During this period, the recession hit California and state funding for gardens dried up quickly. Despite the lack of funding, public support for gardens has grown in the past few years. In 2015, the Los Angeles Food Policy Council's working group on school gardens made expanding assembly bill 1535 a high priority.

While most school gardens depend on state and federal funding, others have flourished with the help of foundations. In 1995, renowned Berkeley chef Alice Waters started the Chez Panisse Foundation when she saw an empty lot next to Martin Luther King Middle School in Berkeley and envisioned a garden. Parents, teachers, and community members came together to turn an old cafeteria into a classroom kitchen and build a chicken coop for chickens and ducks, while students cleared trees and brush. The space became known as the Edible Schoolyard. Today, as the website proclaims, The Edible Schoolyard is a nationwide model for edible education known for its seed-to-table garden and a curriculum that links garden experience with students' math, science, and humanities lessons. Since 2005, the program has expanded beyond the boundaries of the Berkeley School District to other schools across the country, including New York, Los Angeles, and New Orleans. I have visited the Edible Schoolyard's one-acre garden in Berkeley. It is a large, beautiful space, planted with many different crops labeled with bright colors and drawings in both Spanish and English, along with colorful, educational signs that explain the technique being used to improve drought resilience. On one sign, a grasshopper asks, "Have you noticed that these garden beds look a little different? We're using some techniques to increase our drought resilience." It goes on to explain that by covering the garden in straw mulch they conserve water by preventing evaporation and maintaining soil moisture. Alice Waters' work on behalf of sustainable eating, both at her restaurant and through her foundation, earned her a National Humanities Award in 2014. Despite these accolades, Waters points out that the work of her foundation is only the beginning. There is a shift in priorities that needs to happen within federal policy to give garden programs longevity. "Now we need a curriculum that's about ecology and about gastronomy so that we can make sure that children are making the right kinds of decisions for themselves, and for the planet. There's no way to address the issues of obesity unless you let children come into a relationship of food that's positive, restorative and desirable," Waters says.[65]

The White House's vegetable garden has also been a nationwide model for the school garden movement and has led to an increase in the number of school garden programs nationwide. On March 20, 2009, elementary school students in Washington, D.C., and Michelle Obama broke ground on the first vegetable garden at the White House since Eleanor Roosevelt's Victory Garden during World War II. The garden was part of the First Lady's Let's Move Campaign, an initiative she launched to fight obesity by improving children's nutrition and helping kids become more active.[66] In the following years, Michelle Obama has invited hundreds of schoolchildren to the White House to learn where their food comes from and harvest their own fruits and vegetables.

At the same time that Michelle Obama was launching the White House kitchen garden in 2009 and the Edible Schoolyard's program was being replicated in other cities across the country, Caitlin Flanagan published an incendiary article in the *Atlantic*, "Cultivating Failure: How School Gardens Are Cheating Our Most Vulnerable Students," in which she argues that low-income Latino students' time is better spent reading books and learning advanced math than harvesting lettuce and that garden programs will not improve test scores. Flanagan accuses the Edible Schoolyard program of "bestowing field work and low expectations on a giant population of students who might become troublesome if they actually got an education," effectively denigrating working the land and cooking as beneath "respectable middle-class aspiration," to use the words of one of Flanagan's critics, Tom Philpott in an article in the online publication *Grist*.[67] Flanagan begins the piece with the description of a Latino immigrant farm worker's child entering his middle school:

> On the first day of sixth grade, the boy walks though the imposing double doors of his new school, stows his backpack, and then heads out to the field, where he stoops under a hot sun and begins to pick lettuce.

Flanagan considers this student's experience to be a "cruel trick" on the child of hardworking Latino immigrants who have tried to give their child a better life and, as Flanagan suggests, ensure that he can do something more valuable than agricultural work. Flanagan calls the Edible Schoolyard curriculum a "vacuous" experiment that has hijacked the curricula of many schools. She directs her criticism at Alice Waters and the Chez Panisse Foundation and says that the Edible Schoolyard curriculum has done nothing to help students' test scores. Yet, recent studies demonstrate the contrary. Although there is not yet a robust body of quantitative studies of the effects of gardening on students' achievement, more and more studies show that garden-related curricula leads to an improvement in science and math scores and improved fruit and vegetable consumption. A 2005 study, for example, compared the results of a sample group of 647 Texas students in third through fifth grades that participated in gardening activities as part of their science curriculum with a group of students who were taught with only traditional, classroom-based methods. The authors found that the students who participated in school gardening activities scored better on science achievement tests.[68]

The group Flanagan discusses, Latinos, constitutes 49% of California's public school students. Flanagan is correct that there is an increasing achievement gap between Latinos and their white and Asian peers, but what Flanagan fails to realize is that test scores are not the only basis of a good, well-rounded education.[69] Children learn through a variety of modalities such as art, music, and gardening, and thrive in interactive environments. Spending time in the garden is an effective way to make abstract topics such as biology, chemistry, and botany more concrete. Moreover, gardening encourages students to ask questions about how things work, such as: Where does the lettuce come from? How do seeds germinate? What makes plants grow?

In an era in which children spend little time outdoors and, as a result, suffer from what Richard Louv describes on his website as "nature-deficit disorder," spending time planting and harvesting in a garden may have more value than Flanagan believes. Researchers claim that young children who spend too much time in front of the television or computer/video games and too little time playing outside suffer from a wide range of physical and mental health problems, including obesity, diabetes, and attention deficit disorder. How can students with so many physical and mental health issues perform well on state exams? The Centers for Disease Control and Prevention website states that children who eat nutritiously are more likely to perform well in school and have fewer behavioral problems. Tom Philpott responds to Flanagan when he says, "in an age of de-funded, low-quality school lunches and surging diabetes rates among children, Edible Schoolyard has the potential to transform kids' dietary habits."[70]

GARDEN SCHOOL FOUNDATION: A SCHOOL GARDEN TRANSFORMATION

The story of Garden School Foundation is one example of a low-income, predominantly Latino elementary school that has battled children's obesity and lack of access to healthy produce with the creation of a school garden program. In 2003, 24th Street Elementary School, a school located in a low-income neighborhood of South L.A., learned that their school was going to have its playground repaved with new asphalt. The school has a huge plot of land behind it that backs up to the freeway. This was an opportunity to turn asphalt and a chain link fence into something green and beautiful for the children. Over the following years, the garden has grown and flourished. The foundation's website defines their mission as "dedicated to providing an interdisciplinary program of education through garden-based learning in outdoor living classrooms." Over the years, the program has expanded its garden-based nutrition education in collaboration with the Los Angeles Unified School District, acting as a third-party organization. Currently, its programs in six schools serve 2,500 low-income students. With the assistance of stakeholders and donors such as La Brea Bakery, district councilmember Herb Wesson, the Hancock Park Garden Club, the Santa Monica Farmers' Market, the Chez Panisse Foundation, and more, Garden School Foundation has been extremely successful at 24th Street Elementary. Garden School Foundation's website includes a teacher testimony section in which many teachers comment on how engaged and motivated their students are when working in the garden. One teacher, Ted Wakeman, shares the program's impact on the school, community, and on himself:

> It has opened doors to curriculum enhancement and creativity that have slowly been closing due to district mandates and state required programs. It has given the hope back that our students truly can get an amazing education in the midst of an environment that is inspiring for us all.

I regularly take my college students to visit Garden School Foundation to see how elementary school students participate in outdoor learning. The garden consists of various seasonal fruits and vegetables that they harvest and maintain throughout the year. In addition to harvesting their own pesticide-free crops, the students partake in a cooking lesson with a different theme that incorporates the garden's fresh crops every month. The program director Cassie Martinez told my students how they teach the children kid-friendly recipes such as a super smoothie, which contains many different fruits and a few vegetables including kale. Amabilia Villeda, a Guatemalan mother who volunteers regularly in the garden, shared with the students in Spanish the effect the garden has had on her family. She talked about how she and one of her children suffer from diabetes, but since they have been involved in the garden their health and weight have improved. She also talked about how their involvement connected her children to her own cultural heritage since growing foods such as squash, corn, and the Guatemalan spinach tree was an important part of her own upbringing. In a way, Garden School Foundation teaches many of the same lessons as Proyecto Jardín. It unites the community, involves parents, engages youth in outdoor activity, increases access to healthy foods, and improves mental and physical health. The respect the community has for the garden extends beyond the children and their families.

The director told my students about a time when the school was vandalized and graffiti was painted everywhere—except the garden. Outside the wall of the garden someone had painted in black letters "DON'T HURT NATURE."

With new urban farms, school gardens, community gardens, and parkways expanding across the city, the future of urban agriculture in Los Angeles seems brighter. As the city of Los Angeles improves public transportation and increases public housing options—the county supervisors voted in 2015 to set aside up to $100 million a year to construct and maintain affordable housing—urban agriculture will play an increasingly important role. Despite these positive steps, in 2015, the Los Angeles Food Policy Council reported that more than half a million households in Los Angeles County faced food insecurity or hunger. What will the long-term future hold for urban agriculture and low-income residents in this metropolis? I envision Los Angeles as a greener city, a city where each neighborhood takes pride in the bounty from its community garden, where neighbors come together in these spaces for exercise classes and celebrations, where schoolchildren eat carrots and peas they harvest from their own school garden, and where healthy, affordable, culturally appropriate food is not a luxury, but a right available to all residents. Hopefully, this is not just wishful thinking. Current policy and grassroots efforts are on the right track, but only time will tell.

Conclusion

Loncheras, Guerrilla Tacos truck, Guelaguetza, Alta California cuisine—Latino cuisine in Los Angeles is more interesting and innovative than ever. From downtown L.A. to Boyle Heights to Tacos María in Orange County, Latino foods and flavors are captivating American palates and chefs' imaginations. Mexican food is by far one of the most popular, complex, and widely available cuisines, but Southern Californians are also branching out and exploring cuisines from Peru, Argentina, El Salvador, and beyond as well as Mexican-influenced fusion flavors that range from sushi burritos to kimchi *quesadillas*. Proof of how far we have come and the impact Los Angeles' cuisine has made lies in the recent visit of Mexico's most famous culinary star to Los Angeles to eat Mexican food, Chef Enrique Olvera of Pujol. After sampling *tacos* around the city, Olvera declared, "There is a Mexican cuisine that is from Los Angeles, just like there is a Mexican cuisine that is from Oaxaca."[1] Just like all traditions, cuisine transcends borders. It evolves and adapts to its new environment, and Los Angeles' Latino cuisine is no exception.

Immigrants adapt to the cuisines of their new countries, too. Sometimes adaptation and acculturation allow for creative innovations, as in fusion cuisine or L.A.-based Mexican food, but sometimes they have a negative effect. Processed and cheap fast food and a lack of fruits and vegetables have had detrimental effects on generations of Latinos' health. As a result, the number of adults and children suffering from type 2 diabetes and obesity is higher in low-income Latino communities. Who is responsible and how to fix the situation are not questions with easy answers. In this book, I have explored some solutions, but gardens and converted corner stores alone will not solve this enormous problem. It is going to take more than the efforts of the private sector, local nonprofit organizations, and individuals. It will require increased support from our local and national governments to invest more heavily in programs such as the National School Lunch Program, nutrition education programs, EBT (formerly known as food stamps) access for low-income families at *all* farmers' markets, the development of more healthy food retail in underserved areas, and much more. The City of Los Angeles has seen some momentum over the past few years. The Los Angeles Food Policy Council recently announced an initiative to make farmers' markets accessible to all EBT card users by 2017, since 60% of markets still do not accept CalFresh and EBT. As the *LA Times* editorial board wrote, "There's something terribly wrong when Jack in the Box and corner liquor stores eagerly accept EBT, but a farmers market does not."[2] A bright note comes from celebrity chefs Roy Choi and Daniel Patterson who have created a healthy, affordable fast-food concept that they named LocoL. They opened in Watts in January of 2016 and plan to replicate in other underserved, minority communities. The next location in Oakland has already opened. No sodas, fries, or other very unhealthy menu items. While LocoL does not serve Latino cuisine, it does represent the conversion of two worlds: the world of very successful celebrity chefs and the one of low-income, underserved communities of color. Despite the recent progress by the local government, nonprofit organizations, and these famous chefs, the racial and economic divide in food access remains not only in Los Angeles, but in low-income urban and rural areas throughout the United States. So, what does my Magic 8 Ball tell me the future holds for healthy, food access? "Outlook good." "Outlook not so good." Or, "Cannot predict now."

It's August of 2016 and Donald Trump and Hilary Clinton are the Republican and Democrat presidential nominees. Over the course of his candidacy, Trump has made xenophobic, racist, and misogynistic comments that have enraged many Americans. Among his outrageous and incendiary comments, since the inception of his campaign he has proclaimed to his supporters that he is going to have Mexico pay to build a wall between the United States and Mexico. Additionally, when he first announced he was running for president—and many, many times since—he has stated that undocumented Mexican immigrants are "rapists and criminals." While these brash and unfounded statements have elicited thunderous applause and rallied his followers, they have also perpetuated stereotypes of Latinos as dangerous and sexually suspect, stereotypes that were once common about Mexican street vendors—the *tamaleros*—well over a hundred years ago. In today's global world, it is utterly astounding that someone at the level of a presidential nominee would make such xenophobic and racist assertions. Have we not progressed beyond the era of Joaquín Murieta and Gregorio Cortez, mythic *corrido* heroes who were victimized and pursued by the Texas/American authorities, the forced "Repatriation" of Mexican-Americans of the 1930s, and the Zoot Suit Riots of the early 1940s, beyond a past of extreme divisions between the imperial United States and Mexico?

Apparently not. "Poor Mexico, so far from God, so close to the United States," as former Mexican president Porfirio Díaz once said.

In a bid to reach out to Latino voters on Cinco de Mayo, Trump proclaimed in a tweet, "I love Hispanics." He expressed his Cinco de Mayo love with a photo of himself eating a "taco bowl" with a statement that said: "Happy #Cinco de Mayo! The best taco bowls are made in Trump Tower Grill. I love Hispanics!" Not Mexicans, not Mexican food, but Hispanics. And a taco bowl? What is a taco bowl? Trump's questionable taco demonstrates his complete ignorance about Mexican food and about Latinos in general. On a day most Americans mistake for Mexican Independence Day, not only did Trump not even bother to make this distinction he also failed to realize that not all Hispanics are Mexican. Trump's tweet is symbolic of the mentality of his mostly white, conservative followers, voters whose knowledge of Latinos—and their cuisine—has evolved little from the 1960s when Mexican food was first commodified for mainstream American consumers. Yet, the response from some journalists and others on the Internet shows that not everyone shares this backward ideology and can find humor in Trump's absurdity. A Mashable.com article was titled "The 19 Most Offensive Things about Donald Trump's Taco Bowl Tweet." Memes have quickly spread of Trump eating more offensive things than *tacos*. A witty retort came from *Washington Post* reporter Karen Tumulty, who observed, "A taco bowl is just a taco with a big, beautiful wall around it."

Food is symbolic of culture. Misunderstandings about taco bowls represent much bigger misunderstandings about Latinos and Latino food in the United States. The response on social media to Trump's tweet shows that many Americans do understand that. Let's hope that in 2016 and beyond we will be able to bring down walls, not only around *tacos* but also around Latino culture in general.

Notes

INTRODUCTION

1. Anna Brown and Mark Hugo Lopez, "Mapping the Latino Population, By State, County and City," *Pew Research Center Hispanic Trends*, August 29, 2013, accessed February 29, 2016, http://www.pewhispanic.org/2013/08/29/mapping-the-latino-population-by-state-county-and-city/

2. "Food Desert to Food Oasis: Promoting Grocery Store Development in South Los Angeles," Community Health Councils, Inc., July 2010, http://www.chc-inc.org/downloads/Food_Desert_to_Oasis_07-12-2010.pdf

3. United States Department of Agriculture Economic Research Service, http://www.ers.usda.gov/topics/food-nutrition-assistance/food-security-in-the-us/key-statistics-graphics.aspx#insecure

4. Jeffrey Pilcher, "Was the Taco Invented in Southern California?" *Gastronomica* 8.1 (Winter 2008), 26.

CHAPTER 1

1. William Deverell, *Whitewashed Adobe: the Rise of Los Angeles and the Remaking of its Mexican Past* (Berkeley: University of California Press, 2004), 7.

2. Ibid, 8.

3. George Sánchez, *Becoming Mexican-American: Ethnicity, Culture, and Identity in Chicano Los Angeles, 1900–1945* (New York, NY: Oxford University Press, 1993), 91.

4. Ibid, 87.

5. Ibid, 18.

6. Ibid, 18.

7. Gustavo Arellano, *Taco USA: How Mexican Food Conquered America* (New York: Scribner, 2012), 55.

8. Ibid, 55.

9. Gustavo Arellano, "Tamales, L.A.'s Original Street Food," The *LA Times*, September 8, 2011, accessed January 15, 2015, http://articles.latimes.com/2011/sep/08/food/la-fo-tamales-20110908

10. Jeffrey Pilcher, *Planet Taco: a Global History of Mexican Food* (New York: Oxford University Press, 2012),107.

11. George Sánchez, *Becoming Mexican-American: Ethnicity, Culture, and Identity in Chicano Los Angeles, 1900–1945* (New York, NY: Oxford University Press, 1993), 10.

12. William Deverell, *Whitewashed Adobe: the Rise of Los Angeles and the Remaking of Its Mexican Past* (Berkeley: University of California Press, 2004), 4.

13. Ryan Reft, "The Shifting Cultures of Multiracial Boyle Heights," *KCET Intersections*, August 9, 2013, accessed January 27, 2015, http://www.kcet.org/socal/departures/columns/intersections/the-shifting-cultures-of-multiracial-boyle-heights.html

14. David Margolick, "Brooklyn Expatriates in Los Angeles Mourn Fading Reminders of the Past," *LA Times*, April 3, 1994, accessed January 10, 2016, http://www.nytimes.com/1994/04/03/us/brooklyn-expatriates-in-los-angeles-mourn-fading-reminders-of-the-past.html?pagewanted=all

15. Gustavo Arellano, *Taco USA: How Mexican Food Conquered America* (New York: Scribner, 2012), 31.

16. Ibid, 34.

17. Jeffrey Pilcher, *Planet Taco: A Global History of Mexican Food* (New York: Oxford University Press, 2012),110.

18. Gustavo Arellano, *Taco USA: How Mexican Food Conquered America* (New York: Scribner, 2012), 40.

19. Jeffrey Pilcher, *Planet Taco: A Global History of Mexican Food.* (New York: Oxford University Press, 2012),111.

20. Ibid, 114.

21. Ibid, 107.

22. Josh Kun, *To Live and Dine in L.A.: Menus and the Making of the Modern City.* (Los Angeles: Angel City Press, 2015),73.

23. Simpson Methodist Episcopal Church, Ladies Social Circle, *How we cook in Los Angeles: a practical cook-book containing six hundred or more recipes selected and tested by over one hundred well known hostesses including a French, German and Spanish department with menus, suggestions for artistic table decorations, and souvenirs* (Los Angeles: Commercial Printing House, 1894).

24. Encarnación Pineda, *Encarnacion's Kitchen: Mexican Recipes from Nineteenth Century California*, trans. Dan Strehl (Berkeley: University of California Press, 2005), 69.

25. Ibid, 2.

26. Victor Valle, "A Curse of Tea and Potatoes," *Encarnacion's Kitchen: Mexican Recipes from Nineteenth Century California*, trans. Dan Strehl (Berkeley: University of California Press, 2005), 8.

27. Encarnación Pineda, *Encarnacion's Kitchen: Mexican Recipes from Nineteenth Century California*, trans. Dan Strehl (Berkeley: University of California Press, 2005), 48.

28. Victor Valle, "A Curse of Tea and Potatoes," *Encarnacion's Kitchen: Mexican Recipes from Nineteenth Century California*, trans. Dan Strehl (Berkeley: University of California Press, 2005), 8.

29. Ibid,11.

30. Ibid,10.

31. Oddett Garza-Weatherspoon, "An Acquired Taste: How Spanish and Mexican Recipes Helped Shape Early Los Angeles." (master's thesis, California State University, Long Beach, 2007), 87.

32. Victor Valle, "A Curse of Tea and Potatoes," *Encarnacion's Kitchen: Mexican Recipes from Nineteenth Century California*, trans. Dan Strehl (Berkeley: University of California Press, 2005), 8.

33. Carey McWilliams, *Southern California Country: An Island on the Land* (New York: Duell, Sloan & Pierce, 1946), 21.

34. Ibid, 77.

35. Ibid, 77.

36. Charles Fisher, "Rancho San Rafael," *KCET Departures*, October 5, 2010, accessed January 27, 2016, http://www.kcet.org/socal/departures/highland-park/the-highlands/rancho-san-rafael.html

37. Josh Kun, *To Live and Dine in L.A.: Menus and the Making of the Modern City* (Los Angeles: Angel City Press, 2015), 111.

38. Ibid, 109.

39. Ibid, 110.

40. William Deverell, *Whitewashed Adobe: The Rise of Los Angeles and the Remaking of Its Mexican Past* (Berkeley: University of California Press, 2004), 7.

41. Jeffrey Pilcher, "Nachos, burritos, and nationality," *Oxford Wordsblog*, November 2, 2012, accessed March 1, 2016, http://blog.oxforddictionaries.com/2012/11/nachos-burritos-and-nationality/

42. Gustavo Arellano, *Taco USA: How Mexican Food Conquered America* (New York: Scribner, 2012), 56.

43. Ibid.

44. Ibid.

45. Sylvia Ferrero, "*Comida Sin Par*. Consumption of Mexican Food in Los Angeles: Foodscapes in a Transnational Consumer Society." *Food Nations: Selling Taste in Consumer Societies*. Edited by Warren James Belasco and Philip Scranton. (New York: Routledge, 2002), p. 199.

46. Ibid, 203.

47. Jeffrey Pilcher, "Nachos, Burritos, and Nationality," *Oxford Wordsblog*, November 2, 2012, accessed March 1, 2016, http://blog.oxforddictionaries.com/2012/11/nachos-burritos-and-nationality/

48. Carolina Miranda, "The California Taco Trail: 'How Mexican Food Conquered America,'" *NPR the Salt*, April 24, 2012, accessed March 1, 2016, http://www.npr.org/sections/thesalt/2012/04/23/150886690/the-california-taco-trail-how-mexican-food-conquered-america

49. Gustavo Arellano, "The Most Influential Tacos in L.A.," *Firstwefeast. com*, March 8, 2016, accessed March 8, 2016, http://firstwefeast.com/eat/ the-most-influential-*tacos*-in-los-angeles/

50. Alvaro Parra, "Olvera Street: The Fabrication of L.A.'s Mexican Heritage," *KCET Los Angeles*, September 13, 2013, accessed January 10, 2016, http://www.kcet. org/socal/departures/columns/whats-in-a-street-name/olvera-street-the-fabrication- of-las-mexican-heritage.html

51. Jeffrey Pilcher, "Was the Taco Invented in Southern California?" *Gastronomica* 8.1 (Winter 2008), 31.

52. E.N. Anderson, *Everyone Eats: Understanding Food and Culture* (New York University Press: New York and London, 2005), 186.

53. Gustavo Arellano, "Five Authentic Mexican Dishes That Would Make Rick Bayless Scream, Or: For an Aztlanista Approach to the Question of 'Authentic- ity' in Mexican Cuisine." *Orange County Weekly*. Web. October 4, 2010, accessed December 20, 2015, http://www.ocweekly.com/restaurants/five-authentic-mexican- dishes-that-would-make-rick-bayless-scream-or-for-an-aztlanista-approach-to-the- question-of-authenticity-in-mexican-cuisine-6615198

54. Jeffrey Pilcher, "Was the Taco Invented in Southern California?" *Gastronomica* 8.1 (Winter 2008), 26.

55. Ibid, 35.

56. Farley Elliot, *Los Angeles Street Food: A History from Tamaleros to Taco Trucks* (Charleston: American Palate, 2015), 27.

57. Jeffrey Pilcher, "Was the Taco Invented in Southern California?" *Gastronomica* 8.1 (Winter 2008), 26.

58. Gustavo Arellano, *Taco USA: How Mexican Food Conquered America* (New York: Scribner, 2012), 69.

59. Ibid, 61.

60. Jeffrey Pilcher, "Was the Taco Invented in Southern California?" *Gastronomica* 8.1 (Winter 2008), 36.

61. Bill Esparza, "Tacopedia: A Complete Taco Encyclopedia of L.A.," *Los Angeles Magazine*, July 24, 2015, accessed December 20, 2015, http://www. lamag.com/digestblog/tacopedia-a-complete-taco-encyclopedia-of-l-a/

62. Gustavo Arellano, "El Torito Founder Is still the Big Enchilada," *Orange County Weekly*, January 6, 2011, accessed November 14, 2015, http://www.ocweekly. com/2011–01–06/food/larry-j-cano-el-torito-founder/

63. Ibid.

CHAPTER 2

1. Gustavo Arellano, *Taco USA: How Mexican Food Conquered America* (New York: Scribner, 2012), 89.

2. Maria Godoy, "When Chefs Become Famous Cooking Other Cultures' Food," *NPR the Salt*, March 22, 2016, accessed March 22, 2016, http://www.npr.org/sections/the salt/2016/03/22/471309991/when-chefs-become-famous-cooking-other-cultures-food

3. Border Grill website.

4. Ibid.

5. Jonathan Gold, "Border Grill: 99 Essential Restaurants 2011," *LA Weekly*, November 10, 2011, accessed February 6, 2016, http://www.laweekly.com/restaurantsborder-grill-99-essential-restaurants-2011-2172798

6. Diane Kennedy, *Oaxaca Al Gusto: An Infinite Gastronomy* (Austin, Texas: University of Texas Press, 2010), xi.

7. Maite Gomez-Rejón, "Chocolate, the Food of the Gods," *The Online Magazine of the Getty*, February 12, 2015, http://blogs.getty.edu/iris/chocolate-the-food-of-the-gods/

8. Sophia and Michael Coe, *The True History of Chocolate* (New York: Thames & Hudson, 1996), 213.

9. Ibid, 213.

10. Stephen, Lynn, *We Are the Face of Oaxaca: Testimony and Social Movements* (Durham, North Carolina: Duke University Press, 2013), 232.

11. Bill Esparza, "First Mexican Restaurant to Win a James Beard Classics Award," *Los Angeles Magazine*, February 25, 2015, accessed December 15, 2015, http://www.lamag.com/digestblog/guelaguetza-first-traditional-mexican-restaurant-u-s-win-james-beard-classics-award/#sthash.jU2iAvYn.dpuf

12. Gustavo Arellano, *Taco USA: How Mexican Food Conquered America* (New York: Scribner, 2012), 168.

13. Ibid, 170.

14. Jonathan Gold, "Clayuda Me," *Los Angeles Times*, July 28, 1994, accessed March 15, 2016, http://articles.latimes.com/1994-07-28/food/fo-20645_1_black-*mole*

15. Ibid, 166.

16. Ibid, 170.

17. Dana Goodyear, "Grub: Eating Bugs to Save the Planet, *The New Yorker*, August 15, 2011, accessed February 16, 2016, http://www.newyorker.com/magazine/2011/08/15/grub

18. Ibid.

19. Jonathan Gold, "Jonathan Gold Review: Mexicano at the Baldwin Hills Crenshaw Plaza," *Los Angeles Times*, November 20, 2015, accessed January 23, 2016, http://www.latimes.com/food/jonathan-gold/la-fo-gold-mexicano-20151121-story.html

20. Jonathan Gold, "Chichén Itzá: 99 Essential Restaurants 2011," *LA Weekly*, November 10, 2011, accessed January 25, 2016, http://www.laweekly.com/restaurants/chichn-itz-99-essential-restaurants-2011-2172812

21. Daina Solomon, "Rocio Camacho: The Goddess of Mole," *LA Weekly*, May 15, 2013, accessed February 7, 2015, http://www.laweekly.com/restaurants/rocio-camacho-the-goddess-of-*mole*-2896309

22. Jonathan Gold, "Moles La Tia: Beyond the Magnificent Seven," *Los Angeles Weekly*, January 21, 2009, accessed February 27, 2015, http://www.laweekly.com/restaurants/*moles*-la-tia-beyond-the-magnificent-seven-2157938

23. Ibid.

24. Daina Solomon, "Arson damages Rocio's Mole de los Dioses restaurant in Sun Valley," *Los Angeles Times*, August 24, 2015, accessed February 11, 2016, http://www.latimes.com/food/dailydish/la-dd-arson-rocios-*mole*-20150824-story.html

25. Besha Rodell, "In a City with Astoundingly Good Mexican Food, Rocio Camacho's Mexican Kitchen Serves Some of the Best," *LA Weekly*, July 14, 2015, accessed March 1, 2016, http://www.laweekly.com/restaurants/in-a-city-with-astoundingly good-mexican-food-rocio-camacho-s-mexican-kitchen-serves-some-of-the-best-5800538

26. Jonathan Gold, "Jonathan Gold reviews Guisados," *LA Weekly*, September 22, 2011, accessed February 20, 2016, http://www.laweekly.com/restaurants/jonathan-gold-reviews-guisados-2172029

27. Aaron Terrazas, "Salvadorian Immigrants in the United States," *Migration Policy Institute,* January 5, 2010, accessed January 25, 2016, http://www.migrationpolicy.org/article/salvadoran-immigrants-united-states

28. Ibid.

29. Daina Solomon, "Los Angeles Chefs Discuss Downtown L.A. at Aloud," *LA Weekly*, July 19, 2012, accessed February 17, 2016, http://www.laweekly.com/restaurants/los-angeles-chefs-discuss-downtown-la-at-aloud-2383505

30. Rivera website, http://www.riverarestaurant.com/index.php?Modern-South west-Cuisine

31. Jonathan Gold, "Rivera, John Sedlar's Return to the Kitchen," *LA Weekly*, March 25, 2009, accessed January 30, 2016, http://www.laweekly.com/restaurants/rivera-john-sedlars-return-to-the-kitchen-2158956

32. John R. Sedlar, *Food Arts*, September 1995, http://foodarts.com/people/silver-spoon/27396/john-r-sedlar

33. S. Irene Virbila, "The Review: Rivera in Downtown Los Angeles," *Los Angeles Times*, March 32, 2009, accessed February 16, 2016, http://www.latimes.com/food/la-fo-review1-2009apr01-story.html

34. Bill Esparza, "Chef Ray Garcia's Broken Spanish Will Speak L.A.'s Mother Tongue: Mexican Cuisine," *Los Angeles Magazine*, January 15, 2015, accessed February 1, 2016, http://www.lamag.com/digestblog/chef-ray-garcias-broken-spanish-will-speak-l-a-s-mother-tongue-mexican-cuisine/

35. Jonathan Gold, "B.S. Taqueria has a Few Twists Even for This Taco-Centric City," *Los Angeles Times*, June 12, 2015, accessed February 2, 2016, http://www.latimes.com/food/la-fo-gold-bstaqueria-20150613-story.html

36. Gillian Ferguson, "Taco Maria's Carlos Salgado Wants Authentic Tortillas: That means Mexican Maize," *Los Angeles Times*, February 20, 2016, accessed February 20, 2016, http://www.latimes.com/food/la-fo-salgado-corn-20160220-story.html

37. Dave Lieberman, "Taco Maria, Carlos Salgado's Upscale Mexican Truck, Launches," *OC Weekly*, September 14, 2011, accessed February 7, 2015, http://www.ocweekly.com/restaurants/taco-maria-carlos-salgados-upscale-mexican-truck-launches-6610387

38. Gillian Ferguson, "Taco Maria's Carlos Salgado wants authentic *tortillas*: That means Mexican Maize," *Los Angeles Times*, February 19, 2016, accessed February 19, 2016, http://www.latimes.com/food/la-fo-salgado-corn-20160220-story.html

39. Ibid.

40. Victoria Burnett, "Oaxaca's Native Maize Embraced by Top Chefs in U.S. and Europe," *New York Times*, February 11, 2016, accessed February 11, 2016, http://www.nytimes.com/2016/02/12/world/americas/oaxacas-native-maize-embraced-by-top-chefs-in-us-and-europe.html?_r=0

41. Lisa Abend, "Mexico's Chefs Are Fighting a Future of Genetically Modified Corn," Munchies.com, October 13, 2015, accessed February 8, 2016, https://munchies.vice.com/en/articles/mexicos-chefs-are-fighting-a-future-of-genetically-modified-corn

42. Ibid.

CHAPTER 3

1. William Deverell, *Whitewashed Adobe: The Rise of Los Angeles and the Remaking of Its Mexican Past* (Berkeley, CA: University of California Press, 2004), 6

2. Carole Counihan, *The Anthropology of Food and Body: Gender, Meaning, and Power* (Routledge: New York, 1999), 19.

3. Gustavo Arellano, *Taco USA: How Mexican Food Conquered America* (New York: Scribner, 2012), 56.

4. Ibid.

5. Ibid.

6. Erin Glenn, "Taco Trucks on the Street: Where Food and Social Justice Meet," *Los Angeles Public Interest Law Journal*, 2011, http://lapilj.org/wp-content/uploads/Erin-Glenn.pdf, 52.

7. Gustavo Arellano, *Taco USA: How Mexican Food Conquered America* (New York: Scribner, 2012), 164.

8. Jesus Sanchez, "King Taco Got Start in Old Ice Cream Van," *LA Times*, November 16, 1987, accessed February 16, 2016, http://articles.latimes.com/1987-11-16/business/fi-14263_1_ice-cream-truck

9. Farley Elliot, *Los Angeles Street Food: A History from Tamaleros to Taco Trucks* (Charleston, South Carolina: American Palate, 2015), 70.

10. Ibid.

11. Jesús Hermosillo, "A Look at the Stationary Food Trucks of Los Angeles," September 2010, Master of Arts UCLA School of Urban Planning, 8.

12. Ernesto Hernández-López, "LA's Taco Truck War: How Law Cooks Food Culture Contests," *Legal Studies Research Paper Series*, Paper No. 10–29, October 18, 2010, accessed January 6, 2016, 18.

13. Ibid, 5.

14. Patricia Nazario, "The Original Food Trucks," *LA Weekly*, May 10, 2012, accessed December 29, 2015. http://www.laweekly.com/restaurants/the-original-food-trucks-2174867

15. Jean-Paul Renaud, "Curbing East L.A. Taco Trucks," *LA Times*, April 14, 2008, accessed February 1, 2016, http://articles.latimes.com/2008/apr/14/local/me-tacotruck14

16. Rebecca Winters Keegan, "The Great Taco Truck War," *Time.com*, April 25, 2008, accessed January 5, 2016, http://content.time.com/time/nation/article/0,8599,1735104,00.html

17. Erin Glenn, "Taco Trucks on the Street: Where Food and Social Justice Meet," *Los Angeles Public Interest Law Journal*, 2011, http://lapilj.org/wp-content/uploads/Erin-Glenn.pdf, 57.

18. Ernesto Hernández-López, "LA's Taco Truck War: How Law Cooks Food Culture Contests," *Legal Studies Research Paper Series*, Paper No. 10–29, October 18, 2010, accessed January 6, 2016, 8.

19. Jeffrey Pilcher, *Planet Taco: A Global History of Mexican Food.* (New York: Oxford University Press, 2012), 221.

20. Erin Glenn, "Taco Trucks on the Street: Where Food and Social Justice Meet," *Los Angeles Public Interest Law Journal*, 2011, http://lapilj.org/wp-content/uploads/Erin-Glenn.pdf, 58.

21. Ibid, 59.

22. Ibid, 55.

23. Ibid, 60.

24. Ernesto Hernández-López, "LA's Taco Truck War: How Law Cooks Food Culture Contests," *Legal Studies Research Paper Series*, Paper No. 10–29, October 18, 2010, accessed January 6, 2016, 14.

25. Ibid.

26. Garret Thereolf, "Taco Trucks can stay parked," *LA Times*, August 28, 2008, accessed December 17, 2015, http://articles.latimes.com/2008/aug/28/local/me-tacos28

27. Ernesto Hernández-López, "LA's Taco Truck War: How Law Cooks Food Culture Contests," *Legal Studies Research Paper Series*, Paper No. 10–29, October 18, 2010, accessed January 6, 2016, 15.

28. Jeffrey Pilcher, *Planet Taco: A Global History of Mexican Food.* (New York: Oxford University Press, 2012), 222.

29. Crystal Coser, Farley Elliot, Matthew Kang, and Na'ama Landau, "The 18 Essential Los Angeles Food Trucks, June 2015," *Los Angeles Eater*, June 10, 2015, accessed January 13, 2015, http://la.eater.com/2015/6/10/8748817/best-food-trucks-los-angeles-map-essential

30. Bill Esparza, "LA's 25 Best Tacos: The Ultimate Guide to the City's Spirit Snack," *Los Angeles Magazine*, July 2015, accessed January 19, 2016, ttp://media.lamag.com/*tacos*/

31. Deena Prichep and Daniel Estrin, "Thank the Ottoman Empire for the Taco Al Pastor," *PRI's The World*, May 7, 2015, accessed January 23, 2015, http://www.pri.org/stories/2015-05-07/thank-ottoman-empire-taco-youre-eating

32. Ibid.

33. Ibid.

34. Part of this paragraph and the following one were was taken from Sarah Portnoy and Jeffrey Pilcher, "Roy Choi, Ricardo Zárate, and Pacific Fusion Cuisine in Los Angeles." *Global Latin America*. Ed. Matthew Gutmann and Jeffrey Lesser. (University of California Press, 2016).

35. Jonathan Gold, "How America Became a Food Truck Nation," *Smithsonian.com*, March 2012, accessed January 13, 2016, http://www.smithsonianmag.com/travel/how-america-became-a-food-truck-nation-99979799/?no-ist

36. Jonathan Gold, "L.A. Restaurant Review: Guerrilla Tacos Rolls up in High style," *LA Times*, February 21, 2014, accessed February 17, 2016, http://www.latimes.com/food/la-fo-gold-20140222-story.html

37. Hadley Tomicki, "From Teamster to Taquero: Q&A With Guerrilla Tacos' Wes Avila," *Grubstreet.com*, March 11, 2013, accessed January 6, 2016, http://www.grubstreet.com/2013/03/interview-wes-avila-guerrilla-*tacos*.html

38. Russ Parsons, "Wes Avila, from Fine-Dining Track to Fine Guerrilla Tacos off a Truck," *LA Times*, March 13, 2015, accessed January 13, 2016, http://www.latimes.com/food/la-fo-pro-tip-avila-20150314-story.html

CHAPTER 4

1. "Seis de cada diez mexicanos que trabajan están en la informalidad," *La Jornada*, December 12, 2012, accessed February 10, 2015, http://www.jornada.unam.mx/2012/12/12/economia/027n1eco

2. Jeffrey Pilcher, "The Rise and Fall of the Chili Queens," *Planet Taco: A Global History of Mexican Food* (New York: Oxford University Press, 2012), 111–113.

3. Ibid.

4. Mark Vallianatos, "Legalize L.A. Street Vendors," *LA Times*, October 14, 2014, accessed January 6, 2015, http://www.latimes.com/opinion/op-ed/la-oe-valllianatos-los-angeles-sidewalk-vendors-20141015-story.html

5. Stephen Zavestoski and Julian Agyeman, eds. *Incomplete Streets: Practices, Processes and Possibilities* (London and New York: Routledge, 2015).

6. Mark Vallianatos, "Legalize L.A. Street Vendors," *LA Times*, October 14, 2014, accessed January 6, 2015, http://www.latimes.com/opinion/op-ed/la-oe-valllianatos-los-angeles-sidewalk-vendors-20141015-story.html

7. Fazila Bhimji, "Struggles, Urban Citizenship, and Belonging: the Experience Of Undocumented Street Vendors and Food Truck Owners in Los Angeles ." *Urban Anthropology and Studies of Cultural Systems and World Economic Development* 39.4 (2010), 466.

8. Ibid, 467.

9. Robert J. Lopez, "Vendors Protest Against LAPD: Regulation: Street peddlers Accuse Officers of Harassing Them. No Vending Licenses have been issued Since Ordinance Legalizing the Practice was Passed in January," *LA Times*, August 2, 1994, accessed January 15, 2015, http://articles.latimes.com/1994-08-02/local/me-22546_1_street-vendors

10. Henry Grabar, "Los Angeles Renaissance: Why the Rise of Street Vending reveals a City Transformed." *Salon.com*, January 18, 2015, accessed January 18, 2015, http://www.salon.com/2015/01/18/los_angeles_food_truck_renaissance_why_the_rise_of_street_vending_reveals_a_city_transformed/

11. Yvonne Yen Liu, Patrick Burns, and Daniel Fleming, "Sidewalk Stimulus: Economic and Geographic Impact of Los Angeles Street Vendors," *Economic Roundtable*, June 22, 2015, accessed June 24, 2015, http://economicrt.org/publication/sidewalk-stimulus, 4.

12. Fazila Bhimji, "Struggles, Urban Citizenship, and Belonging: The Experience of Undocumented Street Vendors and Food Truck Owners in Los Angeles."

Urban Anthropology and Studies of Cultural Systems and World Economic Development 39.4 (2010), 457.

13. Yvonne Yen Liu, Patrick Burns, and Daniel Fleming, "Sidewalk Stimulus: Economic and Geographic Impact of Los Angeles Street Vendors," *Economic Roundtable*, June 22, 2015, accessed June 24, 2015, http://economicrt.org/publication/sidewalk-stimulus, 9.

14. "Legal Sidewalk Vending: A Tool for Healthy Communities," http://www.oxy.edu/sites/default/files/assets/UEPI/Street-Food-Vending-Factsheet-English-Version.pdf

15. "Council Move to Legalize Street Vending Sparks Opposition in Downtown," *DT News*, June 13, 2014, accessed May 1, 2015, http://www.ladowntown-news.com/council-move-to-legalize-street-vending-sparks-opposition-in-downtown/image_e181f3f6-f347-11e3-8fd5-001a4bcf887a.html

16. Henry Grabar, "Los Angeles Renaissance: Why the Rise of Street Vending Reveals a City Transformed." Salon.com, January 18, 2015, accessed January 18, 2015, http://www.salon.com/2015/01/18/los_angeles_food_truck_renaissance_why_the_rise_of_street_vending_reveals_a_city_transformed/

17. LA County Department of Public Health, website. http://publichealth.lacounty.gov/eh/SSE/StreetVending/strVending.htm

18. "Legal Sidewalk Vending: A Tool for Healthy Communities." http://www.oxy.edu/sites/default/files/assets/UEPI/Street-Food-Vending-Factsheet-English-Version.pdf

19. Emir Estrada and Pierrette Hondagneu-Sotelo, "Intersectional Dignities: Latino Immigrant Street Vendor Youth in Los Angeles," *Journal of Contemporary Ethnography* 40.1 (2011), 103.

20. Daina Beth Solomon, "South LA Street Cooks Could Soon Go Legit." *Intersections: South L.A.*, March 20, 2014, accessed April 20, 2015, http://intersectionssouthla.org/story/street-food-vending-legalization-south-la/

21. Alfonso Morales and Gregg Kettles, "Healthy Food Outside: Farmers' Markets, Taco Trucks, and Sidewalk Fruit Vendors," *The Journal of Contemporary Health Law and Policy* 26.1 (2009), 21.

22. "Vendedores Ambulantes quieren legalizar ventas en Los Ángeles," YouTube video, *KWHY Canal 22 Los Angeles*, February 12, 2014, accessed February 1, 2015, https://www.youtube.com/watch?v=SQGuf0u_3-k.

23. Emily Alpert Reyes, "Legal Team Steps in for Street Vendor Facing Hundreds in Fines." *LA Times*, April 27, 2015, accessed April 27, 2015, http://www.latimes.com/local/great-reads/la-me-c1-street-vendor-court-20150427-story.html#page=1.

24. Jonathan Gold, "Fried in East L.A.: Antojito's Carmen and the Breed Street Band of Mexican Vendors," LA Weekly, November 4, 2009, http://www.laweekly.com/restaurants/fried-in-east-la-antojitos-carmen-and-the-breed-street-band-of-mexican-vendors-2162705, accessed October 15, 2015.

25. Jonathan Gold, "The Hungry Metropolis: from Street Food to Upscale Dining LA Is the Best Place in The World to Eat Now," *Saveur*, February 8, 2010, accessed April 15, 2015, http://www.saveur.com/article/Travels/The-Hungry-Metropolis.

26. Maeve Reston, "Out There: Food Vendors Struggle to Survive," *LA Times*, November 17, 2009, accessed May 1, 2015, http://articles.latimes.com/2009/nov/17/local/me-outthere17

27. Yvonne Yen Liu, Patrick Burns, and Daniel Fleming, "Sidewalk Stimulus: Economic and Geographic Impact of Los Angeles Street Vendors," *Economic Roundtable*, June 22, 2015, accessed June 24, 2015, http://economicrt.org/publication/sidewalk-stimulus, 13.

28. Ibid, 16.

29. "Video Shows Street Vendor Crackdown in L.A.'s MacArthur Park," *CBSLA.com*, March 16, 2015, accessed March 18, 2015, http://losangeles.cbslocal.com/2015/03/16/video-shows-food-vendor-crackdown-in-l-a-s-macarthur-park/

30. Gregory Bonett, P. Scott Chandler, Kevin Whitfield, and Pui-Yee Yu, "Criminalizing the Sidewalk: Why the Los Angeles City Attorney's Office Should Take Action to Reform the Unjust Treatment of Low-Income Sidewalk Vendors," Criminal Defense Clinic of the UCLA School of Law, April 2015, http://webshare.law.ucla.edu/Communications/Criminalizing%20the%20Sidewalk%20-%20A%20Report%20by%20the%20UCLA%20Criminal%20Defense%20Clinic%20-%20April%202015.pdf

31. "UCLA School of Law Report Provides Recommendations to Reform the Unjust Treatment of Sidewalk Vendors," *UCLA LAW*, April 7, 2015, accessed April 10, 2015, https://law.ucla.edu/news-and-events/in-the-news/2015/04/ucla-school-of-law-report-

32. Nancy Cruz, "LAPD Chief Beck Talks Dash Cam Videos, Body Cameras, Street Vendors Protests," *KTLA 5*, April 2, 2015, accessed April 3, 2015, http://ktla.com/2015/04/02/lapd-chief-beck-talks-dash-cam-videos-body-cameras-street-vendors-protest/

33. Gregory Bonett, P. Scott Chandler, Kevin Whitfield, and Pui-Yee Yu, "Criminalizing the Sidewalk: Why the Los Angeles City Attorney's Office Should Take Action to Reform the Unjust Treatment of Low-Income Sidewalk Vendors," Criminal Defense Clinic of the UCLA School of Law, April 2015, http://webshare.law.ucla.edu/Communications/Criminalizing%20the%20Sidewalk%20-%20A%20Report%20by%20the%20UCLA%20Criminal%20Defense%20Clinic%20-%20April%202015.pdf, 9.

34. Emily Alpert Reyes, "L.A. Lawmakers Vote to Reinstate Ban on Park and Beach Vending," *LA Times*, June 16, 2015, accessed June 18, 2015, http://www.latimes.com/local/lanow/la-me-ln-park-street-vending-20150616-story.html

35. Dennis Romero, "Kids Can Buy Coca-Cola at the Park, but Selling Fresh Fruit Is Illegal," *LA Weekly*, June 17, 2015, accessed June 17, 2015, http://www.laweekly.com/news/kids-can-buy-coca-cola-at-the-park-but-selling-fresh-fruit-is-illegal-5695832

36. Joseph Villela, "Los Ángeles le da la espalda a vendedores ambulantes," *La Opinión*, August 3, 2015, accessed August 3, 2015, http://www.laopinion.com/opinion-la-ciudad-de-los-angeles-le-da-la-espalda-a-los-vendedores-ambulantes

37. Emily Alpert Reyes, "Should L.A. Legalize Street Vendors? Stakes Are High for Shop Owners," *LA Times*, September 25, 2015, accessed September 25, 2015, http://www.latimes.com/local/cityhall/la-me-street-vending-battle-20150925-story.html

38. Ibid.

39. Ibid.

40. Debbie L. Sklar, "No Decision on Legalizing Street vending in L.A.," *Mynewsla.com*, October 27, 2015, accessed October 27, 2015, http://www.latimes.com/local/lanow/la-me-ln-street-vendors-cart-seizure-lawsuit-20151028-story.html

41. Ibid.

42. Times editorial board, "How Should L.A. Handle Street Vendors?" *LA Times*, November 4, 2015, accessed November 4, 2015, http://www.latimes.com/opinion/editorials/la-ed-adv-street-vendors-20151104-story.html

43. Leslie Berestein Rojas, "LA Street Vendors Sue City, Business Group Over Seized Carts," *89.3 KPCC*, October 29, 2015, accessed October 31, 2015, http://www.scpr.org/news/2015/10/29/55345/la-street-vendors-sue-city-business-group-over-sei/

44. Ibid.

45. "Lift the Cap on NYC Street Vendors!" Youtube.com. June 28, 2015, accessed November 5, 2015, https://www.youtube.com/watch?v=3HFlIrJm66c

46. http://www.vendyawards.streetvendor.org/newyorkcity/

47. Lucas Peterson, "The Good, the Bad, and the Ugly State of Street Food in America," *Eater.com*, May 21, 2015, accessed November 6, 2015, http://www.eater.com/2015/5/21/8601951/food-trucks-food-carts-street-food-nyc-los-angles-san-antonio

48. Alfonso Morales, "Peddling Policy: Street Vending in Historical and Contemporary Contest," *International Journal of Sociology and Social Policy* 20.3/4 (2000), 76–99.

49. Lorena Muñoz, "Latino/a Immigrant Street Vendors in Los Angeles: Photo-Documenting Sidewalks from 'Back-Home,'" *Sociological Research Online* 17.2 (2012), http://www.socresonline.org.uk/17/2/21.html, Accessed May 1, 2015.

50. Ibid.

51. Lucas Peterson, "Meet the Man Who's Peddled LA's Best Street Corn for 27 Years," *"Los Angeles Eater,"* January 13, 2015, accessed April 15, 2015, http://la.eater.com/2015/1/13/7532441/corn-man-lincoln-heights-dining-on-a-dime-los-angeles-review.

52. A. Martínez and Leo Duran, "Can You Write About Street Food in East LA If You're Not Latino?," *Take Two 89.3 KPCC*. January 22, 2015, accessed April 10, 2015, http://www.scpr.org/programs/take-two/2015/01/22/41201/can-you-write-about-street-food-in-east-la-if-you/

53. Ibid.

54. Gustavo Arellano, "In Defense of Writing About Street Vendors—and Non-Mexicans Writing About Them," *OC Weekly* Blog, January 20, 2015, accessed August 1, 2015, http://blogs.ocweekly.com/stickaforkinit/2015/01/eloteros_street_vendors.php

55. Javier Cabral, "Why This Food Writer Refuses to Review Street Vendors," *Zócalo Public Square*, March 26, 2015, accessed August 2, 2015, http://www.zocalopublicsquare.org/2015/03/26/why-this-food-writer-refuses-to-review-street-vendors/ideas/nexus/

CHAPTER 5

1. Sandy Banks, "#100days100nights Fuels Fear in South L.A," *LA Times*, July 31, 2015, accessed October 3, 2015, http://www.latimes.com/local/lanow/la-me-ln-banks-100days-20150731-column.html

2. Mark Vallianatos, Andrea Azuma, Susan Gilliland, and Robert Gottlieb, "Food Access, Availability, and Affordability in 3 Los Angeles Communities, Project CAFE, 2004–2006," *Preventing Chronic Disease* 7.2 (2010), A27.

3. Ibid.

4. Hing, Julianne, "An Oasis in the South L.A. Food Desert," *Colorlines: News for Action*, October 11, 2013, accessed January 20, 2015, http://www.colorlines.com/articles/oasis-south-la-food-desert.

5. "The Diabetes Epidemic Among Hispanics/Latinos," *National Diabetes Education Program*, last modified December 2009, http://www.ndep.nih.gov/media/FS_HispLatino_Eng.pdf

6. Ibid.

7. Gina Kolata, "Type 2 Diabetes—Symptoms, Diagnosis, Treatment of Type 2 Diabetes," *Health News—The New York Times*, June 28, 2011, accessed January 4, 2015. http://health.nytimes.com/health/guides/disease/type-2-diabetes/overview.html

8. Gail Woodward-Lopez and George R. Flores, *Obesity in Latino Communities: Prevention, Principles, and Action* (Sacramento: Latino Coalition for a Healthy California, December 2006), 2.

9. Michael Goran and Emily Ventura, "Obesity and Liver Disease in the Hispanic Community," *The Huffington Post*, September 14, 2012, accessed November 10, 2015, http://www.huffingtonpost.com/michael-goran/obesity-liver-disease_b_1885337.html

10. Gail Woodward-Lopez and George R. Flores, *Obesity in Latino Communities: Prevention, Principles, and Action* (Sacramento: Latino Coalition for a Healthy California, December 2006), 2.

11. "Trends in Diabetes: Time for Action," last modified November 2012, http://publichealth.lacounty.gov/wwwfiles/ph/hae/ha/Diabetes_2012_FinalS.pdf

12. Michael J. Montoya, *Making the Mexican Diabetic: Race, Science, and the Genetics of Inequality* (Berkeley and Los Angeles: University of California Press, 2011), 4.

13. Gail Woodward-Lopez and George R. Flores, *Obesity in Latino Communities: Prevention, Principles, and Action* (Sacramento: Latino Coalition for a Healthy California, December 2006), 4.

14. Simon Barquera, Lucia Hernandez-Barrera, Carolina Batis, Barry M. Popkin, and Juan A. Rivera. "Food Acculturation Drives Dietary Differences among Mexicans, Mexican Americans, and Non-Hispanic Whites," *The Journal of Nutrition* 141 (2011), 1898–1906.

15. Helen H. Jensen, Grace S. Marquis, and Robert E. Mazur. "Diet and Food Insufficiency among Hispanic Youths: Acculturation and Socioeconomic Factors in the Third National Health and Nutrition Examination Survey," *The American Journal of Clinical Nutrition* 78.6 (2003) 1120–1127.

16. Simon Barquera, Lucia Hernandez-Barrera, Carolina Batis, Barry M. Popkin, and Juan A. Rivera. "Food Acculturation Drives Dietary Differences among Mexicans, Mexican Americans, and Non-Hispanic Whites," *The Journal of Nutrition* 141 (2011), 1898–1906.

17. Ibid.

18. "Latino Hunger Fact Sheet," http://www.feedingamerica.org/hunger-in-america/impact-of-hunger/latino-hunger/latino-hunger-fact-sheet.html?referrer=https://www.google.com/

19. Marion Nestle, *A Place at the Table*, documentary film, directed by Lori Silverbush and Kristi Jacobson (2012; New York, NY: Magnolia Pictures, March 1, 2013).

20. Jennifer Steinhauer, "Farm Bill Reflects Shifting American Menu and a Senator's Persistent Tilling." *New York Times*, March 8, 2014, accessed May 2014, http://www.nytimes.com/2014/03/09/us/politics/farm-bill-reflects-shifting-american-menu-and-a-senators-persistent-tilling.html?_r=0

21. Ibid.

22. M. Kipke, E. Iverson, D. Moore, C. Booker, V. Ruelas, A. Peteres, and F. Kaufman, "Food and Park Environments: Neighborhood-level Risks for Childhood Obesity in East Los Angeles," *Journal of Adolescent Health* 40.4 (2007), 325–333.

23. "By Planting Seeds in His Neighborhood, This Man Got America Talking About Food Deserts," *Takepart*, January 4, 2015, accessed January 20, 2015, http://www.takepart.com/article/2014/12/16/planting-few-seeds-his-neighborhood-man-launched-nationwide-conversation-about.

24. Sánchez, George, *Becoming Mexican American: Ethnicity, Culture, and Identity in Chicano Los Angeles: 1900–1945* (Oxford: Oxford University Press, 1993), 87.

25. Ibid,18.

26. Ibid,14.

27. Kelly Simpson, "The Great Migration: Creating a New Black Identity in Los Angeles," *KCET*, February 15, 2012, accessed February 1, 2015, http://www.kcet.org/socal/departures/columns/portraits/the-great-migration-creating-a-new-black-identity.html.

28. Hector Tobar, "Latinos Move to South-Central L.A.: Drawn by Low Rents, They Replace Blacks." *LA Times,* May 3, 1990, accessed January 15, 2015, http://articles.latimes.com/1990-05-03/news/ti-151_1_south-los-angeles.

29. Ibid.

30. David M. Grant, Melvin L. Oliver, and Angela D. James. "African Americans: Social and Economic Bifurcation," *Ethnic Los Angeles* (New York: Russell Sage Foundation, 1996), 379.

31. Joe Mozingo and Angel Jennings, "50 Years after Watts: 'There is Still a Crisis in the Black Community,'" *LA Times*, August 13, 2015, accessed August 16, 2015, http://www.latimes.com/local/wattsriots/la-me-watts-african-americans-20150813-story.html

32. Sandy Banks, "Shopkeepers Lost Dreams, Livelihoods in Watts," August 15, 2015, accessed August 15, 2015, http://www.latimes.com/local/california/la-me-banks-riots-shops-20150815-column.html

33. "The L.A. Riots: 20 Years Later," April 20, 2012, accessed August 13, 2015, http://timelines.latimes.com/los-angeles-riots/.

34. Paul Lieberman, "51% of Riot Arrests Were Latino, Study Says: Unrest: RAND Analysis of Court Cases Finds They were mostly Young Men. The Figures Are Open to Many Interpretations, Experts Note," *LA Times*, June 18, 1992, accessed August 18 2015, http://articles.latimes.com/1992-06-18/local/me-734_1_los-angeles-riots

35. Anna Almendrala, "Racial Dot Map in LA Highlights Segregation by Neighborhood," August 29, 2013, accessed August 13, 2015, http://www.huffingtonpost.com/2013/08/29/racial-dot-map-la_n_3819252.html

36. Josh Sides, "The Ambiguous Legacies of the 1992 Riots," Planning Los Angeles, ed. David C. Sloane (Chicago: American Planning Association, 2012).

37. Sam Polk, "Op Ed: Friends with Weight-loss Benefits," *LA Times*, January 29, 2015, accessed January 30, 2015, http://www.latimes.com/opinion/op-ed/la-oe-0130-polk-healthcare-gap-social-networks-20150130-story.html

38. Mark Winne, *Closing the Food Gap: Resetting the Table in the Land of Plenty* (Boston: Beacon Food Press, 2008), 88.

39. Lori Siiverbush and Kristi Jacobson, "A Place at the Table." Documentary film (2012; New York, NY: Magnolia Pictures, March 1, 2013).

40. Ali Meyer, "Food Stamp Beneficiaries Exceed 46,000,000 for 38 Straight Months," *CNSNEWS.COM*, January 13, 2015, accessed August 17, 2015, http://www.cnsnews.com/news/article/ali-meyer/food-stamp-beneficiaries-exceed-46000000-38-straight-months.

41. Andrew Khouri and Samantha Masunaga, "Fresh & Easy to close 30 Southland Stores as it Explores New Formats," *LA Times*, March 24, 2015, accessed March 24, 2015, http://www.latimes.com/business/la-fi-fresh-easy-closures-20150324-story.html

CHAPTER 6

1. Alison Hope Alkon and Julian Agyeman, eds. *Cultivating Food Justice: Race, Class, and Sustainability* (Cambridge, Massachusetts: The MIT Press, 2011), 5.

2. Roland Sturm and Deborah A. Cohen, "Zoning for Health? The Year Old Ban on Fast Food Restaurants in South LA," *Health Affairs* 28.6 (November/December 2009), 1088–1097, accessed March 1, 2015, http://content.healthaffairs.org/content/28/6/w1088.full

3. William Saletan, "Food Apartheid: Banning Fast-Food in Poor Neighborhoods," *Slate*, July 31, 2008, accessed March 2, 2015, http://www.slate.com/articles/health_and_science/human_nature/2008/07/food_apartheid.html

4. Jennifer Medina, "In South Los Angeles New Fast-Food Spots Get a 'no thanks,'" *The New York Times,* January 15, 2011, accessed March 1, 2015, http://www.nytimes.com/2011/01/16/us/16fastfood.html?_r=0

5. William Saletan, "Food Apartheid: Banning Fast-food in Poor Neighborhoods," *Slate*, July 31, 2008, accessed March 2, 2015, http://www.slate.com/articles/health_and_science/human_nature/2008/07/food_apartheid.html

6. Robert Creighton, "Cheeseburgers, Race, and Paternalism. Los Angeles' Ban on Fast Food Restaurants," *Journal of Legal Medicine* 30.2 (2009), 258.

7. "Estudio: el veto a la comida rápida en el sur de Los Ángeles no redujo la obesidad." *Fox News Latino*, March 19, 2015, accessed November 1, 2015, http://latino.foxnews.com/latino/espanol/2015/03/19/estudio-el-veto-la-comida-rapida-en-el-sur-de-los-angeles-no-redujo-la-obesidad/

8. Miriam Hernandez, "Is the Fast Food Ban in South Los Angeles Working?" ABC7.com, March 19, 2015, accessed November 16, 2015, http://abc7.com/food/is-the-fast-food-restaurant-ban-in-south-los-angeles-working/565963/

9. "City Mulls Relaxed Ban On South LA Fast-Food Eateries," *CBSLA.com*, April 11, 2013, accessed March 15, 2015, http://losangeles.cbslocal.com/2013/04/11/city-mulls-relaxed-ban-on-south-la-fast-food-eateries/

10. "South LA Fast Food Health Impact Assessment," Community Health Councils, Inc., April 3, 2013, accessed March 1, 2015, http://www.chcinc.org/downloads/CHC_SLA_Health_Impact_Assessment.pdf

11. Miriam Hernandez, "Is the Fast Food Ban in South Los Angeles Working?" *ABC7.com*, March 19, 2015, accessed November 16, 2015, http://abc7.com/food/is-the-fast-food-restaurant-ban-in-south-los-angeles-working/565963/

12. Russ Parsons, "How a Former Gang Member Ended up a Baker at Bouchon Beverly Hills," *Los Angeles Times*, November 13, 2015, accessed November 13, 2015, http://www.latimes.com/food/la-fo-bouchon-homeboy-20151114-story.html

13. "Turning the Corner: Project Seeks to Improve Community's Health by Overhauling Small Markets." *UCLA Public Health*, accessed March 1, 2015, http://ph.ucla.edu/sites/default/files/downloads/magazine/sphmag.6.12.cornerstore.web_.pdf

14. Shirley Ramirez, "Market Makeover: Euclid Market Transformation," *KCET Los Angeles*, December 12, 2013, accessed January 15, 2015, http://www.kcet.org/arts/artbound/counties/los-angeles/public-matters-euclid-market-boyle-heights.html

15. "Turning the Corner: Project Seeks to Improve Community's Health by Overhauling Small Markets," *UCLA Public Health*, June 2012, accessed March 1, 2015, http://ph.ucla.edu/news/magazine/2012/june/article/turning-corner-project-seeks-improve-community-s-health-overhauling, 14.

16. Jordyn Holman, "Here's What Happened When a Troubled Liquor Store Started Selling Fresh Produce," April 7, 2015, accessed April 7, 2015, http://www.huffingtonpost.com/2015/04/07/south-la-healthy-food_n_6992538.html

17. Neelam Sharma, personal communication.

18. Thandisizwe Chimurenga, "Good for Your Body, Good to Your Soul: South L.A.'s Health Food Movement Gains Momentum," *KCET*, October 8, 2015, accessed October 9, 2015, http://www.kcet.org/socal/departures/transforming-south-la/good-for-your-body-good-to-your-soul-south-las-health-food-movement-gains-momentum.html

19. http://www.smgov.net/Portals/Farmers_Market/About_Us/History.aspx

20. Shimada Tia, "Lost Dollars, Empty Plates: The Impact of CalFresh Participation on State and Local Economies," *California Food Policy Advocates*, February 2013, accessed May 21, 2015, http://cfpa.net/lost-dollars-empty-plates-2013

21. Ibid.

22. Ibid.

23. Russ Parsons, "Hunger Benefits Programs Are Vital to Many Farmers Markets," *LA Times*, February 24, 2015, accessed May 23, 2015, http://www.latimes.com/food/dailydish/la-dd-benefits-programs-are-vital-to-many-farmers-markets-20150224-story.html

24. "South LA Fast Food Health Impact Assessment," Community Health Councils, Inc., April 3, 2013, accessed March 1, 2015, http://www.chcinc.org/downloads/CHC_SLA_Health_Impact_Assessment.pdf

25. Russ Parsons, "Hunger Benefits Programs Are Vital to Many Farmers Markets," *LA Times*, February 24, 2015, accessed May 23, 2015, http://www.latimes.com/food/dailydish/la-dd-benefits-programs-are-vital-to-many-farmers-markets-20150224-story.html

26. "Ecology Center Awarded $3.7 Million Grant from USDA to Expand Statewide Program That Supports Farmers & Feeds Families," *Ecology Center*, April 1, 2015, accessed April 3, 2015, http://ecologycenter.org/blog/ecology-center-awarded-3-7-million-grant-from-usda-to-expand-statewide-program-that-supports-farmers-feeds-families/

27. Russ Parsons, "New Grant Adds $1 million in Fresh Produce to L.A. Shoppers' Menus," *LA Times*, April 3, 2015, accessed April 4, 2015, http://www.latimes.com/food/dailydish/la-dd-new-grant-adds-1-million-in-fresh-produce-to-la-shoppers-menus-20150403-story.html

28. Ibid.

29. "Nutrition Incentive Matching Grant Program: Los Angeles," http://www.rootsofchange.org/wp-content/uploads/CNIAstory_LA.pdf

30. Valerie Ruelas, Ellen Iverson, Preston Kiekel, and Anne Peters, "The Role of Farmers' Markets in Two Low Income, Urban Communities," September 16, 2011, accessed January 21, 2015, *J. Community Health*, http://goodfoodla.org/wp-content/uploads/2014/06/The-Role-of-Farmers-Market-J-of-Community-Health.pdf

31. Russ Parsons, "Has the Farmers Market Movement Peaked?," *LA Times*, February 10, 2015, accessed February 10, 2015, http://www.latimes.com/food/dailydish/la-dd-has-the-farmers-market-movement-peaked-20150209-story.html

32. Tracie McMillan, "Why Wal-Mart and Other Retail Chains May Not Fix The Food Deserts," The Salt, *National Public Radio*, October 13, 2015, accessed October 13, 2015, http://www.npr.org/sections/thesalt/2015/10/13/448300139/why-wal-mart-and-other-retail-chains-may-not-fix-the-food-deserts

33. Ibid.

34. Heather Tirado Gilligan, "Food Deserts Aren't the Problem," *Slate*, February 10, 2014, accessed February 20, 2015, http://www.slate.com/articles/life/food/2014/02/food_deserts_and_fresh_food_access_aren_t_the_problem_poverty_not_obesity.html

35. Margot Sanger-Katz, "Giving the Poor Easy Access to Healthy Food Doesn't Meant They'll Buy it," *The New York Times*, May 8, 2015, accessed May 15, 2015, http://www.nytimes.com/2015/05/09/upshot/giving-the-poor-easy-access-to-healthy-food-doesnt-mean-theyll-buy-it.html?_r=0

36. B. Elbel, A. Moran, and L.B. Dixon, "Assessment of a Government-Subsidized Supermarket in a High-need Area on Household Food Availability and Children's Dietary Intakes," *Healthy Eating Research*, February 2015, accessed March 1, 2015, http://healthyeatingresearch.org/research/assessment-of-a-government-subsidized-supermarket-in-a-high-need-area-on-household-food-availability-and-childrens-dietary-intakes/

37. Paula Tarnapol Whitacre, Peggy Tsai, and Janet Mulligan, *"The Public Health Effects of Food Deserts: Workshop Summary,"* (Washington D.C: The National Academies Press, 2009).

38. "Why Making Healthful Foods Cheaper Isn't Enough," *National Public Radio*, March 15, 2010, accessed January 20, 2015, http://www.npr.org/templates/story/story.php?storyId=124610428

39. "For the Love of Money," *The New York Times*. January 18, 2014, accessed January 10, 2015, http://www.nytimes.com/2014/01/19/opinion/sunday/for-the-love-of-money.html?_r=0

40. Sam Polk, "Yuppies Watching Documentaries," *The Huffington Post*, January 6, 2014, accessed January 6, 2015, http://www.huffingtonpost.com/sam-polk/yuppies-watching-document_b_4551095.html

CHAPTER 7

1. Adrian Florido, "LA City Council Approves Curbside Planting of Fruits and Vegetables," 89.3 *KPCC*, March 4, 2015, accessed October 28, 2015, http://www.scpr.org/news/2015/03/04/50192/la-city-council-approves-curbside-planting-of-frui/

2. Jason Mark, "Urban Farming and Rooftop Gardens," *The Sage Encyclopedia of Food Issues* (Los Angeles: Sage, 2015), 1404.

3. Dorothy Blair, Carol C. Giesecke, and Sandra Sherman, "A Dietary, Social and Economic Evaluation of the Philadelphia Urban Gardening Project," *The Journal of Nutrition Education* 23.16 (1991): 161–167.

4. Jill S. Litt, Mah-J Soobader, Mark S. Turbin, James W. Hale, Michael Buchenau, and Julie A. Marshall, "The Influence of Social Involvement, Neighborhood Aesthetics, and Community Garden Participation on Fruit and Vegetable Consumption," *American Journal of Public Health* 101.8 (2011), 1466–1473.

5. Sarah Rich, *Urban Farms* (New York: Abrams, 2012), 14.

6. Ulrich Schmutz, Margi Lennartsson, Sarah Williams, Maria Devereaux and Gareth Davies, "The Benefits of Gardening and Food Growing for Health and Wellbeing," *Garden Organic and Sustain*, April 2014, accessed September 9, 2014, http://www.sustainweb.org/resources/files/reports/GrowingHealth_BenefitsReport.pdf

7. Ibid, 8.

8. Barclay Stone, "Acculturative Stress of Mexican Immigrant Women and the Nature and Role of Social Support," (PsyD dissertation, The Wright Institute, 2011), 2.

9. Olivia M. Espín. "Roots Uprooted," *Latina realities: Essays on Healing, Migration and Sexuality* (Boulder, CO: Westview Press, 1997), 23.

10. Barclay Stone, "Acculturative Stress of Mexican Immigrant Women and the Nature and Role of Social Support," (PsyD dissertation, The Wright Institute, 2011), 3.

11. Kevin A. Lombardi, Susan Forster-Cox, Dan Smeal, and Mick K. O'Neill, "Diabetes on the Navajo Nation: What Role Can Gardening and Agriculture Extension Play to Reduce it?" *Rural and Remote Health* 6.4 (October-December 2006), 640, accessed September 15, 2015, http://www.ncbi.nlm.nih.gov/pubmed/17044752

12. Isías Alvarado, "Migrantes 'sanan' en jardines vecinales de Los Angeles," *La Opinión*, September 3, 2014, accessed October 8, 2015, http://www.laopinion. com/2014/09/03/migrantes-sanan-en-jardines-vecinales-de-los-angeles/

13. Devon G. Peña, "Farmers Feeding Families: Agroecology in South Central Los Angeles," Lecture presented to the Environmental Science, Policy, and Management Colloquium, University of California – Berkeley, October 10, 2005, 3.

14. Deborah Barndt, ed. *Women Working the NAFTA Food Chain: Women, Food & Globalization* (Toronto: Second Story Press, 1999), 206.

15. Jerry Kaufman and Martin Bailkey, "Farming Inside Cities: Entrepreneurial Agriculture in the United States," Lincoln Institute of Land Policy Working Paper, 2000, http://www.urbantilth.org/wp-content/uploads/2008/10/farminginsidecities.pdf

16. Araceli Martínez Ortega, "Granjas urbanas ganan terreno en Los Ángeles," *La Opinión*, March 23, 2014, accessed October 8, 2015, http://www.laopinion. com/2014/03/23/granjas-urbanas-ganan-terreno-en-los-angeles/

17. Patricia Leigh Brown, "In Latino Gardens, Vegetables, Good Health and Savings Flourish," *The New York Times*, January 16, 2010, accessed October 15, 2015, http://www.nytimes.com/2010/01/17/us/17backyard.html?_r=0

18. Jerry Kaufman and Martin Bailkey, "Farming Inside Cities: Entrepreneurial Agriculture in the United States," Lincoln Institute of Land Policy Working Paper, 2000, http://www.urbantilth.org/wp-content/uploads/2008/10/farminginsidecities.pdf

19. Deepa Fernandes, "Group works to Turn South LA Lots into Children's Playgrounds," 89.3 *KPCC*, April 30, 2015, accessed September 20, 2015, http://www.scpr. org/news/2015/04/30/50927/groups-work-to-turn-south-la-lots-into-children-s/

20. CUESA, "New California Law Breaks Ground for Urban Agriculture," October 8, 2013, accessed October 1, 2015, http://ww2.kqed.org/ bayareabites/2013/10/08/new-california-law-breaks-ground-for-urban-farmers/

21. "San Francisco Board of Supervisors President David Chiu, Assemblymember Phil Ting and Supporters Announce State's First Urban Agriculture Incentive Zone Ordinance in San Francisco," San Francisco Board of Supervisors' website, http:// www.sfbos.org/Modules/ShowDocument.aspx?documentid=49421

22. Abby Sewell, "Tomato Garden Tax Break? Backers say it Would Pay off in Better Health," *LA Times*, September 22, 2015, accessed September 22, 2015.

23. Ibid.

24. Noah Wilson-Rich, "Why Urban Beekeeping Is Right for Los Angeles," *LA Times*, October 14, 2015, accessed October 18, 2015, http://www.latimes.com/ opinion/op-ed/la-oe-1014-wilson-rich-urban-beekeeping-la-20151014-story.html

25. Rose Hayden-Smith, "A Brief History of School Gardens," *Kitchen Gardeners International*, February 4, 2011, accessed November 6, 2015, http://kgi.org/blogs/ rose-hayden-smith/brief-history-school-gardens

26. Sam Watters, "Lost L.A.: School Gardens, an Idea Planted a Century Ago," *LA Times*, February 3, 2012, accessed August 27, 2015, http://latimesblogs.latimes. com/home_blog/2012/02/lost-la-school-gardens.html

27. Emma Gallegos, "How School Garden Mania Swept Los Angeles a Century Ago," *LAIST.com*, February 3, 2012, accessed October 29, 2015, http://laist. com/2012/02/03/school_garden_mania_swept_los_angel.php

28. Rose Hayden-Smith, "'Soldiers of the Soil': The Work of the United States School Garden Army during World War I," *Applied Environmental Education & Communication* 6.1 (2007), 21.

29. C.A. Stebbins, "A Manual of School-Supervised Gardening for the Western States," *United States School Garden Army* (Washington, D.C.: Department of the Interior, Bureau of Education, 1920), 49.

30. Rose Hayden-Smith, "'Soldiers of the Soil': The Work of the United States School Garden Army during: World War I," *Applied Environmental Education & Communication* 6.1 (2007), 21.

31. Rose Hayden-Smith, *Sowing the Seeds of Victory: American Gardening Programs of World War I* (Jefferson, North Carolina: McFarland & Company, Inc., 2014).

32. Robert Gottlieb. *Enivronmentalism Unbound: Exploring New Pathways for Change* (Massachusetts: The MIT Press, 2001), 249.

33. Laura Benjamin, "Growing a Movement: Community Gardens in Los Angeles County" (Undergraduate diss., Occidental College, May 2008), 7.

34. Mark Winne, *Closing the Food Gap: Resetting the Table in the Land of Plenty* (Boston: Beacon Press, 2008), 55.

35. Robert Gottlieb and Anupama Joshi, *Food Justice* (Cambridge and London: The MIT Press, 2010), 146–147.

36. Laura J. Lawson, *City Bountiful: A Century of Community Gardening in America* (Berkeley: University of California Press, 2005), 206.

37. Sarah C. Rich, *Urban Farms* (New York: Abrams, 2012), 74.

38. Laura J. Lawson, *City Bountiful: A Century of Community Gardening in America* (Berkeley: University of California Press, 2005), 242.

39. Ibid, 238.

40. Ibid, 244.

41. Jason Mark, "Urban Farming and Rooftop Gardens," *The Sage Encyclopedia of Food Issues* (Los Angeles: Sage, 2015),1405.

42. Devon G. Peña, "Farmers Feeding Families: Agroecology in South Central Los Angeles." Lecture presented to the Environmental Science, Policy, and Management Colloquium, University of California – Berkeley, October 10, 2005, 9.

43. Ioan Voicu and Vicki Been, "The Effect of Community Gardens on Neighboring Property Values," *Furman Center for Real Estate and Urban Policy*, New York University (2006), 1, http://www.urbantilth.org/wp-content/uploads/2008/10/community_gardens_paper_aug3_2006f.pdf

44. Ibid, 2.

45. Robert Gottlieb and Anupama Joshi, *Food Justice* (Cambridge and London: The MIT Press, 2010), 146–147.

46. Dan Barry, "Giuliani Seeks Deal to Sell 63 Gardens to Land Group and End Suits," *New York Times*, May 11, 1999, accessed October 12, 2015, http://www.nytimes.com/1999/05/12/nyregion/giuliani-seeks-deal-to-sell-63-gardens-to-land-group-and-end-suits.html

47. Steinhauer, Jennifer, "Ending a Long Battle, New York Lets Housing and Gardens Grow," *New York Times*, September 18, 2002, accessed October 12, 2015,

http://www.nytimes.com/2002/09/19/nyregion/ending-a-long-battle-new-york-lets-housing-and-gardens-grow.html

48. Nathan Tempey, "Developer Claims It Bought Crown Heights Community Garden Property for $10," *Gothamist*, June 11, 2015, accessed October 5, 2015, http://gothamist.com/2015/06/11/crown_heights_community_garden.php

49. Rachel Holliday Smith, "Judge Throws Out Rogers Avenue Community Garden Eviction Case," *DNAinfo.com*, November 18, 2015, accessed February 13, 2016, https://www.dnainfo.com/new-york/20151118/crown-heights/judge-throws-out-rogers-avenue-community-garden-eviction-case

50. Rachel Holliday Smith, "Threatened Community Garden Could Become Park Through Eminent Domain," *DNAinfo.com*, January 26, 2016, accessed February 13, 2016, https://www.dnainfo.com/new-york/20160126/crown-heights/imperiled-community-garden-could-become-park-under-new-bill

51. Laura Lawson, "The South Central Farm: Dilemmas in Practicing the Public," *Cultural Geographies* 14 (2007), 614.

52. Devon G. Peña, "Farmers Feeding Families: Agroecology in South Central Los Angeles." Lecture presented to the Environmental Science, Policy, and Management Colloquium, University of California – Berkeley, October 10, 2005, 2.

53. Garrett M. Broad, "Ritual Communication and Use Value: The South Central Farm and the Political Economy of Place," *Communication, Culture & Critique* 6 (2013), 20–40.

54. Laura Lawson, "The South Central Farm: Dilemmas in Practicing the Public," *Cultural Geographies* 14 (2007), 614.

55. Tezozomac, "Renewing Agricultural Life in South Central Los Angeles," *on earth*. April 4, 2013, accessed October 15, 2015, http://archive.onearth.org/blog/renewing-our-community%E2%80%99s-agricultural-life-from-loss-in-south-central-los-angeles

56. Tezozomoc biography, e-mail communication on March 1, 2016.

57. "At Stanford Avalon, community gardening gets serious," *LA Times*, March 23, 2011, accessed October 15, 2015, http://latimesblogs.latimes.com/home_blog/2011/03/stanford-avalon-community-garden.html

58. "White Memorial Center: Stop the Displacement of Proyecto Jardín," https://www.change.org/p/white-memorial-medical-center-stop-the-displacement-of-proyectojardin/u/15416818?recruiter=475990014&utm_source=share_update&utm_medium=facebook&utm_campaign=facebook_link

59. Jason Song, "Group Rallies to Secure Stake in Community Garden after Lease Talks Falter," *LA Times*, January 31, 2016, accessed January 31, 2016, http://www.latimes.com/local/california/la-me-proyecto-jardin-20160131-story.html

60. Ibid.

61. Karen Dardick, "'Angeles' Help Children in Garden," *LA Times*, February 27, 1994, accessed October 8, 2015, http://articles.latimes.com/1994-02-27/realestate/re-27755_1_gardening-angels

62. "School Garden Start-Up Guide," http://celosangeles.ucdavis.edu/files/97114.pdf

63. "Cultivate L.A.: An Assessment of Urban Agriculture in Los Angeles County," Prepared for the University of California Cooperative Extension, June 2013, accessed

October 1, 2015, https://cultivatelosangeles.files.wordpress.com/2013/07/cultivate-l-a-an-assessment-of-urban-agriculture-in-los-angeles-county-june-11-2013.pdf

64. Assembly Bill No. 1535, http://www.leginfo.ca.gov/pub/05-06/bill/asm/ab_1501-1550/ab_1535_bill_20060925_chaptered.pdf

65. Krista Simmons, "A New Crop of School Gardens," *LA Times*, July 29, 2009, accessed September 3, 2015, http://www.latimes.com/food/la-fo-garden29-2009jul29-story.html

66. "Let's Move," http://www.letsmove.gov/gardening-guide

67. Tom Philpott, "Thoughts on the Atlantic's Attack on School Gardens," *Grist,* January 14, 2010, accessed October 24, 2015, http://grist.org/article/2010-01-13-atlantic-attack-edible-schoolyard/

68. C.D. Klemmer, T.M. Waliczek, and J.M. Zajicek, "Growing Minds: The Effect of a School Gardening Program on the Science Achievement of Elementary Students," Hort Technology 15.3 (2005), 448–452.

69. Howard Blume, "Achievement Gap Widens for California's black and Latino Students," *LA Times*, September 11, 2015, accessed October 22, 2015, http://www.latimes.com/local/lanow/la-me-ln-achievement-gaps-widen-20150911-story.html

70. Tom Philpott, "Thoughts on The Atlantic's Attack on School Gardens," *Grist*, January 14, 2010, accessed October 23, 2015, http://grist.org/article/2010-01-13-atlantic-attack-edible-schoolyard/

CONCLUSION

1. Gillian Ferguson, "L.A.'s *tacos* Are Filled With a World of Flavors; Chef Enrique Olvera Loves that About Us," *LA Times*, April 15, 2016, accessed April 15, 2016, http://www.latimes.com/food/la-fo-enrique-olvera-taco-crawl-20160416-story.html

2. Editorial, "It's Time for All L.A. farmers Markets to Accept Food Stamps," *LA Times*, March 8, 2016, accessed March 9, 2016, http://www.latimes.com/opinion/editorials/la-ed-0309-ebt-20160308-story.html

Bibliography

Alkon, Alison Hope and Julian Agyeman, eds. *Cultivating Food Justice: Race, Class,and Sustainability* (Cambridge, Massachusetts: The MIT Press, 2011).

Anderson, E.N. *Everyone Eats: Understanding Food and Culture.* (New York University Press: New York and London, 2005).

Arellano, Gustavo. "Five Authentic Mexican Dishes That Would Make Rick Bayless Scream, Or: For an Aztlanista Approach to the Question of 'Authenticity' in Mexican Cuisine." *Orange County Weekly.* Web. October 4, 2010.

———. "El Torito Founder Is still the Big Enchilada," *Orange County Weekly.* Web. January 6, 2011.

———. "Tamales, LA's Original Street Food." *Los Angeles Times*, September 8, 2011.

———. *Taco USA: How Mexican Food Conquered America* (New York: Scribner, 2012).

Barndt, Deborah. ed. *Women Working the NAFTA Food Chain: Women, Food & Globalization* (Toronto: Second Story Press, 1999).

Barquera, Simon., Lucia Hernandez-Barrera, Carolina Batis, Barry M. Popkin, and Juan A. Rivera. "Food Acculturation Drives Dietary Differences among Mexicans, Mexican Americans, and Non-Hispanic Whites," *The Journal of Nutrition* 141 (2011): 1898–1906.

Benjamin, Laura. "Growing a Movement: Community Gardens in Los Angeles County," Urban and Environmental Policy Program, Occidental College, May 2008.

Berezowitz, Claire K., Andrea B., Bontrager Yoder, and Dale A. Schoeller, "School Gardens Enhance Academic Performance and Dietary Outcomes in Children," *Journal of School Health* 85.8 (2015): 508–518.

Bhimji, Fazila. "Struggles, Urban Citizenship, and Belonging: The Experience of Undocumented Street Vendors and Food Truck Owners in Los Angeles," *Urban Anthropology and Studies of Cultural Systems and World Economic Development* 39.4 (2010): 455–492.

Blair, D., C.G. Giesecke, and S. Sherman, "A Dietary, Social and Economic Evaluation of the Philadelphia Urban Gardening Project," *The Journal of Nutrition Education* 23.16 (1991): 161–167.

Broad, Garrett. "Ritual Communication and Use Value: The South Central Farm and the Political Economy of Place," *Communication, Culture & Critique* 6 (2013), 20–40.

Chimurenga, Thandisizwe. "Good for Your Body, Good to Your Soul: South L.A.'s Health Food Movement Gains Momentum," *KCET*, October 8, 2015.

Coe, Sophia and Michael. *The True History of Chocolate* (New York: Thames & Hudson, 1996).

Creighton, Robert. "Cheeseburgers, Race, and Paternalism. Los Angeles' ban on fast food restaurants," *Journal of Legal Medicine* 30.2 (2009).

Deverell, William. *Whitewashed Adobe: The Rise of Los Angeles and the Remaking of Its Mexican Past* (Berkeley, CA: University of California Press, 2005).

Elbel, B., A. Moran, and L.B. Dixon, "Assessment of a Government-Subsidized Supermarket in a High-Need Area on Household Food Availability and Children's Dietary Intakes," *Healthy Eating Research*, February 2015.

Elliot, Farley. *Los Angeles Street Food: A History from Tamaleros to Taco Trucks* (Charleston, South Carolina: American Palate, 2015).

Esparza, Bill. "Tacopedia: A Complete Taco Encyclopedia of L.A.," *Los Angeles Magazine*, July 24, 2015.

Estrada, Emir and Pierrette Hondagneu-Sotelo. "Intersectional Dignities: Latino Immigrant Street Vendor Youth in Los Angeles," *Journal of Contemporary Ethnography* 40.1 (2011).

Ferrero, Sylvia. "Comida Sin Par. Consumption of Mexican Food in Los Angeles: Foodscapes in a Transnational Consumer Society." In *Food Nations: Selling Taste in Consumer Societies*. Edited by Warren James Belasco and Philip Scranton. (New York: Routledge, 2002).

Flanagan, Caitlin. "Cultivating Failure: How School Gardens are Cheating our Most Vulnerable Students," *The Atlantic*, January/February 2010.

Garza-Weatherspoon, Odett. "An Acquired Taste: How Spanish and Mexican Recipes Helped Shape Early Los Angeles." *Master's thesis*, California State University, Long Beach, 2007.

Glenn, Erin. "Taco Trucks on the Street: Where Food and Social Justice Meet," *Los Angeles Public Interest Law Journal*, 2011.

Gold, Jonathan. "Clayuda me," *Los Angeles Times*, July 28, 1994.

———. "Moles La Tia: Beyond the Magnificent Seven," *Los Angeles Weekly*, January 21, 2009.

———. "Rivera, John Sedlar's Return to the Kitchen," *Los Angeles Weekly*, March 25, 2009.

———. "The Hungry Metropolis: From Street Food to Upscale Dining LA Is the Best Place in the World to Eat Now," *Saveur*, February 8, 2010.

———. "Jonathan Gold Reviews Guisados," *LA Weekly*, September 22, 2011.

———. "Border Grill: 99 Essential Restaurants 2011," *Los Angeles Weekly*, November 10, 2011.

————. "Chichén Itzá: 99 Essential Restaurants 2011," *LA Weekly*, November 10, 2011.

————. "How America Became a Food Truck Nation," *Smithsonian. com*, March 2012.

————. "L.A. Restaurant Review: Guerrilla Tacos Rolls up in High style," *LA Times*, February 21, 2014.

————. "B.S. Taqueria Has a Few Twists Even for This Taco-centric City," *Los Angeles Times*, June 12, 2015.

————. "Jonathan Gold Review: Mexicano at the Baldwin Hills Crenshaw Plaza," *Los Angeles Times*, November 20, 2015.

Gomez-Rejón, Maite. "Chocolate, the Food of the Gods," *The Online Magazine of the Getty*, February 12, 2015.

Goodyear, Dana. "Grub: Eating Bugs to Save the Planet," *The New Yorker*, August 15, 2011.

Gottlieb, Robert and Anupama Joshi. *Food Justice* (Cambridge and London: The MIT Press, 2010).

Gottlieb, Robert. *Enivronmentalism Unbound: Exploring New Pathways for Change* (Massachusetts: The MIT Press, 2001).

Grant, David M., Melvin L. Oliver, and Angela D. James. "African Americans: Social and Economic Bifurcation." In *Ethnic Los Angeles*. New York: Russell Sage Foundation, 1996.

Hayden-Smith, Rose. "Soldiers of the Soil: The Work of the United States School Garden Army during World War I," *Applied Environmental Education & Communication* 6.1 (2007), 21.

————. "A Brief History of School Gardens," *Kitchen Gardeners International*, February 4, 2011.

————. *Sowing the Seeds of Victory: American Gardening Programs of World War I* (Jefferson, North Carolina: McFarland & Company, Inc., 2014).

Helde, Lisa. *Exotic Appetites: Ruminations of a Food Adventurer* (New York, NewYork: Routledge, 2003).

Hermosillo, Jesús. "A Look at the Stationary Food Trucks of Los Angeles," September 2010, Master of Arts UCLA School of Urban Planning.

Hernández-López, Ernesto. "LA's Taco Truck War: How Law Cooks Food Culture Contests," *Legal Studies Research Paper Series*, Paper 10–29, October 18, 2010.

Hernandez, Miriam. "Is the Fast Food Ban in South Los Angeles Working?" ABC7.com, March 19, 2015.

Jensen, Helen H., Grace S. Marquis, and Robert E. Mazur. "Diet and Food Insufficiency Among Hispanic Youths: Acculturation and Socioeconomic Factors in the Third National Health and Nutrition Examination Survey," *The American Journal of Clinical Nutrition* 78.6 (2003): 1120–1127.

Kaufman, Jerry and Martin Bailkey. "Farming Inside Cities: Entrepreneurial Agriculture in the United States," Lincoln Institute of Land Policy Working Paper, 2000

Kennedy, Diane. *Oaxaca Al Gusto: An Infinite Gastronomy* (Austin: University of Texas Press, 2010).

Kipke, M, E. Iverson, D. Moore, C. Booker, V. Ruelas, A. Peteres, and F. Kaufman. "Food and Park Environments: Neighborhood-level Risks for Childhood Obesity in East Los Angeles," *Journal of Adolescent Health* 40.4 (2007): 325–333.

Klemmer, C.D., T.M. Waliczek, and J.M. Zajicek. "Growing Minds: The Effect of a School Gardening Program on the Science Achievement of Elementary Students." *Hort Technology* 15.3 (2005), 448–452.

Kun, Josh. *To Live and Dine in L.A.: Menus and the Making of the Modern City* (Los Angeles: Angel City Press, 2015).

Lawson, Laura J. *City Bountiful: A Century of Community Gardening in America* (Berkeley: University of California Press, 2005).

———. "The South Central Farm: Dilemmas in Practicing the Public," *Cultural Geographies* 14 (2007).

Liu, Yvonne Yen, Patrick Burns, and Daniel Fleming, "Sidewalk Stimulus: Economic and Geographic Impact of Los Angeles Street Vendors," *Economic Roundtable*, June 22, 2015.

Lynn, Stephen. *We Are the Face of Oaxaca: Testimony and Social Movements* (Durham, North Carolina: Duke University Press, 2013).

Margolick, David. "Brooklyn Expatriates in Los Angeles Mourn Fading Reminders of the Past," *LA Times*, April 3, 1994.

Mark, Jason. "Urban Farming and Rooftop Gardens," *The Sage Encyclopedia of Food Issues* (Los Angeles: Sage, 2015).

Medina, Jennifer. "In South Los Angeles New Fast-food Spots Get a 'No thanks,'" *The New York Times*, January 15, 2011.

McMillan, Tracie. "Why Wal-Mart and Other Retail Chains May Not Fix The Food Deserts," The Salt, *National Public Radio*, October 13, 2015.

McWilliams, Carey. *Southern California Country: An Island on the Land* (New York: Duell, Sloan & Pierce, 1946).

Montoya, Michael J.. *Making the Mexican Diabetic: Race, Science, and the Genetics of Inequality* (Berkeley and Los Angeles: University of California Press, 2011).

Morales, Alfonso and Gregg Kettles. "Healthy Food Outside: Farmers' Markets, Taco Trucks, and Sidewalk Fruit Vendors," *The Journal of Contemporary Health Law and Policy* 26.1 (2009): 20–48.

Morales, Alfonso. "Peddling Policy: Street Vending in Historical and Contemporary contest," *International Journal of Sociology and Social Policy* 20.3/4 (2000): 76–99.

Muñoz, Lorena. "Latino/a Immigrant Street Vendors in Los Angeles: Photo-Documenting Sidewalks from 'Back-Home,'" *Sociological Research Online* 17.2 (2012).

Parsons, Russ. "Has the Farmers Market Movement Peaked?," *Los Angeles Times*, February 10, 2015.

———. "Hunger Benefits Programs Are Vital to Many Farmers Markets," *Los Angeles Times*, February 24, 2015.

———. "New Grant Adds $1 Million in Fresh Produce to L.A. Shoppers' Menus," *Los Angeles Times*, April 3, 2015.

————. "How a Former Gang Member Ended up a Baker at Bouchon Beverly Hills," *Los Angeles Times*, November 13, 2015.

Peña, Devon G. "Farmers Feeding Families: Agroecology in South Central Los Angeles," Lecture Presented to the Environmental Science, Policy, and Management Colloquium, University of California – Berkeley, October 10, 2005.

Peterson, Lucas. "Meet the Man Who's Peddled LA's Best Street Corn for 27 Years," "*Los Angeles Eater*," January 13, 2015.

Pilcher, Jeffrey. ¡Qué Vivan los tamales!: Food and the Making of Mexican Identity (Albuquerque, NM: University of New Mexico Press, 1998).

————. "Was the Taco Invented in Southern California?" *Gastronomica* 8.1 (Winter 2008), 26.

————. *Planet Taco: A Global History of Mexican Food* (New York: Oxford University Press, 2012).

————. "Nachos, burritos, and nationality," *Oxford Wordsblog*, November 2, 2012.

Pinedo, Encarnación. *Encarnacion's Kitchen: Mexican Recipes from Nineteenth Century California*, trans. Dan Strehl. (Berkeley: University of California Press, 2005).

Polk, Sam. "Yuppies Watching Documentaries," *The Huffington Post*, January 6, 2014.

Ramirez, Shirley. "Market Makeover: Euclid Market Transformation," *KCET Los Angeles*, December 12, 2013.

Rich, Sarah. *Urban Farms.* (New York: Abrams, 2012).

Saletan, William. "Food Apartheid: Banning Fast-food in Poor Neighborhoods," *Slate*, July 31, 2008.

Sánchez, George. Becoming *Mexican American: Ethnicity, Culture, and Identity in Chicano Los Angeles: 1900–1945* (Oxford: Oxford University Press, 1993).

Sanger-Katz, Margot. "Giving the Poor Easy Access to Healthy Food Doesn't Meant They'll Buy It," *The New York Times*, May 8, 2015.

Shimada, Tia. "Lost Dollars, Empty Plates: The Impact of CalFresh Participation on State and Local Economies," *California Food Policy Advocates*, February 2013.

Sides, Josh. "The Ambiguous Legacies of the 1992 Riots," Planning Los Angeles, ed. David C. Sloane. (Chicago: American Planning Association, 2012).

Silverbush, Lori and Kristi Jacobson. "A Place at the Table." New York, NY: Magnolia Pictures, March 1, 2013.

Simpson Methodist Episcopal Church, Ladies Social Circle. *How We Cook in Los Angeles: A Practical Cook-book Containing Six Hundred or More Recipes Selected and Tested by over One Hundred Well Known Hostesses Including a French, German and Spanish Department with Menus, Suggestions for Artistic Table Decorations, and Souvenirs.* (Los Angeles: Commercial Printing House, 1894).

Stone, Barclay. "Acculturative Stress of Mexican Immigrant Women and the Nature and Role of Social Support," (PsyD dissertation, The Wright Institute, 2011).

Sturm, Roland and Deborah A. Cohen. "Zoning for Health? The Year Old Ban on Fast Food Restaurants in South LA," *Health Affairs* 28.6 (November/December 2009): 1088–1097.

Terrazas, Aaron. "Salvadoran Immigrants in the United States," *Migration Policy Institute,* January 5, 2010.

Tirado Gilligan, Heather. "Food Deserts Aren't the Problem," *Slate*, February 10, 2014.

Vallianatos, Mark, Andrea Azuma, Susan Gilliland, and Robert Gottlieb, "Food Access, Availability, and Affordability in 3 Los Angeles Communities, Project CAFE, 2004–2006," *Preventing Chronic Disease* 7.2 (2010).

Valle, Victor. "A Curse of Tea and Potatoes," *Encarnacion's Kitchen: Mexican Recipes from Nineteenth Century California*, trans. Dan Strehl. (Berkeley: University of California Press, 2005).

Whelan, J. S., & Dvorkin, L. "Plants from Many Healing Landscapes: Gathering Information and Teaching Clinicians About the Cultural Use of Medicinal herbs." *Journal of the Medical Library Association*, 94.2 (2006), 223–226.

Whitacre, Paula Tarnapol, Peggy Tsai, and Janet Mulligan. "The Public Health Effects of Food Deserts: Workshop Summary," Washington D.C., The National Academies Press, 2009.

Winne, Mark. *Closing the Food Gap: Resetting the Table in the Land of Plenty.* (Boston: Beacon Press, 2008).

Winters Keegan, Rebecca. "The Great Taco Truck War," *Time.com*, April 25, 2008.

Woodward-Lopez, Gail and George R. Flores. *Obesity in Latino Communities: Prevention, Principles, and Action* (Sacramento: Latino Coalition for a Healthy California, December 2006).

Zavestoski, Stephen and Julian Agyeman, eds. *Incomplete Streets: Practices, Processes and Possibilities* (London and New York: Routledge, 2015).

Index

About the Author

Sarah Portnoy is an Assistant Professor (of Teaching) in the Department of Spanish and Portuguese at the University of Southern California where she does research on food culture and food justice in Los Angeles's Latino communities. She has also developed community-based courses on Latino food culture and food justice. Her Food Studies publications include "Mexican American Cuisine" for the Oxford University Press' *Latino Studies Bibliography* and "Roy Choi, Ricardo Zárate, and Pacific Fusion Cuisine in Los Angeles," an article she co-wrote with historian Jeffrey Pilcher for the edited volume, *Global Latin America*. Information on her current Food Studies research and explorations can be found at sarahjportnoy.com.